AN ILLUSTRATED HISTORY OF THE CHURCH

Guy Bedouelle

An Illustrated History of the Church
The Great Challenges

LTP

LITURGY
TRAINING
PUBLICATIONS

I would like to express my warmest thanks for their work and help to
Father John Langlois, OP (Washington, D.C.); Monsignor Laurence W. McGrath
(Brighton, Massachusetts); Sister Mary Thomas Noble, OP (Buffalo, New York);
Father Paul Philibert, OP (Fribourg, Switzerland); Ms. Lorie Simmons (Chicago,
Illinois); Ms. Ida Richard (Montreal, Canada); and Ms. Jutta Voss
(Fribourg, Switzerland).

International Copyright © 2004
by Editoriale Jaca Book SpA, Milano
All rights reserved

For the main text
International Copyright © 1993
by Amateca, Lugano, and Editoriale Jaca Book SpA, Milano
All rights reserved

ILLUSTRATED HISTORY OF THE CHURCH © 2006 Archdiocese of Chicago: Liturgy Training Publications,
1800 North Hermitage Avenue, Chicago IL 60622-1161; 1-800-933-1800, fax 1-800-933-7094,
e-mail orders@LTP.org. All rights reserved. See our website at www.LTP.org.

Printed in Milan, Italy.

Library of Congress Control Number: 2006922408

ISBN-10: 1-56854-516-9
ISBN-13: 978-1-56854-516-5
ILHIS

TABLE OF CONTENTS

CHAPTER 9
The Church and the Challenge of the Revolutions

CHAPTER 10
The Church and the Challenge of Ideologies

CHAPTER 11
The Church and the Challenge of Cultures

FROM TEXT TO IMAGE
AND FROM IMAGE TO TEXT

Whatever house you enter,
first say, "Peace to this house!"
(Luke 10:5)

At the far end of the apse of the ancient medieval basilica of San Clemente in Rome, a great mosaic shows the cross of Christ literally grasped by the hand of the Father. (See illustration 41, apex of the cross.) From the foot of the cross issues not simply a few branches of a tree of life, but a luxuriant vine with its enormous banderole of shoots curled into circles. Entwined in the vines are figures of some of the Latin Fathers of the Church. Below, six lambs come out from Bethlehem and six others from Jerusalem to meet the Paschal Victim. In between, alongside the stream of living water flowing from Calvary, are figures peacefully going about their occupations, all within the radiance of the glorious cross. We might see here a symbolic representation of the history of the Church. Although the harmony of the scene is not apparent to the actors, it flows from a source, a center, which in faith they must acknowledge.

*   *   *

The purpose of this book is both modest and ambitious. I hope it will be of use to the general public, providing them with a basic and, I hope, not too tiresome overview of the history of the Roman Church through the twenty centuries of its existence. Consequently, this will be a history of the high points. These events, from challenge to challenge, from shocks and tremors to recovery, through conversion and successive integration, give a kind of rhythm to this tale where the believer will always be able to distinguish between the wheat and the chaff and so discover the finger of God writing on the sands of time.

In comparing this book with a wide range of other manuals, it is well to note that its purpose is not to repeat what has already been so well put by many competent historians. Nor is it an attempt to emulate an encyclopedia; hence, neither charts nor chronologies are included. My approach is multiform and my aim is to complement what is generally offered to students, insisting particularly on the revelatory role of art and proposing the choice of an iconography as a mirror reflecting the spirit of an age.

What you have here is a new enterprise, a discussion of the history of Latin Christianity along two parallel and complementary tracks—a conversation in two voices, each with its own specific qualities. If a written sentence necessarily remains incomplete for reasons of brevity, syntax, and coherence, an image will provide a fuller understanding by suggesting the complexity or the relationships of the historical phenomenon. Images will speak with visual symbols, with color and form, and will be better suited to suggest the dimension of mystery. On the other hand, images also need to be explained by writing, either to be situated within a larger whole, as in the chapters of this history, or to have the meaning of their details spelled out clearly, which is the function of the captions that accompany each of the illustrations. Art in all its forms allows us to *see;* historical narration *explains* and leads us to *reflection*. Both of these ways are necessary in order to understand clearly.

The purpose of this book and its 11 chapters is to observe the unfolding of the centuries by considering the way in which the Church related herself to different civilizations, on the one hand, and dealt with her own crises or temptations, on the other hand. This means both challenges from without and challenges from within. The audacity of this enterprise is not incompatible with the modesty of my project which tries to be neither synthetic nor above all exhaustive since, for example, I treat the Eastern churches and the Protestant churches only insofar as they enter into relation or into conflict with the Roman Church. As an historian, I am often called upon to speak to different types of audiences about the overall picture of the Catholic Church as well as about the details of her evolution. Here, I present what I consider the approach that is most characteristic and most worthy of attention for a first glance. For this reason, I dedicate this book to my students at the University of Fribourg.

The English historian Arnold Toynbee (1889–1975), a man sensitive to religious issues, put forward the idea of a *challenge* as the trigger for the growth or for the decline of civilizations. This challenge, which can be of very different kinds—climate, economy, demography, and so forth—generates a civilization by way of responding to the issues. When the energies of creation, response, or invention begin to diminish, the civilization begins to crumble.

At the end of the nineteenth century, a Belgian historian, Godefroid Kurth, without explicating the theme, applied this principle to the history of the Church in the form of these questions: "How did the Church fulfill her mission? Over the course of nineteen centuries, how did she arrive at understanding the many changing problems that lay before her? Did she know how to speak the language of all those centuries through which she passed, and to familiarize herself with the genius of all the peoples whom she encountered on the way? Was she—is she—really the universal society which contains within herself the whole of civilization, or must she remain only one more ephemeral form in which, in any given moment, humanity will have incarnated its internally changing aspirations?"

Let's be clear about this: the project here is not to try to describe or to rediscover some sort of "Christian civilization" that never changes during its passage through history and its contradictions, even if in the Middle Ages it possessed an unquestionable tangible reality that remains a kind of "creative Utopia." Neither is it a question of seeing how Christianity can *pass through* every civilization, but rather how Christianity can *be penetrated* by them. That is the vocation of the Church: She doesn't cast out her nets from outside as if she existed outside of an Incarnation, but rather she acts from within like yeast in the dough— and this Gospel comparison proves to be perfectly fitting here. Moreover, the challenges that the Church encounters from outside herself are often accompanied or even replaced by temptations that she discovers within herself, which is to say that the holy Church is made up of sinners. These internal challenges are not necessarily sins, but rather values that are lesser, secondary, less pure or simply less adequate for her mission to proclaim a salvation that comes from heaven itself.

If then I borrow from Arnold Toynbee this term of *challenge,* which he considered as one of the springs of the history of civilizations, I use it in a little different sense than he does. Nonetheless, it remains a fact that throughout its history the Church often had to reject the image of humanity or of the city or of herself that the surrounding civilization offered to her, even at the price of some wrenching contradictions.

In the logic of the Incarnation, the Church takes seriously the civilizations that she passes through, immerses herself in them, serves them, and most often loves them. Even at those moments when she found the greatest affinity with the surrounding civilization, often because the Church was at that point socially and intellectually predominant, as in the eleventh to thirteenth centuries, her mission obliges her to keep some distance. In a way, then, the Church lives in the midst of humankind as if not fully living there (1 Corinthians 7:29–31): That will always be held against her. But now, let us begin to retrace the steps of this journey.

1. *Frontispiece representing Christ's Ascension (manuscript Apostolic Library of the Vatican, Vat grec, 1162. Homilies on the Virgin of James of Kokkinobaphos, beginning of 12th century). This miniature integrates the event recalled by Saint Luke (Acts 1: 6–11) with a vision of the Church, represented as a Byzantine-style church building. In the pictorial space, the early Church with the eleven apostles and the Virgin Mary, her eyes lifted toward heaven where Jesus is taken by the angels (Psalm 90,13), is framed together with the eternal throne where Christ is seated in glory with these same apostles.*

THE CHURCH AND THE CHALLENGE OF BECOMING UNIVERSAL IN THE CONTEXT OF JUDAISM, HELLINISM, AND NEO-PAGANISM

At its birth, Christianity seemed destined to become nothing more than a small Jewish sect. It was constituted around the year 800 of the Roman calendar under the emperors Tiberias, Caligula, Claudius, and Nero and formed around the disciples of a wonder-worker named Jesus of Nazareth. The members of this sect, who would have coexisted with the Sadducees and Essenes, might have been called Galileans or Nazarenes were it not for the fact that at Antioch on the Orontes in Syria they had been dubbed Christians, perhaps in derision (Acts 11:26).

The challenge that the Church would face in her first three centuries had been made clear to her by Christ himself. The close of Matthew's Gospel recounts the solemn mandate given by Jesus after His resurrection: "Go therefore and make disciples of all nations, baptizing them in the name of the Father and of the Son and of the Holy Spirit" (Matthew 28:19). On the day of the Ascension, the Church knew that her mission would take her "to the ends of the earth" (Acts 1:8). Henceforth she would pursue her own path, rejecting both Judaism and syncretism.

The challenge was to be met successfully at four junctures: the break with Judaism, the confrontation with the religions and philosophies of the ancient world, the adoption of Christianity by the Roman Empire, and the development of a doctrine confessed by all. The Church would thus discover the basis of her religious, intellectual, cultural, and finally, social universality.

The Dilemma of the Relationship with Israel

In view of the goal of becoming a universal Church, the break with Judaism was not something to be taken for granted. Geographically, because of the Diaspora, the Jews had spread far and wide throughout the Roman Empire long before the destruction of the Temple in the year 70 AD. According to

Philo, a contemporary of Christ, there were no less than a million Jews in the city of Alexandria alone. Under the Emperor Claudius (+54), six million Jews lived in the Empire, with less than a third of these in Palestine.[1] This is why the Apostles, and Saint Paul in particular, went forth to preach in the synagogues of the Diaspora. In Jerusalem itself, the Hellenistic Jews mentioned in the Acts of the Apostles (6:1), having returned from the Diaspora, were reading the Bible in Greek, the new language of the Empire in Asia since the conquests of Alexander. As part of Judaism, the disciples of Christ had at their disposal the trump card of a *religio licita,* officially permitted in the Empire and respected at least in its institutions by the conqueror, and a language universal enough to be qualified as common—*koiné,* that form of Greek in which, moreover, the Gospels would be written.

Judaism did not even really threaten missionary expansion among the pagans as long as a kind of intermediary category was accepted, "proselytes of the door" (because they could not cross the threshold of the Temple), or better, "the God-fearing." Circumcision was not required of these people, nor was total observance of the Law. The great Pharisaic teacher of the period, Hillel, gave this instruction: "Love creatures and lead them to the Torah." Jesus had spoken of the intensity of the Jewish mission. "Pharisees, hypocrites! For you traverse sea and land to make a single proselyte" (Matthew 23:15).

Since this was the case, why do we read in Acts that the Apostles, and in particular Peter and Paul, led the first Christian community toward a break with Israel, amid discussions and even deviations from the preferred line of thought? The movement began, at least on the literary level, with the discourse of Stephen, deacon and protomartyr. His speech was an indictment of the obduracy of the Jews as well as a summary of the history of salvation (Acts 7). Then came Peter's vision at Joppa (Jaffa) which abolished the distinction between clean and unclean (Acts 10), the basis of all the prescriptions

of Deuteronomy and Leviticus. Subsequently, we read of the baptism of the centurion Cornelius, who was described precisely as "a God-fearing man."

Following Paul's preaching among the pagans, a controversy arose about circumcision, relations between the Jews and pagans, and the observance of the Law, all summarized in Acts 15. The "Council of Jerusalem" decided to send an apostolic letter permitting ongoing relations between Christian converts from paganism and Judaism. Their conditions were acceptable to the latter group and avoided scandalizing the former. "It has seemed good to the Holy Spirit and to us," they wrote, "to lay upon you no greater burden than these necessary things." Four exceptions then followed (Acts 15:28–29), which reinforced the rejection of idolatry under any form. This had been the stronghold of Jewish resistance, as witnessed in the book of Daniel and the two books of Maccabees.

Although daily life was marked by Jewish rites, it was not primarily because of these that Judaism posed a challenge for the first Christians. The problem was more properly a theological one. Saint Paul shows this in his letters to the Galatians and later to the Romans. If the value of the Law is conferred by faith (Romans 3:31), by faith "all who are led by the Spirit of God are sons of God"(8:14). A new Israel had been born, one which extended its hand to the former chosen people (10:21) and was ready to incorporate them if they recognized Christ as the Messiah awaited by the Patriarchs and Prophets.

By emphasizing the unique "Israel of God" (Galatians 6:16), Paul resolved, transcended, and overcame, so to say, his powerful dialectical opposition between Jews and Gentiles.[2]

He rejoiced in the new People which would take on another dimension and enter a new era—the Christian era. The theologian, Erik Peterson, a Protestant who joined the Catholic Church in 1929, captured the heart of the newness heralded by Paul. Commenting on Romans 9:24 in Germany in 1933, he wrote: "The predestination of the Church to Glory invites Jews and Gentiles to enter the Church. The vocation of the Gentiles to become part of the People of God thus does away with *the Jewish distinction* between Jews and Gentiles. But by this very fact the Jewish idea of election, whereby only one People is chosen, over and against all other peoples of the world, is transcended . . . The call of the Gentiles to become part of the People of God does not signify simply a numerical increase . . . No, if there is to be a call of the Gentiles, the Jewish idea of election must be transcended. But this is only possible in eschatalogical time. In time as reckoned by this world, Israel alone is and remains the Chosen People, and no pagan peoples can ever be received into the People of God, nor even attempt to recapture the reality of the Chosen People. But the time of the Church is that eschatalogical time that began with the Gentiles' call to become part of the People of God."[3]

Theologians of the second century like Irenaeus, Cyprian, or even Tertullian, would prefer to exalt the *Verus Israel*,[4] which seemed to coincide with the Great Church already established. Saint Paul, however, did not overcome the challenge to universality through exclusion or rejection, but through integration, in a theological vision, even while calling for the rejection of the nationalism tainted with messianism that existed in Palestine.

4 and 5. *From the catacombs of St. Sebastian, Rome. On the first tombstone, right to left: the "labarum," which combines the Chi and the Rho, initials of* Christos, *the fish* (ikhthus, *in Greek, initials of Jesus Christ Son and Savior), and finally the anchor of mercy, combined with the letter* Tau, *symbol of the cross. The other inscription represents, as expressed by the inscribed text,* Siricus in peace, *standing in an attitude of prayer in eternal life.*

6. *The apostle Paul, part of a diptych from the 4th century representing Peter and Paul (Museum of Sacred Art in the Vatican Apostolic Library). The iconographic tradition is already established: the Apostle of the Gentiles is depicted with a long face, a large forehead, and bald.*

4

5

2 and 3. *Synagogue in Dura Europos. In this city on the shore of the Euphrates that was a fortress of the Seleucids, then later a Roman fortress, even later captured by the Persians and abandoned by its inhabitants circa 260, was found, in 1921, a remarkable ensemble of religious monuments: pagan temples, a synagogue, and a Christian baptistry. The synagogue, built in 200 of our era and renovated in 244, has the peculiarity of possessing an ensemble of biblical scenes, figurative contrary to Jewish tradition, but executed with the permission of Rabbi Johanan.*

Represented on the west wall (2) (above): the destruction of the temple of Dagon when the Philistines brought in the Ark of the Covenant (1 Samuel 5:1-5) and beneath it, Pharaoh ordering the midwives to kill the male children of the Hebrews (Exodus 1: 16). (3) (above): the consecration of the temple (Numbers 7:1) with the seven-branch candelabrum, animals for the sacrifice, Aaron, the first priest of the Old Law, and trumpet players. (Below): Mordecai's triumph (Esther 6:11) led by Haman, his enemy

6

7

8

The mystery of the call of the pagans, which manifested the universality of the salvation offered by Christ, was profoundly linked to the mystery of Israel. This carried with it the possibility of formidable dangers and called for discernment.

Confrontation with the Religions and Thought of Antiquity

On several occasions, the Acts of the Apostles shows us early Christian evangelization grappling with the exaggerated religiosity of certain popular groups. Take, for example, the enthusiastic welcome given to Paul and Barnabas at Lystra. There, taking them for Zeus and Hermes, the priest and the crowds wanted to offer sacrifice to them (Acts 14:12–14). Gospel preaching had to adapt to the expectations of the pagans, presenting the novelty of Christ with simplicity.[5]

Was Christianity in continuity with ancient cults, or did it, on the contrary, mark a profound break with former attitudes,

ways of being, and behavior? Before answering this question, let us read what Franz Cumont, the great scholar of the history of religions, wrote in 1905. "Suppose that modern Europe should see the faithful deserting Christian churches to worship Allah or Brahma, to follow the precepts of Confucius or Buddha, or to adopt the maxims of *Shinto.* Imagine the great confusion pervading all the races of the world, with Arab mullahs, Chinese scholars, Japanese bonzes, Thibetan lamas, and Hindu pandits all simultaneously preaching fatalism and predestination, ancestor worship and devotion to divinized sovereigns, pessimism and deliverance through annihilation. Picture all these priests erecting in our cities exotic temples in which to celebrate their various rites. This fantasy, which may yet come to be, would closely approximate the religious incoherence of the ancient world before Constantine."[6]

The religiosity of the ancient world, stemming from a proliferation of Asiatic religions almost as a kind of reverse invasion by those who had been conquered by Rome, was

7 and 8. Woman (Florence, Museum of Archaeology) and young man with a golden crown (Moscow, Pushkin Museum). These portraits found in the Fayoum region of Egypt represent the deceased and are painted on the sarcophagi. They are the first expression in painting of the human glance, showing human feeling and anticipating the art of icons.

9. Sarcophagus of a deceased couple (Trinquetaille, Museum of Christian Art, Arles). (Above): Around the central medallion, scenes from the Old and New Testament are depicted. To the left, the creation of Adam and Eve with God between the Holy Spirit and the Son who extends his hand over Eve's head, and, still at the left, the Wisemen with their offerings to Jesus.

9

10

10. Sarcophagus of Anastasia, said to be from Constantine II, from the crypt of Saint Honoratus of Arles, in marble from the end of the 4th century; it was used to bury Bishop Aeonius (+502). The upper part, which is the lid of the sarcophagus, represents the busts of the deceased surrounded by winged figures. The anterior face presents a frieze with the crowned cross in glory; at its foot lie the stricken guards surrounded by the apostles.

both an opportunity and a danger for the religion of Christ. Indeed "the Orontes had flowed into the Tiber," as Juvenal exclaimed (+140). All sorts of mystery cults and their bizarre rites were tolerated. Why make an exception of Christianity? Moreover, had not the Jewish religion, with all its intransigence, won recognition in the Empire as "a licit religion"?

And yet, Christians were not about to be accepted. According to Tacitus, they had no religion. They were "atheists" in the etymological sense: they had no gods. Their "misanthropy" made them a race apart that did not fit into any category in the ancient city and was beyond redemption. Pagans, who could tolerate anything, became intolerant because Christians could not tolerate any other god than their own. A. J. Festugière, OP, gets to the heart of the matter when he asks: Did the pagan contemporaries of the early Christians take no notice of the incredible religious revolution that was being proposed to them—to believe in a God who loved men—or did they recoil from this intellectual scandal?[7]

A certain type of historiography is fond of finding traces of paganism in the first centuries of the primitive Church. There may have been flaws in rites and behavior. However, we have to insist on the rupture that took place with the arrival of the Christian ideal and with the social revolution following the conversion of the Emperor to the new religion.

"Christians often neglected Christian virtues, but Christian attitudes and rewards were publicized to the point where Christians could not simply forget them. They changed the ways in which people regarded life's great encounters, between man and woman and also between people and their gods. They changed attitudes to life's one certainty: death. They also changed the degree of freedom with which people could acceptably choose what to think and believe."[8]

Thus, the conversion of a pagan to Christianity called for renunciations that cut him off from his milieu and ran counter to his education and inmost sensibilities. Must he not give up

11. Mural painting from Herculaneum, from the cult of Isis. At the door of the temple, between the statues of the sphinxes, three priests hold sacred objects. In the center, stands the priest of the sacrifice, armed with a sword. The assistants stir up the fire while the participants extend their hands as a sign of prayer and participation. The flute player accompanies the liturgy.

11

13

12

12. Sidon, Asia Minor, 4th century, marble bas-relief. Mithras, god of light and fire, surrounded by the signs of the zodiac, throws to the ground a bull, symbol of evil and blind force.

13. Silver coat hook from Parabiago (end of 4th century, Milan, city archeological collections). With a diameter of 40 centimeters, this hook represents the mystic nuptials between Cybele and Attis transported in a chariot pulled by four lions. Everything needed for the prosperity of agriculture: seasons, sun and moon, earth, rivers and sea, is rendered symbolically.

14. Dura Europos, votive plaque, 1st century, shows Aflad, son of the god Hadad. He belongs to the pantheon of the pre-Islamic Syrian religion, a god of storms and rain, (a fertility god), mentioned in Zechariah 12:11. He is close to the Baals, whose cult was mocked and condemned by the prophets in the Bible.

14

15

15. *Relief from a sculptural fragment representing Dionysos (Petra, Archeological Museum) who might also be Dusara, principal god of the Nabataean pantheon, his head adorned with vine branches. The commercial civilization of the Nabataeans (sedentary desert nomads in today's Jordan) became strong in the 5th century* BC *until their subjection by Trajan in 106.*

vengeance, luxury, disordered indulgence, magic, and superstition?[9]

Christian authors insisted on a clear understanding of pagan religions and demythologized them. Firmicus Maternus of the fourth century was a master of astrology and had written a treatise on it. Once a Christian, however, he inveighed against "the errors of profane religions." The four divinized elements came under his attack: water or Isis; fire, adored by the followers of Mithra; earth or Cybele, the mother goddess; and air, associated with the cult of Juno, the heavenly goddess.

It is possible that the oriental cults contributed to preparing the soil where Christianity was to flourish by accustoming Western piety to a daily solar or seasonal rhythm. As some have asserted, they may have inculcated the notion of a suffering and saving god such as Tammouz, the Babylonian god so similar to the Greek Adonis. They also may have opened the Western mind to the significance of mystical or "occult" piety.[10]

Beyond popular religiosity, there was the intellectual pagan world. The apostles had wanted to reach this world and win it over. This was the role of the most brilliant and cultured of

them, Paul of Tarsus, as we see in his famous sermon at Athens, which even then was the cultural capital of the ancient world. The year was 50 AD. In his learned and skilled manner, Paul quoted the poets Epimenides of Knossus and Aratos. The latter had been quoted by Cleanthes, the Stoic philosopher of the third century BC and author of a "Hymn to Zeus." His attempt to persuade his hearers to recognize in Jesus their "unknown god" (Acts 17:23) failed, however, when he brought up faith in the resurrection of the dead, so foreign apparently to the ideas of the bystanders crowding around him (Acts 17:21). Yet a small group of Athenians did meet with him later, and he had great success at Corinth. Since the sensibilities and origins of the Corinthians had been more influenced by the Orient, they had, perhaps, a greater aptitude for religion than the rational or rationalistic Greeks.[11]

Thus, beginning with Chapters 17 and 18 of Acts we see Christianity engaged in an intellectual dialogue with the two cities that represented in a symbolic way the philosophical side of Hellenism on the one hand and its religious sensibility on the other: Athens and Corinth. For Luke, "the nations"—the

16. Temple of Apollo at Corinth. The city of Corinth, already a commercial center during the Hellenic period, had the reputation during the Roman epoch of being a place where ideas were exchanged the same way market goods were. At the Temple of Apollo where a god of the arts was worshipped, conversions to Christianity were numerous, and the community experienced the conflicts that Paul attempted to settle in his two epistles.

17. Mosaic, 1st century Pompeii (Naples, National Archeological Museum): The Seven Philosophers. From left to right are represented: Heraclitus Ponticus, giving a speech; Speusippus, Plato's nephew and his successor, Plato himself, who points to the celestial globe; maybe a disciple of Plato who ordered the mosaic; Eudoxius of Cnidus; Senocrates, Plato's second successor, and finally Aristotle.

Gentiles—were not lacking in a certain joyous, natural knowledge of God, because they could give thanks when their hearts had been "satisfied with food and gladness" (Acts 14:17). In graver and more solemn tones, Saint Paul affirmed this natural knowledge of God. "Ever since the creation of the world, his invisible nature, namely, his eternal power and deity, has been clearly perceived in the things that have been made" (Romans 1:20). In claiming to be wise, had men become fools, had they become futile in their thinking (Romans 1:22–23)? Or can we find a "preparation for the Gospel" in the efforts of the wise? The debate was heated in the early days of Christianity, and has in fact continued so throughout history.

Theophilus of Antioch, in his "Apologia to Autolycus" at the end of the second century, and Tertullian, at the beginning of the third century, rejected pagan culture. However, a different attitude was seen earlier with Justin, who after a long intellectual journey had been converted to Christianity around 130. Having in a sense exhausted the possibilities of the philosophical systems of his time, he felt "a fire kindled in his soul"—the Truth of Christ. For him, this meant fulfillment rather than a rupture. The philosophies he was familiar with were incomplete, but what they possessed of truth and justice were in fact "the seeds of the truth." It was the Word of God, the Logos, who had from eternity sown these seeds of light and truth.[12] Denounced as a Christian by a philosopher, perhaps of the school of the Cynics, Justin died a martyr in the year 165 during the reign of the Emperor Marcus Aurelius who, imbued with stoicism, was a philosopher as well.

Justin's approach was admirable and it is important to weigh its significance. A persistent calumny has tried to claim that Christian apologists, among whom Justin is included, were not the first forgers eager to adapt, betray, and reduce the Gospel to Greek philosophy. They were not working toward conciliation, however, but toward the integration of the wisdom of the ancients into the mystery of the Word of God. What was at stake was nothing less than the universality of the message: the meeting of the reality of thought and of the world with the reality of the Christian mystery. The affirmation is ontological: it has to do with what we believe about the very nature of man. Every human being, because human, has kinship with the Creator Word, and is therefore empowered to receive the Word, to be capable of God. This tremendous theme would be taken up by Clement of Alexandria (+c. 215), who presented Christ as the Teacher of the moral life.

These authors were therefore very much aware of all these "preparations for the Gospel," to borrow again the expression of a later historian/theologian, Eusebius of Caesarea (c. 340);

18. *The Theater of Dionysius (Bacchus for the Romans), in Athens. The god of wine was also the god of the theater and was worshipped with special attention in the large city of Athens where the Bacchanalia were celebrated, days of orgies and release.*

yet they met with pagan rejection. In the middle of the second century, Celsus, whom Origen refuted, had reaffirmed against the Christians the "True Logos."

Actually, early Christian theology had adapted the Semitic religious categories of the Old Testament to the cultures of its time. The Stoic terminology that we find in Pauline thought helped Christian intellectuals to account, for example, for the ineffable generation of the Word. Plato would naturally have had an influence on Christian thought. A theologian as profoundly biblical as Origen (+254) was indebted to the Neo Platonism of his period for his doctrine of the Logos. Central to the research of the Fathers of the Church was the discovery of a "Christian Plato" seen above all in the *Timaeus.*[13]

Primitive Christianity did, in fact, take great care to avoid anything that looked like contamination or syncretism. From a philosophical viewpoint, it had to struggle against a most subtle and dangerous enemy, Gnosticism, with its multiple ramifications. Irenaeus, bishop of Lyons (+c. 200), referred to it as "that bed of poisonous toadstools" in his *Treatise against Heresies,* in which he affirmed all the great Christian principles in opposition to the recurring dualism of human thought. In the following century, Origen fought with all his might against the infiltration of Gnosticism. Reading his exegesis of Saint John, we see the difference between the clear teaching of salvation in Christ and the syncretistic dreams of a Gnosticism which was continually cropping up.[14]

There was constant tension, then, between the discernment needed in order to avoid an insidious infiltration of doctrines incompatible with Revelation, and a sympathetic attentiveness to what could prefigure Christ. The Sibyl, Apollo's prophetess, with her mysterious oracles, remains the poetic symbol of all that prefigures Christ.[15] Christian art illustrates here for us early Christianity's efforts to achieve integration.

By way of example we might take the representation of Christ drawing all people to Himself that is painted on a ceiling in the catacomb of Saint Calixtus in Rome. He is depicted as Orpheus, a poet and musician charming the animals, son of eloquence, with two doves perched in a nearby

19. Coin from the Roman Republic representing the Sibyl (Rome, Roman National Museum). The Sybils were soothsayers or prophetesses, about ten in number, who were recognized in the Empire and played an important role in pagan religious life. The Sibyl from the city of Cumes is exalted by Virgil (Aeneid 6, 77–102), and the Latin poet, in his fourth eclogue, made her pronounce an oracle on a child who "makes the golden race spring up," an oracle that the Christian tradition applied to Christ.

20. Monumental block at the entrance of the funeral chamber of the tomb of Wardian, Roman epoch (Alexandria Museum). The bust of the god of the shepherds is located in a rustic sanctuary surrounded by metal grills. To the right, a shepherd carries his ewe on his shoulders.

19

20

21 and 23. The Good Shepherd. (21) Marsa Matruh statue (4th century) (Greco-Roman Museum, Alexandria) who carries the shepherd staff or crook (pedum). (23) Mosaic pavement (Aquilaea, South Aula Teodoriana) that combines the Gospel parable with one about Orpheus and his lyre and with the poetic image from Psalm 42,1 (Hebrew) summing up the work of the Redemption: "This Good Shepherd found the lost sheep; carried it on his shoulders, shoulders that bore the wood of the Cross, and after having taken hold of it, took it back to the heaven" (Homily of Gregory Nazianzen).

21

22

23

22. *Mosaic from the 3rd century, found in the caves of the Vatican. Christ is represented as a solar divinity. The Roman emperor, following the spread of solar cults coming from the East, took the title "Unconquered Sun" (sol invictus), but the Christian artist indicates that his resurrection allows it to apply to Christ. The horses are symbols of strength, but the wheel probably also evokes Elijah's chariot (2 Kings 2:11).*

tree, emphasizing the resemblance to the Good Shepherd. We find the same thing at Ravenna in the mausoleum of Galla Placida, around 450.

When we realize the symbolic importance of Orpheus in Hellenism, as the victor over the forces of evil in the world beyond, we can measure Christianity's power of integration in finding in him a poetic prefiguring of the One who rises again from hell.[16] Again, we can think of the Christ-Helios in the Vatican cemetery. Henceforth, "Great Pan" is dead. The man-beast has been replaced by the Man-God.[17] It is the end of the pagan world.

Christians and the Empire

Before the recognition of Christianity by the Empire, Christians truly had to use this world as though they used it not (1 Corinthians 7:31).[18] There were many things in pagan society that were repugnant to them, but which they either tolerated or ignored with a kind of social nonconformity. However, they could not bring themselves to sacrifice to idols and to the emperor, divinized since the time of Augustus. This was the very test imposed on them by Pliny the Younger when he was governor of Bithynia.

Throughout the history of the Church, we encounter this radical impossibility of accepting the divinization of the state, whatever it might be. Christianity has never preached rebellion against civil authority, as is witnessed in Romans 13. There was simply a desire to share in the peace of the Empire. The only thing Christianity could not accept was idolatry, even a purely formal or benign type. For Emperor Decius in 250, however, and for Diocletian in 304, this refusal was seen as an attack on the dignity, and therefore the security, of the State. It was a period of persecution—not continual, for there were respites—but carried on in bloody outbursts. Yet, as Tertullian said, "the blood of martyrs is the seed of Christians."[19]

The development of Christianity went hand in hand with the growth of imperial pretensions in the religious domain. From Nerva (+98) to Septimus Severus (+211), people went so far as to deify the emperor during his lifetime. Rumors circulated about Christians and their so-called secret and bloody gatherings and stirred up public opinion, giving rise to constant, systematic accusations of treachery.

There were several great waves of official persecution.[20] Early Christian historiographers such as Lactantius and

24

25

24. A portrait of Virgil, Codex Vergilus Romanus, 6th century (Apostolic Library of the Vatican). The poet, in his Roman toga edged with purple, the imperial color, holds in his hand a scroll of his works, probably the Aeneid, whose episodes were re-read by the Christians as an announcement of the foundation of the eternal Rome.

25. Roman Forum, Arch of Septimus Severus. It was erected in 203 to honor this emperor and his two sons who were seated on the upper part of the arch, on a bronze chariot pulled by six horses, to celebrate their victory over the Parthians.

26. Lyon, Roman amphitheater with a stake fixed at the presumed location of the martyrdom of Saint Pothin, Lyon's first bishop, and of Saint Blandina, a young slave, and of forty-six other Christians, probably in 177.

Orosius, in his *History against the Pagans* (417), tended to number them at ten, to match the ten plagues of Egypt.

The first attack came from Nero. In the year 64, he blamed the Christians for the fire that devastated the city of Rome. The repression did not apparently continue outside of Rome, but it targeted Christians for public blame for the first time. The martyrdom of Peter and Paul dates from the years following this event.

Domitian persecuted both Jews and Christians in 94 and 95 AD. He sentenced Flavia Domitilla of the imperial family to execution, as well as Nereus and Achilleus, who were perhaps her servants, and Manius Glabrio, who had been consul in 91. This indicates that Christianity had already penetrated into the upper echelon.

After the threats and trials revealed in the letter from Pliny the Younger to Trajan in 112, and in spite of the tolerance of Hadrian and Antoninus the Pious, many isolated cases of martyrdom can be seen. It was under the Stoic Emperor Marcus Aurelius that the persecution of the martyrs of Lyons took place in 177.

But it was only with Decius that persecution became general and systematic. In January 250, he ordered the execution of Fabian, Bishop of Rome, and decreed in June that all subjects of the Empire must offer sacrifice to the official gods under pain of death. The measure obviously targeted chiefly the Christians. Many apostatized or obtained certificates of sacrifice to the gods. Pressure relaxed after Decius' death in June, 251. His successor, Valerian, forbade Christians to

26

assemble in 257 and had a large number of bishops and laity arrested. Gallienus suspended these measures in 260.

Finally, the last great blow came from Diocletian, who had shown a certain tolerance on coming to power in 284. On February 23, 303, at Nicomedia, he ordered the destruction of the churches and the scriptures, a decision influenced by Galerian, whom he had raised to power. In the following year, a general persecution took place. This anti-Christian policy continued after Diocletian's death, particularly in the East. In 311, Galerian, who was near death, revoked the edicts.

The situation changed totally when the emperor—if not the Empire—was won over to the Church. The era of the martyrs came to an end, although the evangelization of the nations and the great conflicts with secular power would result in violence and deaths throughout the history of the Church.

There are wonderful records of the period of persecution in the Acts of the Martyrs, resulting in the martyrs rapidly becoming the object of veneration. The assimilation of the martyr to the suffering Christ found expression in poetic symbols. Saint Ignatius of Antioch (+107) compared the chains used to drag the prisoner to death to "spiritual pearls."[21] Polycarp (+155), bishop of Smyrna, likened them to diadems.[22]

Saint Clement (+96) in his Letter to the Corinthians did not hesitate to pray at length for the prosperity and health of those who ruled the Empire, as seen in this text that followed closely upon the persecution of Domitian. "Make us subject, Lord, to your all powerful and holy Name, as well as to those who govern and guide us in this world. It is you, Lord, who by

27

27. Rome, San Clemente. Mass of this holy bishop of Rome, considered the fourth successor of Peter. The fresco is from the 11th century and represents, to the left, the donors Beno de Rapiza and his wife Maria Macelleria, who paid for the restoration of the church after the fire in 1094. The fresco on the right recalls the punishment of the pagan Sisinius, who became blind after trying to force his wife Theodora, who was Christian, to leave the Church.

your magnificent and ineffable might have given them power to exercise their authority. Knowing that it is from you that they have received the glory and honor we see them enjoying, may we be subject to them and never oppose your will. Grant them, Lord, health, peace, concord, and stability, so that they may exercise without hindrance the sovereignty you have entrusted to them."[23]

This prayer of Christian loyalty to the Empire, which is equivalent to the forgiveness of enemies, shows how generations of Christians desired peace and concord. They would not obtain it until the conversion of Constantine to Christianity.

When the Emperor Constantine defeated his rival Maxentius at the Milvian Bridge on October 28, 312, he adopted as his military emblem, whether through self-interest or conviction, the monogram of Christ, the *Labarum*.[24] This event, rather than the official date of his personal conversion, signaled that the "universal" Roman Empire had become Christian. Christianity definitively emerged from hiding and from the glory of martyrdom. It could now enjoy the "Constantinian peace" and develop its institutions in broad daylight. Eusebius of Caesarea, one of the earliest Church historians and a rather indiscreet eulogist of the Emperor Constantine, sang the praises of the new era of this triumphant peace which allowed the Church to carry on her spiritual mission.

In 313, Constantine and Licinius (+325), his pagan co-emperor, granted to Christians, in a document incorrectly called the "Edict of Milan," freedom of worship and the restitution of their confiscated goods. From 324 on, when Constantine became the sole emperor, the Church of Christ was recognized throughout the vast territories subject to Rome. The new capital, Constantinople, or the city of Constantine, founded in 330, would be the Christian city par excellence. In ancient Rome, the construction of the great basilicas began.

There is a historiographical myth that attributes to Constantine the first decadence of the Church, which, according to the idea, was too well "established" in this world not to fall victim to the corruption of wealth. This myth, originating it seems in a few verses of Dante's *Inferno* (19:115), where he alludes to Constantine's legendary donation to Pope Sylvester, has become commonplace, droning on through the years ever since.

Ah, Constantine, what evil fruit did bear
Not thy conversion, but that dowry broad
Thou on the first rich Father didst confer.[25]

30

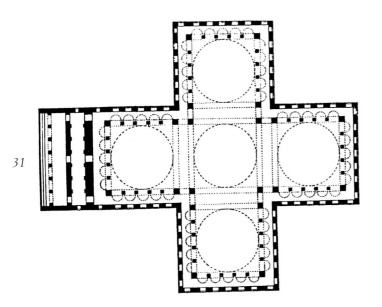

31

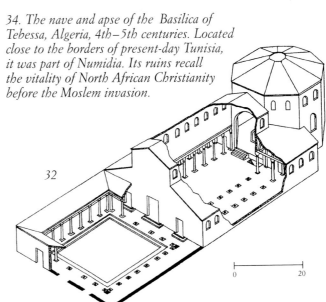

32

34. The nave and apse of the Basilica of Tebessa, Algeria, 4th–5th centuries. Located close to the borders of present-day Tunisia, it was part of Numidia. Its ruins recall the vitality of North African Christianity before the Moslem invasion.

0   20

33

34

35. *The triumph of Christ and of the Church (Rome, Basilica of Santa Sabina, historic door of the 5th century). Contemporary with the construction of the church, this door was initially composed of 28 panels, alternating scenes from the Old and the New Testament. In this one, the Church on earth is surrounded by Saints Peter and Paul who lift over her head a sort of halo; notice the stars, the moon and the sun. In the upper part, the triumphant Christ in a mandorla surrounded by symbols of the four evangelists is the alpha and the omega.*

We should note, first, that the Church faced the threat of a return of the fire of persecution at the time of the apostasy of the Emperor Julian (361–363). It was only with the reign of Theodosius and the banning of paganism in 391, that the Church finally knew true supremacy. The "established" Church, if such it was, was actually Theodosian rather than Constantinian. But we should note above all that the Church, in her teaching and in her attitude toward authority, did not change. Grateful and admiring though she might be, she had acquired the right to be bold as well. The Fathers of the fourth century spoke with incredible severity in the face of social injustices and even of political crimes. Here we might recall the words of Ambrose of Milan in 390, rebuking Theodosius for the massacre perpetrated at Thessalonica! The Church had become the partner of the Empire.

The "imperial" peace was decisive for the rooting of Christianity, the training of the baptized, the ratification of doctrine, and the spread of conversions, all of which advanced a deeper universality. The advance was also evident, as a sort of counterbalance, in the development of monasticism. This was not merely a substitute for martyrdom. Saint Anthony the Great, father of monks, withdrew into the Egyptian desert long before the end of the third century. The flowering of

36. The Four Crowned Saints (Rome, Chapel of Saint Sylvester). In this narrative cycle concerning Constantine and Pope Sylvester (1246), Constantine offers the insignia of his imperial authority to Sylvester. These frescoes belong to the legend of the Donation of Constantine, an apocryphal document (9th century) that claimed territorial privileges given to the successor of Peter as bishop of Rome by the first Christian emperor.

37. The San Vittore Chapel "with the golden sky" (Milan, Basilica of Saint Ambrose). Saint Ambrose seems to be wearing the toga or the chasuble.

38. Saint Paul of Thebes and Saint Anthony the Great (fresco from Saint Macarius monastery in the region of Scete, Wadi Natrum, Northern Egypt). The holy hermit-founders of the Christian monastic life are represented with arms upraised in prayer.

38

monasticism demonstrated, rather, Christianity's capacity for detachment now that it was free from harassment. And, despite the fierce opposition of rigorists, the Church also had the ability to forgive and reintegrate those who had formerly lacked the courage to resist persecution.

In the East, Church and Empire would ally themselves, or tear each other apart, so that Christianity might enjoy another kind of universality, that of thought and of the confession of faith.

The Universality of the Catholic Faith

When evangelization began in the apostolic age, the "good fight of the faith" or the "good profession" of faith that Paul had recommended to Timothy (1 Timothy 6:12), was carried on through preaching and teaching. Questions about the life of the Church relating to faith, such as the reconciliation of Christians who had betrayed their baptismal promises during the persecutions, or again the validity of Baptism conferred by heretics, were treated collegially at Rome, Antioch, or Carthage. Heretics and schismatics were condemned.

In the West, in the years following the conversion of Constantine, bishops representing more and more regions were brought together in "councils" or "synods," such as the council held in Arles in 314.

Then came the period of "ecumenical" councils which also responded to the challenge of universality: the formulation of affirmations concerning the entire Church. It is impossible within the scope of this book to describe the unfolding of the seven councils that all Christian confessions recognize as universal.[26] Their main lines can be found in textbooks dealing with the Trinity and Christology. All ecumenical councils, in fact, either directly or indirectly, judged and condemned heresies regarding the divinity or humanity of Christ, or the unity of His person. We can grasp their universality and their "ecumenical thrust" from the Greek word *oikouméné,* meaning "all the inhabited world."

The Council of Chalcedon in 451 was the first to give the title "ecumenical" to the assembly held at Nicea in 325, "the great and holy Council."[27] We find this word in the synodal letter announcing to the Bishop of Rome, Leo the Great, that the Council had adopted his theological conclusions on the two natures and one Person of Christ. In its "Definition of Faith," the Council described itself as a "great, holy, and ecumenical Synod . . . assembled at Chalcedon, a metropolis in the province of Bithynia."[28]

Although at Nicea Eastern bishops were greatly in the majority, the Council could be considered an assembly of the universal episcopate because the West was represented by the two legates of the Bishop of Rome. Thus, in the anathema that follows its Creed, the Council of Nicea presents itself as "the Catholic and apostolic Church." It was indeed the faith of the entire Church that the great Athanasius would defend in the midst of so many trials.

The Council of Constantinople was also "canonized" by Chalcedon along with its Creed, which had confirmed that of Nicea. The Cappodocian Fathers Gregory of Nyssa and Gregory of Nazianzus took part in it. The Council proceeded in the midst of great confusion. How could an assembly that was not ecumenical either in intention or in fact become so? "A kind of universal consensus of the Church recognized in the Council of Constantinople this retroactive ecumenicity."[29]

At Ephesus, the legates from Rome were present. Nestorius was condemned here "by the authority of the apostolic See and the unanimous (*consonans*) decision of the bishops."[30] At Chalcedon, Leo's role was predominant. The Pope sent three legates who this time would preside over the Council, and he presented in his letter to the patriarch Flavian a doctrine that

39

40

he judged should be "accepted by the universal Church." Actually, the celebrated Christological definition of the Council was the object of numerous contestations and was ignored by entire sections of Eastern Churches. It became, however, the touchstone of orthodoxy up to the seventh century, as we see in the struggle against monothelitism of Maximus the Confessor, for example.

The case of Constantinople II is very odd, since it was celebrated in the absence of Pope Vigilius, yet was convoked by the Emperor Justinian. It was therefore only later on that Rome acceded to the definitions of Constantinople II, that is, to the consensus of the other Churches. Constantinople III was recognized without problems, having been preceded by the dramatic events that ended with the martyrdom of Pope Martin I in 655.

As for the Second Council of Nicea on sacred images, it was certainly accepted by the Pope but its ecumenical character as well as its teaching was challenged by Charlemagne and his theologians. It is interesting to note that Nicea II, in opposing the iconoclastic pseudo-council of Hieria in 754, refuted Hieria's ecumenical character and thus clarified the conditions for universality. It was stated that "the Bishop of

41

Rome should 'collaborate' in a Council by sending legates or a letter, and that the other Patriarchs should give their consent." It is, moreover, in the interpretation of Nicea II in the East that we find the origin of the theory of the "Pentarchy," whereby the ecumenical character of a council was established by the consent of the five Patriarchs.[31]

The turbulent, dramatic—complicated, if you will— history of ecumenical councils, illustrates the development of the Church through two thousand years and shows how the universality of the faith must be unceasingly built up, redis-covered, and discerned. The Latin West also endeavored, dur-ing these first centuries, to provide criteria for this universality and assure the means of its preservation.

Saint Vincent of Lerins (+ c. 450) in his *Commonitorium*, written in 434, sought to determine the conditions of the true faith which rested upon the true interpretation of Sacred Scripture. It is in this text that he enumerates the three con-ditions of his celebrated "canon": Catholic tradition consists of whatever has been believed everywhere, always, and by all Christians (*ubique, semper, ab omnibus*).[32] Here we have a way of transcending the geographical notion of universality and of understanding it rather as "catholicity," just as the idea of

41. Apotheosis of the Cross and of the Church (Rome, San Clemente, mosaic of the apse and triumphal arch). Realized in the 12th century, it gathers together an almost excessive assortment of symbols of the history of salvation. The cross is in the center with Mary and John, and God's hand points to it. Twelve doves cover it, symbol of the peace that is the fruit of the cross. The vine branches that seem to spring from the burning bush enfold the Doctors of the Church, many persons of all kinds who are God's people, and some animals, because creation, too, is renewed. Below, twelve sheep surround the mystical Lamb while the Latin inscription combines Luke 2:14 and Revelation 4:9.

42

42. Istanbul, exterior of Santa Sophia. The basilica of the Holy
Wisdom, who is Christ, was built at the order of the Emperor
Justinian and consecrated in 538. It is one of the most perfect
examples of Byzantine architecture, with its dome and 40 windows
that light the ensemble. It was transformed into a mosque when
the Turks conquered Constantinople in 1453.

43

43. Lerins. View of the island of St. Honoratus near the medieval
tower. Around 419, Saint Honoratus built a monastery on this
island in the Bay of Cannes that had a considerable influence,
particularly because of Saint Vincent of Lerins and Saint Caesarius,
bishop of Arles.

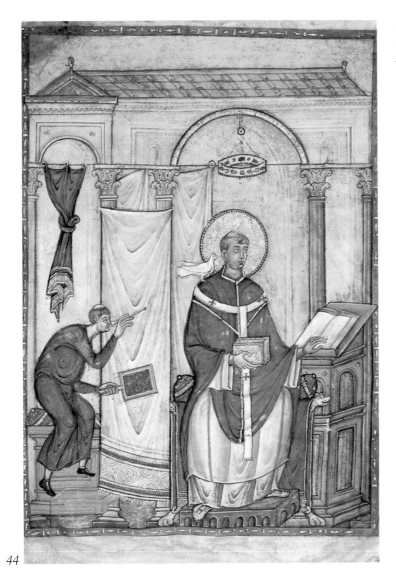

44

45. *Manuscript Vindob. 324,* Tabula peutingeriana *(Vienna, National Library). Detail from a map showing Rome as a feminine figure holding the attributes of sovereignty. She is* Caput mundi, *"head of the world."*

45

44. *Registry of Pope Gregory the Great (Manuscript of the State Library, Trier, 983, correspondence collection). The pope, wearing the chasuble and pallium and showing his monastic tonsure, inspired by the Holy Spirit represented by a dove, dictates to a cleric one of his numerous letters through which he governed the Latin Church and sustained his missionary enterprises.*

ecumenism in conciliar matters is broader than the simple representation of the bishops of the entire world. Beyond the opinions of schools or theologians, there is a catholic faith characterized by the tradition of what has been believed in the universality of space, time, and unanimity.

The means of discerning this "catholicity" of faith are diverse and encompass very varied forms such as prayer,[33] and sacred art, the bearer of faith. The question still stands: who is ultimately responsible for declaring in a sovereign manner the object of this discernment? In the West, the Petrine principle, so influential in the history of the Church, surfaced at this time.[34]

Gregory the Great (+604) claimed for himself and for all bishops of Rome the universal title that "had been given them by the venerable Council of Chalcedon."[35] The role of the Papacy, already preeminent from the time of Leo, was to acquire considerable weight in the Church's consciousness henceforth. According to traditional historiography, this marked the beginning of the Middle Ages.

With Gregory we are already in a new era of Church history, which will depend on what has been achieved, sometimes at great cost in blood and tears, in order to meet the challenge of universality. According to Lactantius, Rome had been "the City which conserves and sustains all." But Rome, the imperial City, the head of the Empire, was no longer herself at the time of Gregory, a native of the city and its most illustrious citizen. For the Church had already entered into the era of a new challenge, that of the Barbarians.

1

1. Missorium, silver platter for serving at table, found in Badajoz, ancient Roman city in Spain, celebrating the Emperor Theodosius, a halo around his head. He is surrounded by the Augusti, by Arcadius and Honorius, his sons, who shared his power. Theodosius is the last emperor who reigned first successively, then, simultaneously, in the East and the West from 379 to 395. Baptized when he became emperor, he consolidated the supremacy of Christianity as the religion of the Empire, even accepting the penance imposed by Saint Ambrose in 390 after the massacre at Thessalonica.

2. Hypothetical reconstruction of Hadrian's Wall. Hadrian was emperor from 117 to 138. This long defensive line, incessantly reinforced, covered more than 500 km from the North Sea to the Danube.

2

THE CHURCH AND THE CHALLENGE OF THE BARBARIANS

If we fix the reign of Theodosius (379–395) as the date of Christianity's real integration into the Empire, we see that the Church had very little time in which to enjoy the *pax romana.* The barbarians camping impatiently at the frontiers of the imperial state became more and more of a threat, not so much in themselves as because they were being driven forward by the Huns, who had come from the steppes to settle on the Danube. Preceded by the Visigoths in 376, Vandals, Sarmatians, Alani, and Suebi crossed the Rhine near Mainz at the beginning of the fifth century.

Who were these tribes whom we call barbarians? We still call them that, the name the Greeks, and later the Romans, gave to everyone except themselves. Indeed, we have to distinguish several succeeding waves of them. Two centuries before our era and two centuries after, Germanic tribes were kept beyond the frontier of the Empire, at its gates, symbolized by the *limes,* or fortified trenches by means of which Hadrian separated them from the Roman world. But already infiltrations and migrations had led to these "Germans" serving in the army. Then from the fifth to the sixth century there were tidal advances called "the great invasions." This was followed by the slower advance of the Slavs, while the Vikings and Muslim Saracens made brutal onslaughts in repeated fits and starts. Meanwhile, the first wave had been incorporated in the birth of a new world that was to grow and ripen into medieval Christianity.

Here again the choice to incorporate the barbarians was not made without rifts, without nostalgia even, nor without the dizziness of a leap into the unknown. Faith dictated this choice, which Western history would have to ratify, and we know now that Western history itself was determined by the decision. Reciprocity was at work. We must look in greater detail at this new risk and response to the challenge of the barbarians, every bit as audacious as the preceding one.

A Time of Bewilderment

Theodosius had succeeded in placing at his service, Alaric, chief of the Goths. But Theodosius's son, Honorius, now emperor of the West, after lengthy political and financial negotiations with Alaric, yielded to the game of intrigue and breach of promise. This was all Alaric needed. He determined to make an example of the betrayal and sacked Rome on August 24, 410. His was a mighty victory.

All who called themselves Romans were crushed, shaken to the depths of their being. Among them, Christians suffered the keenest shock, because they felt that the fate of their religion was linked with that of the brilliant Latin civilization. Had it not allowed them the freedom to become a universal Church?

It was the "provincials" who seemed most attached to the capital. This phenomenon of attachment to a distant fatherland is recurrent in history. It is quite understandable, and worthy of respect. Saint Jerome (+420), in his grotto at Bethlehem, had just finished his commentary on the prophet Isaiah when news of Rome's fall arrived. This Ciceronian who had been baptized in Rome and had served as secretary to his bishop, Pope Damasus, was not mistaken concerning the significance of the sack. "An ancient city has collapsed, she who was for so many centuries mistress of the world."[1] "The Roman Empire, or rather, the whole world was decapitated when Rome fell."[2] Petrified, rendered speechless, overwhelmed by the news of massacres brought to him by an influx of refugees, Jerome, a few years later (414–417), felt that "the universe had collapsed."[3]

The Spaniard Orosius, in his history "against the Pagans," describes well the feelings of a typical citizen of the Empire. For him, to be a Roman was to enjoy "that peace and tranquillity" which the Church pleaded for in her prayer. "I was a Roman among Romans, a Christian among Christians, a man among men. The common law protected me; I was at home everywhere." Yet already he asks the question: As a result of

3

so much devastation, will other nations perhaps come into contact with the power of the Gospel?[4]

But it was the African, the Berber Augustine, bishop of Hippo, who spoke most profoundly, rising up to render a theological judgment. Augustine loved Roman civilization with both body and soul. With his *Confessions* (397–401), he became in his time a master of Latin literature. He too could have said along with the pagan Rutilius Numantius, "The mother of the world has been assassinated." Clearly, he did not draw the same conclusions from the catastrophe as did the still vigorous adversaries of Christianity. In their view, Rome fell because she had deserted her ancient gods. More precisely, according to Augustine, "The pagans reproach our Christ for being the cause of the fall of Rome, for in former times her gods of wood and stone had protected her."[5]

It was against this background that *The City of God* was written. Augustine's great treatise of apologetics and theological history was to demonstrate that on the contrary, the Empire had become fragile because its inhabitants had not been Christian enough. Augustine invited his readers to a personal conversion. Christianity, in fact, held out hope beyond the crumbling of civilizations. As he remarked in a homily on "the devastated city," "Perhaps Rome has died so that the Romans themselves might not perish!" Men mattered more than institutions and works of art. He never ceased urging them to arise to new life. "Do not remain bound to the old world, do not refuse to grow young in Christ."[6]

Once the time of bewilderment was behind her, Christianity recovered hope. Whatever legitimate, noble, and grateful attachment the Church might have for the civilization that had welcomed her, she knew that this was a human sentiment. She must rise above her distaste for barbarian crudity.[7]

This is why the Church kept up her courage through the fifth century, amid the trials the barbarians inflicted on the ephemeral restorations of the Western Roman Empire. Augustine died in 430 while Hippo lay under siege; soon the Vandals would devastate it. Thanks to the intervention of Leo the Great, bishop of Rome, Attila and his Huns consented to return to the East, but with the promise of a large tribute.

In 476, Odoacer, head of the small Germanic tribe of Rugians, found himself by good fortune in a position to depose the last emperor, an adolescent who somewhat ironically bore the name of Romulus Augustulus, redolent of the grandeur of heroic, mythical Rome. He was exiled to the Campania with a pension of six thousand gold pounds. The imperial insignia were sent to Zeno, emperor of the East. This was not done out of contempt, but rather as a sign of great respect. The gesture

4

5

was an expression of the esteem the barbarians had for the Empire and the ideal of unity it symbolized—a sign, doubtless, that they had every intention of preserving this unity.[8]

A little more than twenty years later Clovis, king of the Franks, would indicate by his entrance into the Church a better way of integrating and fusing together what was left of the Roman character with the new and overwhelming vigor of the barbarians. In contrast, the Vandals came in as destroyers and the Goths as conquering heretics.

The Church, Melting Pot of Civilization

The barbarians were pagans, though some were Arian Christians, thanks to the bishop, Ulfilas (+383), who had evangelized the Goths and had translated the scriptures into their language. They now found themselves confronting an empire which had linked its destiny with Catholicism, but in which there still remained some resistance on the part of the last families attached to the ancient gods. Although it had become decadent, the Empire still fascinated them with its unity, grandeur, prosperity, and culture.

Furthermore, a fusion had already begun to form. The peasants at times saw the barbarians as liberating them from imperial taxes; at other times they simply resigned themselves to new masters. They did this all the more willingly because the land had become once more their true wealth and the Germanic juridical structure lent itself quite well, at social and familial levels, to the needs of a society which was less urban and more economically independent. The barbarians, prepared to "Romanize" themselves, encountered Romans who were disposed to accept or recapture structures that tended to be tribal or familial rather than state-controlled and centralized.

The Church consciously and effectively facilitated this reconciliation of conquerors and conquered. Thus, like Rome, "victoriously vanquished" by Greece, the conquering barbarians would themselves be conquered by all that made up the soul of Rome. Was it not true that their conversion would be the sign of becoming civilized, along with the fact that the bishop would be seen as the sole defender of the city? By entering the Church they inserted themselves, psychologically and culturally, into a life regulated by a coherent organization based on monarchy and hierarchy and unified by the prestigious Latin language. The barbarians were peoples without a past, without any other justice than the right of might, and without stability. Now Rome's privileges, culture, history, and written tradition, all those social acquisitions so cruelly lacking to them before, could be theirs.

Let us consider a few examples of this fusion between conquerer and conquered, this integration desired by the Church. It would take her several centuries to achieve it fully, but "Rome itself was not built in a day." There were plenty of hesitations and opposition. A Sidonian, Apollinaris (+ c. 480), bishop of Clermont in Gaul, was nostalgic for Virgil and Horace, whom he used as poetic models. But he also feared for the Catholic faith itself, because of the Arianism of the conquerors.

This is why the conversion of Clovis, who became king of the Franks in 481, had such symbolic value. His marriage to the Burgundian Catholic princess, Clotilda, was a decisive influence in the midst of many political and military factors. Between 496 and 499, he was baptized by Remigius, bishop of

10. Boethius, The Consolation of Philosophy, *in Dutch translation (manuscript from Ghent 1492, Paris, Bibliothèque nationale). Philosophy is an old woman dressed in colorful clothes. To her left stand two muses, and to her right Lady Fortune, crowned, an allegory of destiny rather than chance.*

11. Codex amitianus *(Florence, Laurentian Library). This manuscript copied and illuminated in the Jarrow Abbey workshop in England around 700 is a refined representation of the scribe Ezra, who collects manuscripts in the large cabinet next to him. Ezra is given credit for collecting the 22 books of the Old Testament (Ezra 7:1, 11). This codex is related to a biblical manuscript by Cassiodorus.*

6. The Baptism of Clovis. *Detail from an ivory bookbinding plaque, 9th century (Amiens, The Museum of Picardy). Immersed in the baptistry fountain, the French king received the imposition of hands and pouring of water that seem to be accompanied by a divine hand. To the left, Queen Clothilda.*

7 and 8. Golden medallion from Theodoric, used as a fibula (clasp) *(Rome, National Roman Museum). The inscriptions honor the Ostrogothic king who became master of Italy, as pious prince, victor of nations.*

9. This mausoleum of Theodoric the Great (Ravenna) *is an architectural witness to the barbarians' assimilation: It recalls the shape of the nomads' tents and constitutes a monumental symbol of a new civilization.*

Reims, together with three thousand warriors. The "new Constantine," as Gregory of Tours called him,[9] appeared to the Gallo-Romans as a defender of the Church and the preserver of Latin culture. It was not without significance that he chose as his capital the ancient imperial residence of Lutecia, soon to be known as Paris. Making Gaul "the eldest daughter of the Church," an oft-repeated expression, Clovis inaugurated the practice of supervising and directing the nomination of bishops, which was to become so frequent and problematic through the Middle Ages and beyond.

At the same time Theodoric the Great (+526), founder of the Gothic kingdom of Italy, adopted all the structures of Roman administration, including the Senate, and enjoyed an amazingly firm and prosperous reign. Romans and barbarians lived side by side, and Theodoric established a clever political balance between Arians and Catholics. Some of the Catholics, such as the philosopher Boethius (+524), who is considered the last of the philosophers of antiquity, enhanced his reign. Cassiodorus (+583), the first "humanist" if you will, succeeded in transmitting ancient knowledge to the early Middle Ages through the copying of manuscripts in his monastery of Vivarium. He thus saved from destruction the Roman *civilitas* to which he was so attached.

But Theodoric, irritated by the anti-Arian policy of the emperor of the East, persecuted his Catholic subjects beginning in 523, even wanting to use Pope John to further his designs. This meant the failure of that integration which could only be built around the orthodox faith. If we wish to find witnesses in art, however, to the fusion of barbarians and Christians, we should doubtless turn to Ravenna with its double baptistry, one for the Orthodox and one for the Arians, or to the curious "tomb of Theodoric." The latter gives a very strange impression: Is it intended to reproduce, as has been suggested, the curved roof of a barbarian tent? These

12. Mosaic and marbles (Ravenna, San Vitale, apse). In this context where hieratic style, sobriety, and magnificence are combined, the interaction of Byzantine imperial ceremonial and Christian liturgy are apparent. Christ's vestments and his posture in the cupola mosaic are similar to the famous representations of Justinian, emperor of the East from 527 to 565, lower left, and of the Empress Theodora surrounded by their court.

13. Left side and campanile from Sant' Apollinare Nuovo (Ravenna). This basilica was built by Theodoric for the Arians whom he favored, and then was given over to Catholic worship. The patronage of Saint Apollinarus only came a few centuries later. The basilica is a privileged witness to Christian art at the end of antiquity, particularly because of the mosaics it contains.

14. Ambo of Bishop Agnello (Ravenna mid 6th century) The decoration of the ambo, called a "tower" (pyrgus) by the inscription, gathers the animals of God's creation in horizontal series (fish, birds, deer, peacocks, and lambs).

12

13

14

monuments of the end of the fifth century and the beginning of the sixth, with their marble and mosaic decorations, show how Greek and Roman elegance could be combined with the ruggedness of the conquerors.

Scarcely a century later, a Pope, Gregory the Great (+604), organized and developed throughout the Church as a whole the definitive integration of Roman tradition and barbarian vitality. This former civil servant of "the eternal city," in fact the highest official in Rome, became a monk at the time of his conversion and soon found himself at the head of the Church through his elevation to the episcopal See of Peter in 590. He was a true "consul of God" as his epitaph states.

Within a few years, Gregory succeeded in making the papacy the veritable axis of the barbarian West. The peace he concluded in 592 with the Lombards, the new invaders, was achieved apart from the emperor of the East, who was the sovereign of Italy in name if not in reality. With his wholly spiritual personality, Gregory, shepherd of Christians, knew

15. *Marble slab (Brescia, St. Julia, City Museum) The peacock depicted on this slab combines several influences. The theme is from classic antiquity: it is the goddess Juno's bird. The framing is of Byzantine style and the interlace at the bottom is of Irish inspiration. The peacock was at first a symbol of pride, but its other symbolism as a figure of immortality, due to its reputation of possessing incorruptible flesh, prevails in Christian art.*

16. *Cover plate of the binding of the* Gospel Book of Theodelinda. *Theodelinda was the wife of two Lombard kings whom she converted to the Catholic faith at the end of the 6th century. Monza, Treasury of the Collegiate Church. This Gospel book, containing pericopes intended to be sung in the liturgy, probably a gift from Pope Gregory the Great, is a good example of Lombard art.*

15

16

how to adapt himself everywhere to the humble preachers of "learned ignorance." He stands out in history as the most important of the popularizers of Christian thought. In this capacity, he was one of the founders of the popular medieval sentiment born of the fusion with the barbarians.[10]

He who, beginning in 591, called himself "bishop not of the Romans but of the Lombards,"[11] used his brother monks, formed in the school of Benedict of Nursia whose life he wrote, to transmit the faith to the most distant lands where hordes of barbarians had succeeded one another.

Let us take for example England. Here we see a conflict between two attitudes. The first consisted in a refusal to accept the challenge of the barbarians. This was the position of the Celts in Great Britain, soon relegated to the western-most extreme of the civilized north, to Wales and then beyond the sea to Armorica. This Breton Christianity, which had been formed by the evangelization of the second century as the Empire penetrated into these regions, confined itself to an exaggerated patriotism and refused to pass on to its conquerors, the Angles and Saxons, the benefit of the faith. It was this intransigence that Bede the Venerable (+735), historian of the new Christianity, described as an unspeakable crime.[12]

17. Canterbury, Trinity Chapel in the Cathedral. At his arrival in 597, Augustine consecrated an already existing Roman basilica as cathedral; it was then rebuilt in a Norman style in the 11th century after being destroyed by a fire.

18. The Fahan stele from Donegal county, Ireland, where Saint Mura founded a monastery in the 7th century. It shows two crosses intertwined with one another. Two figures whose heads form a D are represented on each side. The stele has a Trinitarian Greek inscription.

19. The Book of Durrow, named after the place where it has rested since the 17th century. The initial from the Gospel according to Saint Mark, with its odd figure, provides another example of Irish art a bit earlier than the famous Book of Kells (9th century). The interlaces, spirals, and curves that intertwine like ribbons are probably an adaptation of Celtic or Germanic pagan art.

18

19

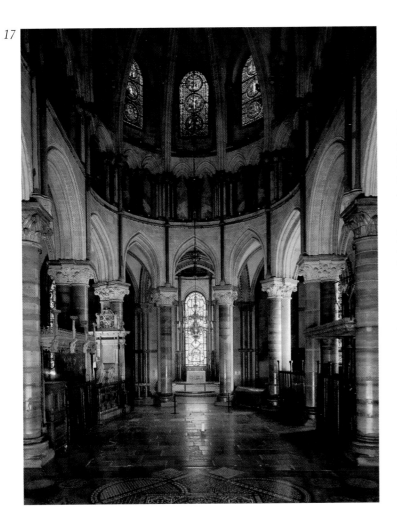

17

This atrophy in regard to the past and the determination to monopolize the Word of God in the name of one civilization went counter to the ideal of Saint Gregory. He suggested that princes and pastors adopt a different attitude. We find this in the very detailed orders he sent to Augustine, his brother in the religious life, accompanied by a cohort of monks. Augustine was soon to be consecrated a bishop.

Like Clovis a century earlier, Ethelbert, king of Kent, was converted to Christianity, thanks to the efforts of Augustine. He was baptized at Canterbury, the new cradle of English Catholicism. Bertha, the king's Catholic wife, like another Clotilde, lent her assistance. Thus Gregory and Augustine of Canterbury proposed to the barbarians that they enter the Church without any other condition but that of faith. This was clearly expressed when, in instructions to missionaries in 601, Gregory ordered the Abbot Mellitus to destroy the idols but not the temples, and even to explain that the sacrificial rites that had been paid to the devil should now be offered to the one true God. It was hoped that "the new Christian people, accustomed to their temples, would come to them as usual, but in order to adore the true God there."[13]

This shows a remarkable flexibility and desire for integration, reminiscent of our modern idea of "inculturation." We should not, however, disguise the fact that Christianization was a long and exacting task. It took years in Gaul, England,

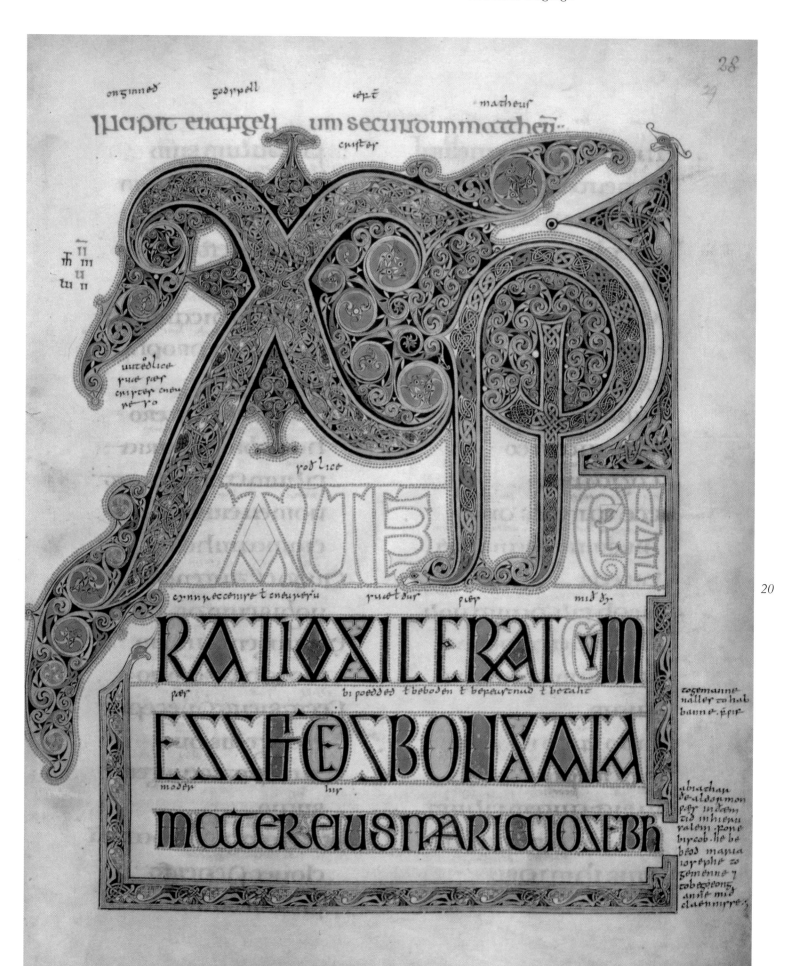

20

21. Crypt of Saint Paul at the Abbey of Jouarre, France (Seine-et-Marne), 7th century, intended to shelter the remains of a rich family. The cornices of the columns are a Merovingian adaptation of antique style. The sculptures on the sarcophagus at the back show people surrounding Christ and lifting their hands to heaven, awaiting the Resurrection. On the right, decorations shaped like shells.

21

22

22. Jouarre. Sarcophagus for the bishop of Paris, Agilbert, brother of the abbess Teodechilde. A beardless Christ is shown in a mandorla, holding the Book of the Gospels and surrounded with the symbols of the four evangelists.

and elsewhere. In some places there would have to be a definitive victory over Arianism, as in the Visigoth kingdom; elsewhere, in Germany for example, missionary work would still be carried on at the beginning of the 8th century.

National Churches were set up and were often dependent upon rulers. Historians have referred to a "barbarization of Christianity," which was doubtless the price of choosing integration. It is true that Merovingian times, as reported by Gregory of Tours in his *History of the Franks,* were filled with

THE CHURCH AND THE CHALLENGE OF THE BARBARIANS

23. *The cross of the parish church at Ruthwell in Dumfries, England; vertically it evokes the episodes of* The Dream of the Cross, *an Anglo-Saxon poem on the victorious cross, with inscriptions in runic characters, the ancient alphabet of Germanic and Scandinavian languages.*

24. *The Cross of Saint Cuthbert, Bewcastle, Cumberland, is a stele designed as a tree of life sheltering animals in its curves.*

25

26

horrendous, bloody incidents. A primitive system of justice often resorted to trials by ordeal, which were considered to be "judgments of God." In Ireland, even monastic life, which ought in principle to calm the passions, remained fiercely attached to extreme forms of asceticism. Benedictine life tended to appear as a center of peace in "the world" where vengeance reigned. It was a place of stability at a time when the barbarians were scarcely settled, and an enterprise setting a high value on manual labor and agriculture when warriors tended to look down on peasants.

At the same time, a new type of power began to take shape. Issuing from the reaction to the challenge of the barbarians, this power so clearly labeled "Germanic Roman," and based on a deliberate reclassification of social functions, would come to be known as feudalism. The Church would contribute to its fashioning, but would at the same time never cease to moderate it, or in a word, to convert it.

23   24

25 and 26. *Steles from Konigswinter-Niederdollendorf near Bonn, Germany (Bonn, Landemuseum). These 7th century blocks are examples of popular sculpture. The first one represents a victorious Christ holding a lance in his hand (Ps. 45:4), and the second one, a deceased person with a big dagger (scrasamax) fighting a serpent with a head in the front and in the back, symbol of the underground world. There is a flask at his feet.*

27. *These remains of the* presbyterium *of Saint Pierre aux Nonnains, Metz, 7th century (Metz, Museum of Art and History) offer an example of Merovingian religious art, probably originating from the North of Italy. The motifs are diverse— vegetables, animals, and geometric forms—as are the inherited influences— antique, Eastern, and Germanic.*

27

29. *Marginal illustrations from a psalter at the end of the 9th century (Chloudov manuscript, Moscow, Historical Museum) are themselves attacks against the iconoclasts. The Greek inscription compares the soldiers, who, in the upper part, abuse the Crucified Christ, to those in the lower part who appear to want to erase the representation of his face.*

28

29

28. *Christ* Pantocrator *(icon from the monaastery of St. Catherine, Sinai, 6th century). It establishes a style in the representation of Christ that will prevail in the Eastern tradition.*

31

30

32

31 and 32. In the nave of the Basilica of the Nativity, Bethlehem, are represented, in a non-figurative way, the holding of provincial and ecumenical councils. Beneath the cross in the center of each are inscriptions of the articles of faith along with some architectural motifs.

1. *The Bible of Saint Martial of Limoges, Paris, Bibliothèque Nationale, Ms lat. 8. This colorful miniature represents the two forms of holiness: on the right, the bishop, in his rich garments and crowned with a miter, a halo edged with purple around his head, the staff in his hand, stool under his feet, and blessing with three fingers in the name of the Trinity; on the left, the lay saint blesses with two fingers and wears simple clothing.*

Chapter 3

THE CHURCH AND THE CHALLENGE OF FEUDALISM

During the first third of the eighth century, the papacy grew weary of incessant conflicts with the Byzantine emperor. Without seeing all that was at stake, it also had a premonition of the gravity of the quarrel over iconoclasm which had just begun in the East, and decided to turn westward. Pope Gregory II stated this explicitly in a severe letter to Emperor Leo III around 730. He decided on "a journey to the western-most regions,"[1] knowing that the barbarian chiefs wanted his patronage. The Church had not only met the challenge of the barbarians but had also collaborated with them in building a society known in history as feudalism. Strange as it may seem to us, the organization of feudalism definitely reflects a traditional, primitive structure incorporated in myths and the collective unconscious.

Three Roles Assigned to the Three Estates

The earliest mention of the medieval division of society into three estates seems to go back to a phrase of Alfred the Great (+899), king of the Anglo-Saxons, in his translation of Boethius' *Consolation of Philosophy.* He speaks of those who pray, those who fight, and those who work. We find this division again in texts attributed to Aelfric the Grammarian, an English Benedictine who died around 1020.[2] And at the beginning of the eleventh century, there were at least two versions of the division in the north of France. The one which is better known and is always cited is taken from a poem of Adalbero, bishop of Laon in 1030, addressed to king Robert the Pious.[3]

Inspired more or less remotely by Saint Augustine's *City of God,* and confronted with the realities of his time, Adalbero made several distinctions according to a basic division which can be translated in more modern terms as Church and State. In the Church there was only one body, in which all were equal according to grace. This was manifested by the equal respect shown to Church ministers, who were not allowed to engage in any secular occupation, lest they be influenced by worldly values. In the State, ruled by human law, there were two classes: first, the free men or nobles, that is to say the warriors, protectors of churches and guardians of the people; and second, men who were not free. They provided money, clothing, and food for all, things without which free men could not subsist.

Furthermore, Adalbero continued, there was a distribution of tasks in the city of God (identified here with Christianity): the *oratores* (those who prayed), the *bellatores* (those who fought), and the *laboratores* (those who worked). They all lived together and could not imagine being separated. Each group supported the other two. In this way peace would reign. This was the foundation of medieval and feudal society.

From the twelfth century on, texts of this type multiplied, especially in the vernacular. At the end of the century, a certain Stephen of Fougères wrote in old French:

The clerk should pray for all,
The knight should promptly defend and honor the others,
And the peasant should work.

It should be noted that at this time, the distinction between those who were free and those who were not had disappeared.

Ethnologists and historians of religion and literature have noted this triple division of roles in many Indo-European myths, particularly in India, where in one of the great sacred poems, the *Mahabharata* (the history of the descendants of Bharata), there is a classification of the gods and the hierarchy of a system that we incorrectly call the caste system.

Georges Dumézil, a famous historian of religions, made the connection in his major work, *Mythe et Epopée,* or *Myth and Epic,* which carries as its subtitle, *The Ideology of the Three Roles in the Epics of the Indo-European Peoples.*[4] As he sees it, we have to admit a common origin. It has often been

*2. Temple of Shiva, 8th century (Prambanan, Java, Indonesia).
A sculptured representation of the* Ramayana, *one of the mythic epics that set in place the social and mental structures of the three Indo-European castes. Baratha, Rama's brother, sits on the left. A Brahman pours water on his head and body, the equivalent of a royal anointing. Other Brahmans recite formulas, and the dancers mime war, a royal prerogative.*

3. The Great Conquest of the Crusader Kingdom, ordered by Sancho IV the Brave (+1295,) king of Castille and Leon (Madrid, National Library). The Christian warriors and the infantrymen fulfill the defensive and offensive function of the feudal system.

4. Codex of Egbert (Trier, Stadtbibliothek, Ms 24). Egbert (+993) was a famous personality in Otto II's court before being named Archbishop of Trier. This Gospel book gives us an idea of the culture around the year 1000 and pays homage to Egbert's monastic reforms.

objected that these three functions or roles were so universal as to have no significance. His response was that very few peoples drew an explicit or implicit ideology from this natural structure. It was therefore a question of a theory or ideal, or as Dumézil puts it, a "privileged dream." The division was not always accompanied by such subdivisions in actual reality. It is important, moreover, neither to be to be too rigid nor to oversimplify a system that, in fact, was very complex.

It has been necessary to point out the primitive origin of feudal society in order to see it more clearly as an ordering of the world. It was a structure to which the medieval world was attached and which the Church tried to safeguard, at the same time purifying and humanizing it.

What was feudal society like, concretely speaking? It was built on the ruins of the Roman Empire, on the disintegration of the public power reserved to the state, on the state's monopoly of the right to wage war, to the benefit of a new class, the landed gentry. Because of the absence of centralization and their distance from the reigning power, the members of the propertied aristocracy, who distributed territories among themselves, remained free either to preserve the peace or to make war.

In peace as in war, these lords depended upon the masses, who can be called "rural dependents." It is true that there were a few small free property holders *(juniores)* and some townspeople who were merchants or artisans, but at the end of the first millennium they were not very numerous. The majority of the population consisted of peasants who were free in theory and who were called colonists or tenants of the great landlords. Finally, there were the serfs, perhaps descendants of former slaves. These were few in number at the end of the Empire. Christianity had not abolished their state, which the New Testament does not condemn, but had affirmed their personal dignity. Contrary to former customs regarding slavery, however, serfs were not a commodity and had rights at times, even though they could be sold.

Under the Carolingians, free dependents became less free. The colonists (or tenants) were treated rather badly by the judiciary, itself subject to the landowners. These last were all the more powerful because for the most part they had bought back from the king the military obligations of their peasants. Serfs, on the contrary, became more and more "classed" as it was called; that is, they were tenured and regrouped for better surveillance because the bond of servitude consisted essentially in the personal dependence of one man to another.

This personal bond constituted the main nerve of feudal society by means of vassalage. It was a matter of organizing protection according to a hierarchical order and of exchanging it for financial or military service. Kings increased the number of their direct vassals *(vassi dominici)* as much as possible. They gave them privileges and lands, and urged the fairly modest landowners to ally themselves with them. In this

5. Vienna, Austrian National Museum. Typical work through the months, ms. from the early 9th century. Work in the fields, harvesting, and hunting are done by the third estate of the Indo-European society, made up of laborers who feed the clergymen and nobles in exchange for celestial and temporal protection.

6

way, feudal society was organized by a chain of oaths, at the end of which was the sovereign. The medieval order thus established was based implicitly on the three classes, on respect for one's promise, and on the protection of security and peace.

How would the Church react to this order found nowhere in the Gospel? She would maintain the form of a Christianity that consolidated this social order and at the same time received its unity from it. The challenge confronting her did not result from the political and social structure itself—this she willingly accepted—but from its deviations. The Church realized that excesses or imbalances held the risk of either binding or corrupting her.

In order to preserve her freedom of action, the Church needed to affirm unceasingly her specific character within the framework of social life. Above all, she would never stop showing that all divisions of functions rested upon one great distinction. There was the city of God, which she represented or incarnated, and then there was the earthly and temporal city. This terminology, taken from the great work of Saint Augustine, has at times been distorted and used in a too literal sense.[5] There was, on the one hand, the *Sacerdotium,* or Church, as represented chiefly by the Pope, bishops and clergy, and on the other hand, the *Regnum,* including emperor, kings, and lords. Except during periods of subservience, the Church in the West never ceased to affirm the distinction between these powers and the primacy of the spiritual.

The Church Ensnared by Feudalism

The reign of the early Carolingians, from Pepin the Short (+768) to Charles the Bald (+877), was, at two important moments, a period of political reconstruction and a return to culture. This was so evident that the period has been loosely referred to as "the Carolingian Renaissance." The dynasty issued from Charles Martel, who drove the Muslims back at Poitiers in 732 and thus saved the Germanic and Latin integrity of the West. For a time, the early Carolingians reestablished the unity of the empire that had disappeared in the West and enjoyed an unequaled prestige in Europe. The coronation of Charlemagne at Rome by the Pope in 800 is its best known symbol. It became the model for every consecration of monarchical power.[6]

The Church contributed powerfully to this era of peace and to the emergence of a civilization which Alcuin called the *regnum christianitatis.* The Carolingians knew that it was in their interests to involve the religious authority in political government. This sense is what lay behind the coming of

8. A reconstruction of the exterior of the Palatine Chapel at Aachen, south view (sketch by Felix Kreusch). The architecture of this chapel combines forms from Roman antiquity and Byzantine monuments, showing the double patronage of the ancient Latin Rome and the new Greek Rome (Constantinople).

9 and 10. (9) The evangelist Saint Luke and his symbol (the winged ox), the Lorsch Gospels, from the Palatine school of Aachen, around 810–815 (Vatican Library, Ms. Pal. Lat. 50). (10) The evangelist Saint Matthew, The Coronation Gospels, end of 8th, beginning of 9th centuries, (Vienna Art Historical Museum). The stylized representations of the Gospel's authors in manuscripts of the sacred texts show the interest in the Bible on the part of the leaders of the Carolingian Renaissance, among whom Alcuin was the most famous.

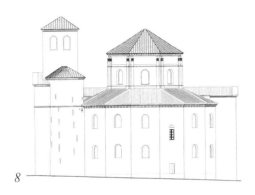

8

9

a cleric (a bishop) and a layman (a count) as imperial delegates or *missi dominici*. They would journey through regions, serving as intermediary wheels or cogs for the functioning of the central authority. In principle, they incarnated the symbiosis or collaboration of the spiritual and temporal powers. More often than not it was a case of officials doing double duty, for what we see happening is that clerics were becoming vassals. The prince or lords considered Church property (benefices) to be at their disposal. Ever since the time of Louis the Pious, the son of Charlemagne, who was emperor from 814 to 840, all bishops and certain abbots had to become vassals of the crown. In 860, Hincmar, archbishop of Reims, denounced the rite of the oath of fidelity imposed on bishops and refused to take it himself. But the high clergy became more and more closely associated with the lay aristocracy to the point of belonging to the same families. The institution of the tithe received by the State for the profit of the Church caused it to fall into administrative traps that held it captive for a thousand years.

Actually, the emperor felt he was responsible for all of Christian society in its search for a unity that had disappeared with the Roman Empire. Agobard of Lyons wrote of Louis the Pious in 840: "May it please almighty God to grant that, under a very pious king, all men may be governed by one

10

11. Saint Benedict of Nursia, 13th-century fresco by Master Conxolus (Subiaco, Sacro Speco, lower church). The father of western monks is represented holding his Rule that will win over all the monasteries of Europe. The right hand of the one whose name means "the Blessed" is extended in a large gesture of blessing.

11

single law. This will promote justice and the peace of the City of God."[7]

The papacy no longer enjoyed the unifying role that it had once filled so well. The Pope received from Pepin the Short territories taken from the Lombards which constituted the first Papal States. Through this transaction, guaranteed by the apocryphal text of "The Donation of Constantine" to Pope Sylvester I, supposedly dating from the fourth century, the Pope became himself a temporal sovereign, a development with incalculable consequences through the centuries.

It is true that the Carolingian Renaissance, by the unification of law, the development of education, and the general "Romanizing" of the liturgy, contributed greatly to the spread and development of Christianity. But it was principally with the unity of monastic life around the Rule of Saint Benedict of Nursia that a model of holiness began to radiate. This was due to the work of Saint Benedict of Aniane at the beginning of the ninth century. The development contained within itself the remedy so greatly needed by a Church subjected to feudalism.

With the dissolution of the Carolingian Empire at the end of the ninth century and the arrival of the dynasty of German emperors with Otto the Great in 962, the Church was integrated within the feudal system and subjected to all its political and familial hazards. In 862, the Count of Auvergne drove out the bishop of Clermont, replacing him with a candidate of his own choice. In 925, the Count of Vermandois had his five year old son Hugh elected to the archbishopric of Reims. In 990, the Viscount of Beziers, not having a son, gave the bishopric of Agde to his wife! This is the time of lay investiture—the act whereby the new bishop was invested with his powers by laymen, who bestowed upon him his cross and ring.

After the death of the very firm and authoritarian Pope Nicholas I (+867) and throughout the tenth century, kings and then Germanic emperors took over the nomination of popes. One of the most terrible symbols of these dark ages was the posthumous trial of Pope Formosus (+896). Nine months after his death, he was disinterred and despoiled of his pontifical insignia. The "cadaver" council of January 897 marked the beginning of a tragic era for the Church. She was delivered up to Roman factions ruled by a shrew, the infamous Marozia, mistress of a Pope (Sergius III), mother of a Pope (John XI), grandmother of a Pope (John XII) and aunt of a Pope (John XIII). It may well be that the later legend of a "Pope Joan" can be traced back to this era.[8]

The only thing to be remembered from this scandalous period is the Church's total integration in the feudal system. She was handed over to the cupidity of the powerful. Bishoprics, as well as parishes, went to the highest bidders. This would be called simony, after Simon the Magician, who in the Acts of the Apostles, wanted to pay Peter for the power coming from the imposition of hands (Acts 8:18–20). It was also the era of priestly concubinage and immorality, called "Nicolaitanism." This is a reference to Revelation 2:15 which speaks of a sect that had reestablished pagan rites. Owing mainly to the appointment of lay abbots, decadence invaded even monastic life. Yet it was from the monasteries that renewal was to come and that the challenge of feudalism would be met. Monks made profession in the hands of the abbot with the same gesture as that of a vassal's homage, but for them it was an expression of their obedience to God. Monastic life was to bring the feudal order back to its source, and the purity of Gregorian chant, some beautiful examples of which date from this period, allows us to hear, as it were, the source of the renewal.

12 and 13. Master of the Registrum Gregorii (letters of Saint Gregory), 10th century (Chantilly, Condé Museum). The emperor of the Holy Roman Germanic Empire, surrounded by his four provinces, is dressed in Byzantine imperial purple. He holds the scepter and the globe of the universe, marked with a cross. He also wears the imperial crown, an example of which (13) has been preserved (Vienna, Weltliche Schatzkammer).

12

13

14

14. Bronze door of the Cathedral of Gniezno (Poland) second half of the 12th century. Otto II (+983) holding the imperial scepter entrusts the episcopal staff to Saint Adalbert (+997). Behind Otto, an officer holds the sword representing the temporal order. This example of lay investiture of a clerical office will become one of the issues of the Gregorian reform.

ART FROM
THE YEAR 1000

15. Manuscript commissioned by
Ferdinand I and Dona Sancha of
a commentary on the book of
Revelation (Madrid, National
Library vitr. 14.2). Image loosely
representing Revelation 15: The
seven angels holding the last
plagues, a crystal sea mingled with
fire over which those who were
victorious over the Beast
(accompanying themselves with
harps) chant the canticle of the
Lamb who was slain (pierced by
the Cross). The Middle Ages
incorporates this symbolic image
taken from the New Testament
into its vision of human history.

16

18

16. *Ivory (Milan, Castello Museum). Christ in glory, surrounded by the Virgin ("Saint Mary") and Saint Maurice, is paid homage by a prince and a bishop who offer him a child, probably the young Otto III, with his mother Theophano, a Byzantine princess, and his grandmother Adelaide, who were his regents.*

17. *The charter of New Minster (London, British Library, ms Cotton Vespasian A VIII). Edgar (+975) king of the Anglo-Saxons, surrounded by the Virgin and Saint Peter, presents to Christ in glory (symbolized by the mandorla supported by angels) the charter decreed in 966, that transfers Winchester Cathedral from the secular canons to the Benedictine monks as requested by Saint Ethewold (+984). It is an affirmation of royal legislative power, but also an indication of a desire for stricter religious life.*

18. *Statue of Saint Foy (Conques, treasury of the abbey). The Abbey of St. Foy, a masterpiece of 11th-century art, shelters this reliquary called Saint Foy in Majesty, containing the relics of a girl martyred at Agen (+303). It is an example of the splendor with which the Middle Ages honored the relics around which great religious structures were built.*

17

19 and 20. (19) A longitudinal section of Cluny II, reconstruction of a vanished structure, part of a huge ensemble of buildings. (20) After the devastations of the French revolution, only a few buildings, surmounted by two towers, remain at Cluny.

21. Glory Portico, 12th century (Cathedral of St. James of Compostella). A vision of the heavenly Jerusalem from the Apocalypse: surrounding Christ as Judge, Christians on their earthly pilgrimage are given a vision of the Church triumphant.

19

20

The Church's Struggle for Independence

In fact, if not by law, the Church had become the vassal of lay power. Her efforts to disengage herself took place during a period of fear and confusion at the dawn of the second millennium.

In 909, William, Duke of Aquitaine, founded a monastery which he offered "joyously and spontaneously" to the holy apostles Peter and Paul. This was his way of bestowing ownership on the ones whose relics were venerated there. As the abbatial church was, so to speak, the shrine of this reliquary, so the monastery that enclosed it became its case. A particular clause specified that the monks gathered together here under the rule of Saint Benedict would not be subject to "the yoke of any temporal power, neither ours, nor our parents, nor that of the king, nor of a secular ruler, nor of bishops, nor even of the Roman Pontiff."[9] This meant the creation of an island of temporal independence. It was from Cluny, coming under the jurisdiction of Rome in the religious domain, that renewal would come.

The great good fortune of Cluny was that it had, from the beginning, a series of exceptional abbots. The founder of the abbey, Berno, abbot from 909 to 927, came from the monastery of Baume, which he had reformed. He was followed by

Saint Odo (927–942), and then by Saint Majolus, who enjoyed a veritable abbatial reign of forty-six years from 948 to 994. Saint Odilio, ruling the abbey for fifty-five years from 994 to 1049, was the founder of the Cluniac Order, leaving sixty-five houses at his death. Finally, under the abbacy of Hugh, which lasted for sixty years from 1049 to 1109, Cluny reached its peak, symbolized by its three churches, one of which was the largest of Christendom.

Cluny offered a model for reform. In the first place, the Cluniac Order was distinguished for its centralization, since each monk, wherever he might be in Europe, was considered a professed monk of Cluny, having promised obedience and conversion of life in the hands of the abbot. Cluny also demonstrated a desire to return to essentials. The ministry of charity was exercised through works of mercy, almsgiving, and hospitality to the poor and pilgrims. That of prayer consisted in the continual public praise of the divine office.

This return to virtue and prayer was preached, practiced, and disseminated by the monks of Cluny. It enabled the Church to meet the challenge of feudalism. It was from a Cluniac monastery that the first thrust of energy came in Gerbert (+1003), who had grown up in Aurillac in the center of France. Gerbert's meeting with the Emperor Otto I around

21

970 would help put him at the highest level of Christianity. Otto III had him elected Pope in 999, and he chose the name of Sylvester II to emphasize his alliance with this new Constantine. A person truly eminent for his learning and political courage, Gerbert guided the Church through the shock of the year 1000.

A little later, Cluny gave impetus to that movement so decisive for ecclesial renewal, the Gregorian reform. This received its name from its most celebrated artisan, Gregory VII. It has been clearly shown that the reform had been set in motion by the preceding Popes. The first one, Bruno of Toul, had as bishop supported his clergy in their efforts for moral purification. Chosen Pope by the will of the Emperor Henry III, Bruno took the name Leo IX (1048–1054). He then decided to reestablish the Church's precedence and to reverse the customary manner of nominating the Roman pontiff. At Toul, he wore the garb of a pilgrim and retained his title of simple bishop until he was acclaimed as Pope by the cardinals and the people of Rome. Thus he became Pope by election and not by the emperor's investiture.

Leo IX and his successor Stephen IX (1057–1058), abbot of Monte Cassino—who did not even solicit the imperial consent—and then Nicholas II (1059–1061) and Alexander II (1061–1073), began a reform of the Church by means of various ecclesiastical assemblies that firmly condemned simony and Nicolaitanism. They were aided by the prestige and action of the austere Peter Damian (1007–1072) who, in his appropriately entitled *Book of Gomorrah,* stigmatized clerical concubinage. But behind the reforming action of the Popes from Stephen IX on was one of the most outstanding men in the history of the Church: Hildebrand. Born around 1021, he had been archdeacon of Rome since 1059, and upon his election as Pope in 1073, he took the name of Gregory VII.

This Pope was convinced that reform should be effected through the reinforcement and above all the independence of the pontifical power. It is in this sense that we should understand the celebrated text of the *Dictatus papae,* a kind of catalogue of the privileges of the Roman pontiff.

Through centralization around the Apostolic See and the commissioning of emissaries who enjoyed his confidence, Gregory took in hand certain local Churches whose bishops were most often creatures of political power. The institution of permanent legates of the Holy See was an indication of this strategy. One of these men, Hugh of Die, can be seen as the veritable head of the Church in France. Everywhere, Nicolaitanism was hunted down. Gregory VII never ceased

22. Donizone (The Life of Mathilda of Canossa) *(Vatican Library ms lat. 4922). In a long poem about the family of the Lords of Canossa, the Benedictine Donizone eulogizes the countess Mathilda at the end of her life (+1115). The miniature does not represent the well-known scene of the Emperor Henry IV asking for pardon in front of Canossa Castle, but rather the hospitality that Mathilda granted him at the request of the abbot Hugh of Cluny, following the Christian rules of honor extolled by feudalism.*

to reaffirm the obligation of ecclesiastical celibacy, which met with enormous resistance in Germany and France.

Lay investiture remained the most difficult obstacle to overcome. It was the cause of the major conflict that placed Gregory VII in opposition to Emperor Henry IV of Germany. After an initial struggle over the archbishop of Milan, in which Henry IV unilaterally deposed him in 1076, Pope Gregory VII excommunicated the emperor, and Henry IV addressed to the Pope a letter of incredible insolence, in which he challenged the validity of the Pope's election and demanded his resignation. We should note that at this period, excommunication absolved the subjects of a prince from their oath of fidelity and thus threatened the entire political order. But we should also add that to attack Milan was to threaten the Patarenes, members of the lay movement which, in Milan, was most closely allied to the papacy.

Changing his tactics, Henry presented himself in the garb of a penitent and publicly begged forgiveness before the castle of Canossa in January 1077. Gregory VII saw clearly, as a politician, that this was a maneuver, but as a priest he could only grant forgiveness. It was a matter of the holiness of the sacrament of Penance and the spiritual independence of the one who forgave. Rarely was the conflict between the immediate interest, which called for the maintenance of the excommunication, and the spiritual principle, which called for the granting of the forgiveness of Christ, so acute.

Gregory VII therefore granted pardon. His allies considered his action treason. Henry IV quickly resumed his political and military initiative, took possession of Rome in 1083, exiled Gregory VII, and set up an anti-Pope. The Gregorian re-affirmation of spiritual power over temporal power, which was to be known as the theory of "the two swords" in the service of "theocracy," seemed to have met with failure.

But some ten years later, the reform of the episcopate and the general reform of the Church were viewed as a posthumous triumph for Gregory VII. The successors of the two protagonists of the great conflict now heading the papacy and empire were more flexible in temperament and succeeded in finding a solution agreeable to both parties. On September 23, 1122, in two separate declarations, Pope Calixtus II (1119–1124) and Emperor Henry V concluded the "Concordat of Worms."[10] Henry promised to restore the properties confiscated during the death struggle between Church and empire, and to assure the freedom of episcopal and abbatial elections. Pope Calixtus agreed to allow the emperor to bestow on the one chosen, not the cross and ring, but investiture "through the sceptre" for

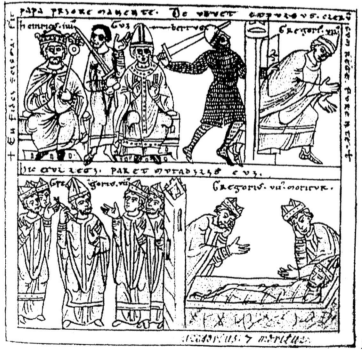

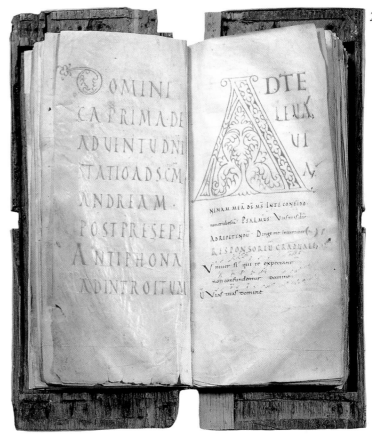

23. Chronicle of Otto of Freising *(Ms Iena, Bose 9). A few scenes from the life of Gregory VII: the Emperor Henry IV expels the legitimate Pope and replaces him with the antipope Guibert, but in return Gregory VII excommunicates the bishop-supporters of Henry, and dies in exile in 1085.*

secular affairs. This was also a victory crowning the work of the canonists, most particularly Bishop Ivo of Chartres (from 1091 to 1116), who emphasized the necessary cooperation between the two powers.

The challenge of feudalism had been overcome. The papacy did indeed take refuge behind a partial reading of *The City of God,* identifying it improperly with the visible Church, while the temporal power was likened to the terrestial city,

24. *Latin song book from the time of Abbot Hartmann (922–925), Abbey of St. Gall, foundation of the diocese of St. Gall. Pictured here is the introit antiphon for the First Sunday of Advent. The Latin liturgy was made possible by the* scriptoria *from the monasteries and collegiate churches.*

25. *Cluny III capital (Cluny, Farinier Museum). Certain capitals from the largest church in Christendom represented the eight tones from the Gregorian Chant (named after Gregory the Great, +604, even though it actually dated from more than a century later). Pictured here is the symbol of the first tone.*

26 27

26. *"Moralizing" Bible,
beginning of the 13th century
(Vienna, National Library, Ms
2554). Christ, the divine
architect, creates the world with
the help of a compass, The text
from Genesis, illustrated by the
miniature, is written in French.*

27 and 28. (27) *Psalter Map
(13th century). This geography
of the world, protected by
Christ who blesses it and rules
over it, places the earthly
Jerusalem at its center. The
circle shape is indicative of
perfection: the Jerusalem
circle is the reproduction
of the circle of the universe,
microcosm in the cosmos.*
(28): *Almost two centuries
later, the Benedictine Andreas
Walsperger, in 1448, represents
the earth and the spheres in
a more complex manner, but
Jerusalem remains in the center
of the known world.*

28

29. *Beatus of Liébana,
Imago mundi (Paris,
Bibliothèque Nationale).
This map of the inhabited
world was drawn up for
the Cistercian monastery of
St. Andre de Arroyo
(Palencia, Spain) at the
request of the King of
Castille and Leon, Saint
Ferdinand III, between
1219 and 1235. The plan,
totally horizontal, describes
paradise with its
distribution of rivers
(Genesis 2, 8–14) and the
presence of Adam and Eve
after the Fall. Immediately
beneath them is Jerusalem
but on the other side of
the river that flows
vertically, one notices the
place given to Rome and
Constantinople. The
known islands are
distributed on the marine
border outside. The
mountains are spread out
across the map.*

29

30

31

which for Augustine was the city of the damned. Mysticism was turned into politics. "Political Augustinianism," as it was called,[11] introduced the idea that the two swords of Christendom, spiritual and temporal, were in the hands of the Pope. The Vicar of Christ could use the temporal sword when necessary for the sake of Christian order. It was unthinkable that lay power could accept this theory permanently and this would be the next challenge to face the Church.

The entrenchment and deviations of feudalism had been countered by a return to what was seen as the order willed by God. The balance consisted in a clear distinction between the Church and the temporal power. At the same time, the pre-eminence of the spiritual, that is to say the Church, was maintained; it retained the primary role, the most dignified position in Christendom.

The concept of a natural and a supernatural order (the order of the cosmos), which is disturbed and damaged by sin and restored by grace—that concept is expressed in all Romanesque art. The basilica of Vézelay is one of its highest achievements. The nave dates from the middle of the twelfth century. If we study the great tympanum in the narthex we can read there a figurative inscription in stone of the concept of medieval order. In the outer arc around Christ in His mandorla, surrounded by apostles and crowds of people, are the signs of the zodiac. These are accompanied by various temporal activities carried on through the cycle of the seasons, such as the harvesting of wheat and of grapes.[12]

This natural order is affirmed and assured by grace. Perhaps the most moving symbol of it at Vézelay occurs on June 24, the Solemnity of the Nativity of John the Baptist. It also is the summer solstice. The sun is at its zenith and traces a royal path through the basilica from the sculpted John the Baptist on the column of the portal beneath the tympanum to the altar in the choir. Through the center of the nave runs this royal but fleeting path, sprinkled with spots of luminous color.[13] The church faces due east in order to allow for the annual occurence of this symbol. It manifests the presence of the divine promise and recapitulates and restores the cosmic order, incorporating and spiritualizing it.[14] The Church, responding to the challenge of the social structures of its time, wished both to incorporate them and to preserve their spiritual meaning.

30, 31, and 32. *The architecture of the Basilica of St. Mary Magdalene, Vezelay, a masterpiece of Burgundian Romanesque art, is inserted into cosmic reality. At the zenith of the sun, on the day of the summer solstice, the Solemnity of the Nativity of Saint John the Baptist, the path of the light in the center of the nave indicates the itinerary of salvation across time, from the statue of Christ's precursor in the central portal to the relics of Mary Magdalene, who announced the Resurrection.*

32

33

34

35

33. The Bayeux Tapestry (circa 1077). More than 70 meters long and, attributed by legend to Queen Mathilda of Flanders, the wife of William the Conqueror, this embroidery narrates the Norman invasion of England in 1066. This document shows the violence of the combat, but the stiffness of the figures and the strange animals in the upper part of the tapestry are a clue to the mythic aspect of the tale.

34 and 35. The medieval bestiary leads into an imaginary world that science and observation will dissipate. Taken from the Bible, from antique mythology, and from Celtic and Germanic legends, these animals play their role in the enchantment of the world in which medieval religion was at home. (34): Church of St. Clement in Tahull, Catalonia: an animal whose body is covered with eyes (maybe from Revelation 9:19) and (35): Church of St. Martin, Zillis in the Graübunden, Switzerland. On an extraordinary ceiling painted in this Romanesque church (circa 1130), we find this being that is part beast, part fish, and which represents Evil.

36

37

36. Cathedral of St. Martin, Lucca, copy from the 13th-century original. Saint Martin of Tours (+397) is one of the most popular characters of the medieval West, as is evident from the great number of locations or families named after him. The episode of the gift of half of his soldier's cloak to a poor man is presented as a model of charity and prudence.

37. Mosaic, Ganagobie Monastery, Alpes-de-Haute-Provence, France. The archangel Michael wears the medieval knight's breastplate and fights the dragon, which is split in several pieces (Revelation 12:7)— the final victory of the angelic forces over evil.

38

38. Bishop's throne (St. Sabin Cathedral, Canossa). According to the inscriptions on this monumental marble throne, Ursone, bishop of Bari and Canossa, ordered Romuald (1079–1089) to make it. Surmounted by a pine cone, sign of abundance, decorated with small eagles, and supported by two elephants, male and female, this throne is more symbolic than practical, and, despite the cross, more secular than religious.

THE CHURCH AND THE CHALLENGE OF FEUDALISM

1

2

3

1. *Fresco, circa 1200 (Romanesque church, Cressac, Charente). Figure of a knight with a cross on his pennant and shield is honored in this representation made at the time of the fourth crusade.*

2. *Illustration from* The Romance of the Grail *of Chretien de Troyes (Florence, Laurencian Library). The Knights of the Round Table, grouped about King Arthur, are taking an oath at this table that also evokes Christ's Last Supper and the chalice he used. The knights will go and search for it in a mystic quest, the same quest that inspired the Crusades and the pilgrimages.*

3. *Reims Cathedral. This double sculpture of a priest giving communion to a knight is also a figure of the meeting between Melchisedech, mysterious "priest of God Most High," and Abraham (Genesis 14:18). It symbolizes the two powers: The spiritual, in giving the supreme good of the Eucharist, dominates over the temporal power.*

THE CHURCH AND THE CHALLENGE OF SECULAR THOUGHT BETWEEN THEOCRACY AND NEO-CAESARISM

The protracted efforts of Gregory VII and of the Popes who had preceded him seemed, if not defeated, at least arrested, on the death of the one whose name we associate with the "Gregorian" reform. But as happens with almost every period, the harvest and fruits were gathered some twenty years after the planting and pruning. And so for us, the twelfth and thirteenth centuries seem like the greatest period of medieval Christianity, its apogee, its "high noon" as Léopold Génicot puts it.[1]

But we need to be on our guard. For the believer, it is merely a question of the success of a civilization that was truly inspired by Christianity. He admires it, but sees it simply as one stage, like so many others, in the journey of the city of God. The historian is wary of idealizing the subject of his study. Behind this apogee, he detects many shortcomings and structural flaws, which will increase with time. Every period is a balancing point. The controversies of the fourteenth and fifteenth centuries were already present in the undeniable success of the age of monasteries and cathedrals in the West, the twelfth and thirteenth centuries.

The Apogee of Christianity

It seems that the Church had in some way succeeded in sublimating the fighting instinct and warrior role in that astonishing institution, chivalry, in which nobility found its Christian vocation. Animated by a human ideal of courage and liberality—signs for detachment and magnanimity—chivalry was in fact rooted in mysticism. This was evident in the search for the Holy Grail, that immense tree of medieval literature with its varied branches. Its principal theme was the fraternity of the Knights of the Round Table, who set out in search of "the chalice, or cup of Jesus Christ of Holy Thursday." Pilgrimage, search for the Eucharist, quest for communion— all of these gave chivalry its true dimension, which is mystical.

This was expressed first and foremost in the famous night-long vigil which preceded the ceremony of the dubbing of the knight. Then, at the beginning of the fifteenth century, when Konrad Witz, the great painter of Basel, wished to depict the episode of the meeting between Abraham and Melchisedech, he clothed the patriarch in armor while the mysterious priest, clearly representing the Church, offered the Eucharistic species to the knight.

We may indeed envisage the great medieval enterprises from the viewpoint of this chivalric ideal, provided we reinsert them in the social and even economic context of the period. The West was then at the start of a demographic surge that began at the end of the eleventh century and was to last until the thirteenth. It is believed that in Europe, between 1150 and 1250, the population increased by close to twenty million people—which meant that there were sixty million in Latin Christendom—while in the preceding century there had been an increase of only four million.[2] It is important to keep in mind the background of this demographic explosion when discussing the Crusades.

Misunderstood or maligned because of its questionable features, the phenomenon of the Crusades, extending over two centuries (1096–1291), took on the character of both a military undertaking and a pilgrimage to rescue the tomb of Christ. This adventure, typical of an itinerant people who journeyed to Compostella and then to Rome, can be seen primarily as the most grandiose of the Church's efforts to create and maintain institutions of peace. The Church had long proposed truces whenever possible—during liturgical seasons and from Thursday to Sunday—these were known as the "peace of God." She had denounced the murderous violence of tournaments (for example at the Second Lateran Council in 1139) and of mercenary armies (as at the Third Lateran Council in 1179). The Crusades thus represented a tremendous effort on the Church's part to channel and divert the internal violence that stemmed from incessant conflicts

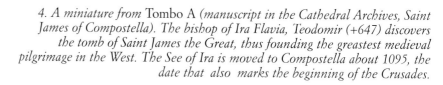

4

5

4. *A miniature from* Tombo A *(manuscript in the Cathedral Archives, Saint James of Compostella). The bishop of Ira Flavia, Teodomir (+647) discovers the tomb of Saint James the Great, thus founding the greastest medieval pilgrimage in the West. The See of Ira is moved to Compostella about 1095, the date that also marks the beginning of the Crusades.*

5. *Hans Gieng, statue of Saint James the Greater, Fribourg, Notre Dame Hospital, 1520. The saint himself wears the insignia of the Compostella pilgrims: the staff, the hat adorned with the shell, and the Gospel. The pilgrim's status had to be visible for him to be recognized and respected.*

6. *From* The Pilgrimage Book of Ricoldo of Montecroce *(Paris, Bibliothèque Nationale, ms. fr. 2810). The pilgrimage "par excellence" remains the one to Christ's tomb, the Holy Sepulchre in Jerusalem. In a stylized holy City, Christian pilgrims are received after paying a tribute to a Muslim wearing a hat with an Islamic crescent on top. The doorkeeper opens the sanctuary. Peaceful visits to the Holy Places were the norm before the 11th century.*

7 and 8. *These two examples of architecture at the times of the Crusades, St. John of Acre and the citadel of Marqab, show the importance of the "Latin" military sites in Palestine. Conquered, lost, and recovered, the citadel of St. John of Acre will be the last bastion of the crusaders resisting until 1291.*

9. *Church of St. Romanus (Toledo). This composite architecture, incorporating arches from the synagogue of Santa Maria Blanca, expresses, in a way, the cultural coexistence (not always peaceful) of the three religions of medieval Spain: Judaism, Christianity, and Islam. This* mudejar *art, the name given to Muslims under Christian authority, combines their non-figurative decoration with the representation of persons, preferred by the religion of Incarnation.*

70

6

7

8

9

10. *Woodcut by Peter Metlinger, Dijon, 1491. Pope Callistus II recognizes in 1119 the Cistercian Order, represented by Robert of Molesme, Stephen Harding, and Alberic, but also by Saint Bernard, who is not a founder but its most illustrious personality. The illustration intends to show the importance of the Cistercians as agents of the Pope in the 12th century.*

11, 12, and 13. *The abbey church and monastic buildings of Fontenay in Burgundy, founded by Saint Bernard in 1119, the year of the approbation of the Charter of Charity. Cistercian architecture reveals the ideal and the splendor of monastic simplicity, and provides the framework for its work and prayer.*

10

11

12

13

Saint James

The Templars

Alcanatara

Hospitallers of Saint John

14. Icon of Saints Sergius and Bacchus, last quarter of the 13th century (Monastery of St. Catherine, Sinai). These two elegant Roman army officers were denounced as Christians and executed in Syria. They are considered the protectors of the Byzantine armies.

15. Insignias of the Hospitaller and military orders, which were born in the context of the Crusades to serve as models of Christian chivalry in the conquest and occupation of the territories of the Near East. The Order of Alcantara was created for the reconquest of Catholic Spain from Islam.

16. Miniature from The Roman de la Rose *by Jean de Meung (14th-century manuscript at Chantilly, Condé Museum). Heloise and Abelard (the remarkable and strange couple whose fate forced them apart to embrace clerical and monastic life) discuss philosophy and theology.*

14

15

between kings and nobles confined in territories too small to provide sustenance for so many people.

Yet unintentionally, the Crusades would upset a certain balance that had been established in Europe between the three monotheistic religions. Spain provides the most paradoxical example of this. The *Reconquista* against Islam was accomplished by stages and brought about the cohabitation of Christians, Muslims, and Jews in numerous regions. Between the decisive dates of 1094—the capture of Valencia by the Cid (that is, the Lord) Campeador—and 1212—the victory of Las Navas of Tolosa—Alphonsus VI, king of Castille (+1109), still called himself "king of the three religions." But it is precisely from the time of the Crusades that we can date the unleashing of aggression against the Jews. They had lived peaceably not only in Spain but throughout all of Europe, and particularly in the north of France, where they formed brilliant intellectual centers. Now, in order to affirm itself, Christianity becomes exclusive.

If any man could typify and incarnate the apogee of Latin Christianity, it was Bernard of Clairvaux (1091–1153). The preacher of the Second Crusade at Vézelay in 1146 was the protector of the first Templars, an institution that epitomized all the audacity of the twelfth century. An Order at once military and monastic, the Templars had as their mission the protection of pilgrims to the Holy Land. Saint Bernard was above all, if not the founder of Cîteaux, at least the one who gave the veritable impulse to this reform of monastic life, carried out in the name of renunciation and poverty. The Cistercians broke away from the Cluniac monks, deeming them decadent with their lengthy liturgical observances and their works of charity, which caused them to administer immense domains. The new group turned toward total retreat, silence, and the mystical life. We know that Cistercian influence on the quest for the Holy Grail was great.

Saint Bernard stood out as a giant in his century, present in all combats, fighting wherever Christianity seemed to him threatened. This knight, monk, and priest, teeming with energy and genius, fought as valiantly for the true Pope, against the usurper Anacletus, as he did for the true faith, particularly against Abelard. That brilliant and heretical precursor of a more dialectical and rational theology has been characterized as "the first modern man" by M. D. Chenu. Abelard's dramatic reputation has tended to make us forget the greatness of the learned Héloise, the one who was always loyal to him, and whose fate raises the question of the position of women in the Middle Ages.

16

17. *Scene from the* Life of St. Thomas Becket, *circa 1310–1320 (London, British Library, Ms Royal 2 B. VII). The Archbishop of Canterbury, appointed by Henry II of England himself, has to cross the English Channel to escape the tyrannical power of the king and maintain the Church's freedom in the face of pressure from the temporal power.*

18. *Fra Angelico,* Saint Lawrence Giving Alms, *detail from the Vatican Chapel fresco. An old beggar, accompanied by a blind man, leans toward the holy deacon who, by reason of his ministry, takes care of the poor. It is a reminder of the Church's charities throughout history, especially when a money economy becomes more important.*

17

18

But what does Citeaux and its enormous success tell us? The Cistercian Order bore witness that the call of the Gregorian reform for a return to evangelical poverty had been heard. The Church renewed herself from within, showing that love of God has primacy over love of the world. Is this to say that the other goals of the Gregorian reform, rejection of the benefits of feudalism and retention of the Church's independence in the face of temporal power, had been achieved? The "murder in the cathedral" of Canterbury of the archbishop Thomas Becket in 1170, on the thinly veiled order of his sovereign friend turned worst enemy, Henry II of England, demonstrates that tensions were still alive. But the Pope who canonized Thomas three years after his assassination, Alexander III, was the one whom the Germanic emperor Frederick Barbarossa (+1190) so violently opposed. The Church could only resist the permanent challenge of the state because of the integrity restored to her, after the Gregorian reform, by Saint Bernard's formulation of the theory of the two swords held in the Pope's hand,[3] and also by the personalities of the succeeding pontiffs.

The importance of the persons heading the Church in the thirteenth century, especially during its first half, is obvious. If we compare Innocent III (1198–1216), Honorius III (1216–1227), and Gregory IX (1227–1241), we have to admit that the first certainly left the most profound mark on the Church. In this age of the Gothic cathedrals, which were just beginning to soar due to the "miracle of the ribbed vault,"—buildings such as St. Denis of Paris, "madly conceived and wisely executed"— harmonious constructions would be built throughout the realm.[4] In 1215, at a time when cities were beginning to flourish, bishops from all corners of Western Christendom gathered at the Fourth Lateran Council. There they formulated pastoral

19. *Giotto,* The Dream of Innocent III, *circa 1295–1300 (Asissi, upper church nave). Thomas de Celano related how, in a dream, the Pope saw his Lateran Cathedral collapsing, and how a frail religious kept it from falling over. This is why he was so quick to give Francis of Assisi permission to found a community. Eighty years later, Giotto makes Francis look significant and gives him a halo.*

20. *Taddeo Gaddi,* Francis' Meeting with the Egyptian Sultan Malek-el-Kamel. *This meeting, which probably took place in the beginning of September 1219, is authentic. Saint Bonaventure reports on Francis' conversations with Muslim theologians and his proposal to prove his faith to the Sultan by walking on burning coals.*

19

21. *Saint Dominic, detail of the Perugia Triptych by Fra Angelico (Perugia National Library). Fra Angelico depicts the founder of his order holding his attributes, the New Testament opened to 1 Timothy 4: "preach in season and out of season," the lily of virginity and chastity, and in the halo, the evening star that still reflects the light of Christ, the Sun.*

21

20

legislation, building upon the work of Gratian who in the middle of the twelfth century had codified canon law.[5]

Innocent III knew how to channel the vast movement of a return to Gospel poverty. After the relative falling off of the Cistercians, Europe was adrift amid forms of this movement that ranged from the most admirable types, (heremetical life especially), to the strangest and most heretical aberrations. Innocent realized the threat posed by the Waldensians, with their challenging of religious practices. But these reformers were relatively moderate. The Church dialogued with them and tried to reintegrate them. The Cathars, a sect that took hold through southern France and Italy, used evangelical and Christian language while in fact perpetuating the ancient Manichean heresy that rejected matter and creation. Innocent III gave complete freedom to two exceptional men, contemporaries and friends in spite of their very different temperaments: the Italian, Francis of Assisi, following a lay spirituality and vowed to mendicant poverty, and the Castilian, Dominic, clerical founder of an Order of Preachers of doctrine who would very soon become mendicants also.

22

23

From the movement of evangelical poverty, the papacy drew apostles in the service of a truly ecclesial ideal and supported the independence and responsibility of masters and students of universities established in Paris, Oxford, and Bologna. And at the end of the century, from the combined influence of the new Franciscan and Dominican mendicant orders and of the universities being established in Europe, there rose up cathedrals of a new kind, the theological Summas of dogma and morality. While Bonaventure, Minister General of the Franciscans, followed the more traditional and Augustinian line, Thomas Aquinas inaugurated a kind of intellectual revolution. He integrated the concepts of the ancient Aristotle, who had been rediscovered thanks to the translations that Jews and Muslims had made into Arabic. This gigantic work of integration provided Thomas with an instrument capable of explaining revelation by clearly distinguishing between the realms of faith and reason, and of grace and nature, which is never destroyed, but rather transformed, after having been assumed.

It is quite possible to maintain that the height of Latin Christianity can be placed—in terms of civilization and the history of ideas—at the end of the twelfth century and the greater part of the thirteenth. This incontestable Western success owed its origin to multiple factors, but from a theological and philosophical point of view its roots may be traced to the mutual dependence of distinction and balance. This era coincides almost miraculously with an ideal of harmony between things hitherto carefully separated, precisely in order that they might the better be joined and reunited: the distinction between faith and reason, the supernatural and the natural, God and Caesar, contemplation and action. A solid theology of creation, seen as distinct from the uncreated Creator, also permitted, within the optimism of a humanism founded in God, the execution of the command to "rule the earth" (Genesis 1, 26), which was given to man formed in the image and likeness of God. We must understand at the same time that such a synthesis, based on a balance between so many elements, could not last. And yet it stamped the Western mentality forever, giving it its fundamental optimism, leading it toward technical research, and inspiring its missionary thrust. We know likewise that it has ever since had its admirers, torn between nostalgia, imitation, and re-invention.

This synthesis appeared in many forms. The audacious architecture of the Summa Theologiae, subtle and scholarly,

23. Jean Fouquet, the descent of the Holy Spirit (Etienne Chevalier Heures, breviary, New York, The Lehman Collection). The 15th-century artist evokes the coming of the Spirit on numerous disciples, probably the mendicant orders, who will evangelize the city of Paris, depicted here as the Ile de la Cité and Notre Dame, while the demons of error and heresy take flight.

24. Master of the Saint Ursula Legend, St. Bonaventure, circa 1510 (Cologne, Wallraf-Ritchartz Museum). The minister general of the Friars Minor has become the bishop of Albano and a cardinal. But, under the splendor of the cope, one can see the rope of the Franciscan habit and the bare feet of the one who had to legislate on poverty for his order.

25. The Basilica of St. Francis of Assisi was erected over the tomb that Brother Elias had built to shelter the stigmatized body of Saint Francis. It is formed by two superimposed churches in which frescos by Cimabue and Giotto exalt the life of the saint so as to inspire the devotion of the pilgrims who come in great numbers—a sign of Francis' great popularity in Italy.

26. Fra Angelico, Triptych of St. Peter Martyr (Florence, San Marco Museum). Detail of Saint Thomas Aquinas, recognizable by his face, both noble and full-featured, represented in the Dominican habit. He presents the text of Psalm 103:13, on which he made a famous commentary.

27. Dominican church, called the Church of the Jacobins, Toulouse. In this city where Saint Dominic founded the first priory of the Preachers, after the area's integration into the Kingdom of France in 1271, this church with two naves was built, one nave for the religious and the other for preaching to the laity. The two naves join in an immense palm-shaped vault, an architectural symbol of the Catholic faith. Saint Thomas' body is buried here. He gave a magisterial account of the complexities of Catholic doctrine in his Summa Theologiae.

24

25

26

27

28

28. *The creation of the stars, detail from the Creation mosaic (Monreale Cathedral, Sicily). Here, through a theological interpretation of the story from Genesis, the sky and its stars are created by Christ, the Word of God, who, as one of the persons of the Trinity, is also Creator of the world.*

29. *Latin manuscript of Saint Hildegard called* Homo quadratus *(State Library of Lucca, Ms 1942). Hildegard of Bingen, seen in the lower left, contemplates the man created in perfect harmony. This strange image prefigures Renaissance speculations on the physical and moral dignity of the human being, who is a microcosm of reality.*

29

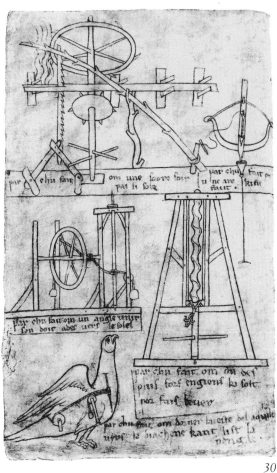

30

30. *Villard de Honnecourt, drawings of medieval machinery, circa 1220–1250 (Paris, Bibliothèque Nationale, ms fr. 19093). The 13th century brings about the first developments of technology and experimental science, as testified, for example, by Roger Bacon.*

THE CHURCH AND THE CHALLENGE OF SECULAR THOUGHT

31

32

33

34

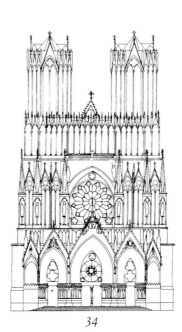

might be seen at the century's close as a reflection of the splendid art of contemporary cathedrals, Chartres at the beginning of the century, Notre-Dame of Paris in mid-century, and Reims at its close, all of them converging with a social consent. As Elie Faure says, in phrases more lyrical than precise, "The cathedral, and all Gothic architecture, concretized the balance between the new popular forms and the metaphysical monument whose setting Christian philosophy had been preparing for some thousand or twelve hundred years. But as they developed, these forces completely broke out of their settings and shattered them."[6]

How amazing it is also to see the two greatest thinkers of the thirteenth century summoned in 1274 to the Second Council of Lyons, whose task was to reconcile Eastern and Western Christianity. Aquinas died on the way; Bonaventure died at the Council itself. The same ideal of unity and of defense of the Church had animated Saint Louis, king of France, who had died a few years before in the Crusades (1270). His ardent yet humble manner of acting seemed to seal the union between spiritual and temporal power; and we may envision him as the authentic lay Christian, before the "laicist" rupture of the following century.

To nuance this too beautiful picture, we should contrast Saint Louis with a contemporary sovereign who foreshadowed the fragility of the edifice of Christendom. Frederick Hohenstaufen II (1194–1250), godson of Pope Innocent III,

35

37

36

38

THE CHURCH AND THE CHALLENGE OF SECULAR THOUGHT

39

39. *Prague, Cathedral of St. Veit (1344), completed in the 20th century. The splendor of Gothic architecture's expression of sacred space.*

40, 41, and 42. *The Europe of the cathedrals. In the second half of the Middle Ages, these stone vessels seem not to be inserted into the cities; rather, the cities are built around them. (40) In England, Lichfield, 13th century; (41) in Germany, Cologne, the largest Christian cathedral, reconstruction on the site of an earlier building begun mid-13th century; (42) in Castille, Burgos, 13th century, completed in the 18th century.*

40

41

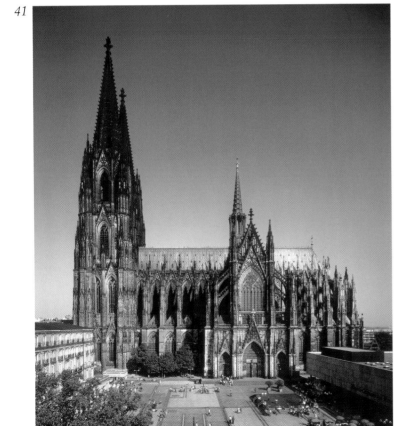

42

THE CHURCH AND THE CHALLENGE OF SECULAR THOUGHT

43. King Roger's bedroom (Palermo, Royal Palace). These mosaics combine several styles, typical of the complex society of Sicily. The Moslem style of non-figurative decoration, that exploits Mediterranean vegetation and almost African-like fauna, does not prevent the reference to Greek mythology with the centaur.

43

44

45

46

was to prove himself the cleverest and most astounding of medieval sovereigns. This emperor preferred negotiation to the Crusades and did not hide his sympathies for Islam, which he had encountered in Sicily where Latin, Byzantine, and Muslim civilizations rubbed shoulders. His independent politics won him excommunication on several occasions. He was, as it were, the genial and complex precursor of all those sovereigns who would confront the Church with a new challenge usually called "the lay spirit."[7] This challenge was based on the secular resistance of the state to the pretensions of the Church, which thought it had reestablished the equilibrium of "the two Cities." It was based also on new conditions, which would appear in the fourteenth and fifteenth centuries.

47

48

Things Fall Apart

In 1284, the daring vaults of the cathedral of Beauvais collapsed. Beyond a simple error of construction, some have seen in this the symbol of an ancient ideal that was about to fall to ruins.

In fact, already at the end of the thirteenth century, the new mendicant Orders shared in this collapse. In order to facilitate the repression of heresy, the Pope, bishops, and sovereigns instituted the procedure of the Inquisition, which was soon transformed into a tribunal, around the years 1230–1235. This jurisdiction, which did not follow the customary legal arrangements, was entrusted chiefly to the mendicant Dominican and Franciscan friars because it was considered to be a form of preaching. Its purpose was to bring those who had deviated from the faith to a recognition of their errors and inconsistencies regarding the teaching of Christianity. No one in the Middle Ages was shocked by this procedure nor by the

sanctions that could follow from it, but the Church incontestably put itself on the defensive.

It must be admitted that the Franciscan source, so pure and limpid in the time of Saint Francis and Saint Clare, became at times rather muddied with successive generations. An entire branch of the Franciscan Order turned toward an apocalyptic spiritualism originating with Joachim of Fiore. This degenerated in the fourteenth century into what could well be called a number of different sects, such as the Fraticelli.

The secular masters of the universities, particularly in Paris, where William of Saint Amour (+1272) won his notoriety, rose up against these dangers posed by the new orders. Directly attached to the Pope, the new orders threatened the ecclesiology of the secular masters, which was by contrast more episcopal or local, if not national. Curiously, the emperor, whose only logic was to oppose the papacy, supported the current of the Franciscan spirituals, who themselves rebelled against the Pope. They did this in the name of the ideal of absolute poverty, which they claimed to find in a literal interpretation of the Testament of Saint Francis.

The end of the thirteenth century witnessed intransigence on all sides. Harassed by Philip the Fair, King of France, Pope Boniface VIII published a text reaffirming "theocracy" with extreme vigor. The bull *Unam Sanctam* of 1302 was based, as its title indicates, on the concept of the unity of Christendom, represented by one head, "not two heads as a freak would have, Christ *and* Peter, the vicar of Christ *and* the successor of Peter." Even from a temporal viewpoint, the supremacy of the Pope was operative "if temporal power should veer off course."

The turning point of the fourteenth century seemed marked by the hegemony of the papacy, symbolized by the enormous success of pilgrimages to Rome. This inspired Boniface VIII, in the year 1300, to institute the Holy Year,

49. Sandro Botticelli, illustrations for The Divine Comedy, *1482– 1490. Hell, Canto XIV (Vatican, Apostolic Library.) Dante's odyssey takes him to the regions of the dead in 1300, the year of the Jubilee that grants a plenary indulgence—a forgiveness coming from the merits of Christ and of the Church.*

a Jubilee with a plenary indulgence remitting all temporal punishment due to sins. Dante, who perhaps went to Rome during this year himself, has left us a description of it (*Inferno* XVIII, 29). But the evolution of Dante's thought, as we see it in *De Monarchia* (1312–1313) and in *The Divine Comedy,* shows us the contradictions to which the Church was subject after the spiritual triumph of the Jubilee.

The Rise of the Lay Spirit

Three years later, following upon the conflict with Philip the Fair, the French jurists, that is to say the king's jurists, opposed the theocracy defended by Boniface VIII. William of Nogaret, allying himself with the Roman family of the Colonna, insulted the Pope on September 7, 1303, in his castle at Anagni. Boniface VIII refused to put himself "under the protection of the king of France" as had been suggested to him. On the contrary, he prepared to excommunicate the king. A month later, under the shock of these events, the Pope died.

In 1305, Bertrand of Got, Archbishop of Bordeaux, was elected as Clement V, and in 1309 he was installed in Avignon, on the borders of the kingdom. The papacy was indeed under the protection of the French king. Not only had forces changed camps in favor of temporal power, but theological justification was to precede and follow this national and royal claim to autonomy.

The great medievalist, Ernst H. Kantorowicz, who died in 1963, showed in his classic work written in 1957 the shift toward a mystical concept, operative at levels ranging from ecclesiology to politics.[8] The Church's most profound definition regarding the Eucharist, *Corpus mysticum,* was applied by extrapolation and a shift in meaning to the leading national monarchies. The "mystical Body" referred also to the state which, by means of this symbol, achieved a certain abstraction and could demand obedience and sacrifice. Henceforth a person could "die for the fatherland," with a real disregard for the state itself and the individual king. The king had "two bodies," his physical body, personal and mortal, and the body that survived him. This is precisely the meaning of the famous French saying, "The king is dead, long live the king!"

The national monarchy was exalted in almost theological terms. It had its theoreticians, but to the German emperor's advantage, they were opposed to the pontifical plenitude of power. *The Defensor Pacis,* drawn up in 1324 by Marsilio of Padua (+1342) and John of Jandun, of the University of Paris,

(50) Detail of a fresco of the prophets in the grand audience room of the Palace of the Popes in Avignon, painted by Mateo Giovanetti about 1353. Note that the texts chosen for the scrolls of the prophets (with chapter references) become more important than the figures of the prophets. (51) This enormous palace was as much civil as ecclesiastical, intended as the seat of an effective administration.

50

51

supported the subordination of Church to state. They held that the ecclesiastical institution ought to be limited to the distribution of the sacraments. This was a direct attack on Pope John XXII who had opposed Louis of Bavaria, the elected emperor. Here we have a kind of inverted theocracy, since the "defense of peace," which pertained, in Augustine's view, to the City of God, was now being entrusted to the emperor.

In keeping with his position on ownership and poverty, which was at the heart of the Franciscan debate, and of his conflict with the papacy, William of Ockham (+1347) would,

52

53

52. The Effects of Good Government *(1338–1339), Ambrogio Lorenzetti (Siena, Public Palace, Room of the Nine). In a purely civic public building, the artist depicts a utopian ideal of urban order and prosperity that has no need for any religious dimension as such.*

53. Giovanni di Paolo, Saint Catherine of Siena in the presence of a Pope, *around the second half of the 15th century (Madrid, Thyssen Bornemisza Foundation). The artist from Siena represented the Dominican tertiary either at Avignon in 1375 before Pope Gregory XI, to convince him to return to Rome, or with Urban VI, newly elected in 1378 and rejected by a part of the Sacred College.*

54. Saint Bridget as a pilgrim *(15th century, xylography). Bridget was the widow of an important Swedish lord. On the basis of revelations she received, she started her pilgrimage to Avignon to convince Gregory XI to come back to Rome, his diocese, as bishop. She wears the hat and carries the staff of a pilgrim and also the cross that identifies her as the foundress of the Order of the Holy Savior (Brigittines).*

54

a few years later, give this political doctrine a more theological dimension. His nominalist trend of thought cast doubt on the value of mediation, through a kind of rejection of universality. The emperor held his temporal power by the direct delegation of God, through the consensus of nations. There was then a declericalization of the world and of power. The fresco painted by Lorenzetti for the City Hall of the Piazza del Campo in Siena, representing good government, does not include clerics. Was not God also the God of the laity?[9]

All other things being equal, this was surely Dante's position: "The authority of the temporal monarch comes down to him directly from the universal source of all authority" (*Monarchia* III, XVI, 15). The two great lights which had formerly combined to illumine the world could no longer be united, for the one had extinguished the other when the crosier was aligned with the sword (*Purgatorio* XVI, 106–111). Dante chose to defend the rights of universal monarchy. This was the challenge known as neo-Caesarism. While political philosophy and a theology stamped with the new spirit were

advancing toward confrontations more radical than those of the fourteenth century, the Church met rather ineptly the practical challenge hurled at her by sovereigns. She was on the verge of a major crisis in her history, first through servitude, and then through division.

The Crisis of the Church

Dominated by the king of France, the institutional Church entered into servitude. She was held captive even physically at Avignon. Already at the Council of Vienne (1311–1312), certain measures, such as the condemnation or suppression of the Templars, had signaled the revenge and retaliation of Philip the Fair. The French Popes, especially those from Languedoc, or the "Limousins," were entrenched in Avignon, while all around them the Hundred Years' War between France and England raged (1337–1453). The "companies," irregular troops of thieves and murderers in the pay of the

56

55

English, fought ruthlessly, and epidemics of the plague devastated Europe. The "black death" decimated perhaps one third of the population in the fourteenth century.[10]

Imperturbably, and in the end courageously, the French papacy set up a remarkable administrative and fiscal system, with a consistorial government and a series of juridical and institutional reforms leading to centralization.

Gregory XI, exhorted by the mystics of his time, Saint Brigid of Sweden and Saint Catherine of Siena, both of whom had a keen sense of ecclesiology, decided on a return to Rome in 1378. His almost immediate death caused a terrific shock: The Spouse of Christ, "one and holy," was now to be divided by the Great Western Schism. From 1378 until 1417, Christendom witnessed first two, then three lines of Popes, that of Rome, of Avignon, and finally, that of Pisa with the unworthy John XXIII. Each Pope created his own cardinals, who were supported by their national countries of origin. The Church was reflecting in her government the confrontation of national monarchs, and her powerlessness in the hands of secular politics. Regions were sometimes divided. Religious orders, almost always torn apart, had two heads. Even saints were divided in different camps.

Plans to resolve the schism failed after a whole series of unsuccessful attempts. The most symbolic of these was the abortive meeting of January 1408, when Benedict XIII, the Avignon Pope, found himself at Portovenere near La Spezia and Gregory XII, the Pope of Rome, at Lucca, fifty kilometers distant. Things remained at an impasse.

The end of the schism came with the convocation of the Council of Constance in 1417, summoned at the initiative of Emperor Sigismund of Hungary. The Council led to the election of Martin V of the Colonna family in 1417. Martin was a native Roman, so the bishop of Rome was returning to his own city. The consequences of the schism, however, were incalculable. Some were psychological, as the reciprocal excommunications and the danger of dying without the sacraments during this period of ever-present sudden death haunted people's minds. There were also ecclesiological

57

consequences. In their distrust of the papacy, bishops and sovereigns henceforth put their confidence in a council. This meant that the government of the Church was thrown off balance by conciliarism. Finally, there were theological consequences with the rise of John Wycliff (+1384) in England and John Huss (+1415) in Bohemia. These clerics adopted in some way the theses of the lay spirit. The martyrdom of John Huss, burned at the Council of Constance, served only to stir up Czech nationalism, with Huss as its hero.

During these years of trial and sorrow, the people of God held fast, prayed, and found solutions that would not be without their own repercussions. The Church was a mass of men and women abandoned by their pastors. The challenge of the lay spirit in the fourteenth and fifteenth centuries was taken up by the people of God.

Responses of the People of God

Christians managed, somehow, to transcend the rude shocks that the Church was experiencing. Wounded as they were, psychologically, in their adherence to the Church—because of the desertion of their pastors or, at the least, because of their falling into disrepute—Christians were left indubitably to their own devices.

This is how we have to interpret that taste for the concrete, the intimate, the reassuring, which took the form of renewed devotion to relics. Relics could be touched; the people could carry them on their persons for protection. Whatever was concrete, such as counting one's prayers in reciting the Rosary, accumulating merits, or collecting indulgences, reassured people. These things could preserve them from the violent death which, according to the belief of the period, would precipitate them into Purgatory. The concrete also meant seeing. Isolated in huge churches where Latin was the norm, the Christian people asked "to see God" as they put it. They wanted to contemplate and adore the Eucharistic Host, soon to be celebrated by the feast of Corpus Christi. This celebration became generalized at the beginning of the fourteenth century. Konrad Witz represents the concept well, as he pictures the Church holding the host and chalice and supported by the processional cross.

But there was more. To appease this appetite for the concrete and the intimate, spiritual writers proposed a devotion, which was called modern because it was new, the Flemish *devotio moderna*. It was based on the loving contemplation of the Incarnation of God, on Jesus the Man, close to us, so close

58

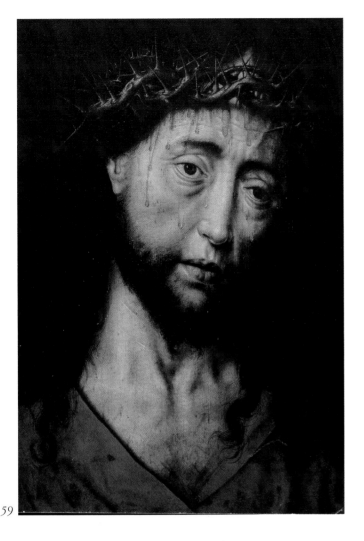

59

60. Ruysbroek, The Spiritual Tabernacle and Other Treatises, *Groenendael, Brabant, circa 1420 (Brussells, Royal Library, ms 19295–97). John Ruysbroek transcribes his interior illuminations on a tablet under the inspiration of the Spirit hovering in the center of the illustration, while a brother writes them on a manuscript. The illustration conveys the interior and exterior calm of this Flemish mystic as well as the studious atmosphere in which he worked.*

61. Thomas a Kempis (+1471), a manuscript of his writings. This Canon Regular to whom tradition attributes the most widely read of all Western books of spirituality, The Imitation of Christ, *is the representative of the spirituality called the* Devotio moderna, *characterized by a conformity to the Christ in the Gospels.*

that one might, in fact, imitate him. This was proposed in the greatest spiritual text of this period, *The Imitation of Christ* by Thomas a Kempis (+1417).[11] Finally, Christians of this period, in order to escape from their too great solitude, gathered devoutly in innumerable confraternities of Friends of God, to use the term originating in the schools of Rhineland mysticism. This mystical movement later was at the opposite pole from the *devotio moderna,* and served as a prior counterbalance. We are in the era of fraternities, whose role was, perhaps, to help people overcome their anxiety and mitigate their loneliness.

For there was yet a second shock for Christians. The anguish of death and the horrors of the macabre had entered their world. These were elicited by powerful sermons on hell and the last judgment, preached throughout Europe by the Dominican from Valencia in Spain, Saint Vincent Ferrer

60

61

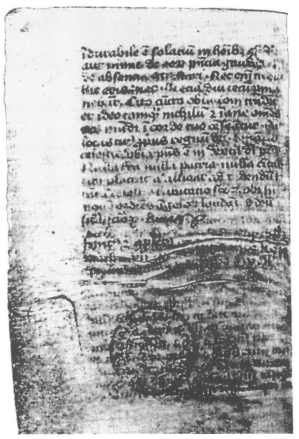

62. The Black Death, *Giovanni Sercambi, miniature from the beginning of the 15th century (Lucca Chronicle, Lucca State Archives). The omnipresence of death, symbolized by the skeletons holding scythes, dominates consciousness at the end of the Middle Ages because of the plague epidemics that decimated Europe.*

63. Chronicle of the World, *written in Constance. German miniature, 14th century (Munich, Bavarian State Library). Given the calamities of the times, a spirit of penance characterizes the most fervent groups, who, by means of impressive processions, make a public spectacle of self-flagellation to invite their contemporaries to conversion.*

62

63

64

(+1419). Death's gruesome dance made its way into cemeteries where the terrible equality of all souls in death was depicted. Popes, kings, townspeople, and peasants matched steps in the dance of the skeletons. Violent death, from plague or war, was omnipresent.

Accompanying all this came a new thrust of heroism, springing from the lowest social levels. Where horror abounded, holiness abounded all the more. Devotions proliferated. We can think of the fraternities of undertakers who buried the repulsive corpses that spread disease. There was also the heroism of Saint Rocco who died in 1327 in Montpellier while caring for the plague-stricken. He was to become such a powerful protector against sickness that his relics would be stolen and brought to Venice where his confraternity engaged the painter Tintoretto in 1562 to illustrate the saint's miracles. There was the devotion of the great mystic Tauler at Strasbourg in 1348, and so many other hidden instances of heroism. The theology of the Assumption of the Blessed Virgin, which received new emphasis at this time, gave Christians the hope of transcending the macabre rotting away of their bodies

through faith in the preservation of Mary's body and in their own resurrection.

Finally, the people of God, involved in struggles between nations, found a way to give a broader, more ecclesial and evangelical significance to the concept of the nation. Here again, it was the saints who pointed out the way. Joan of Arc "drove the English out of France" because for nations, too, there is a justice, a right, a vocation. But she encountered the ecclesiastical caricature of priests in the pay of kings, like Cauchon, bishop of Beauvais, or the conciliarist and soon Gallican theologians, such as those of the University of Paris, of whose number Gerson alone had sufficient genius to be convinced of her innocence. The paradox of Joan of Arc, burned at the stake in 1431 at the age of nineteen, was that it sanctified the earthly nation in its relationship to the heavenly Kingdom and that she was condemned by those who, entrusted with incarnating the City of God, were instead enslaved by worldly politics.

Fifty years later, in December 1481, a peasant hermit and mystic of the Trinity, Nicholas of Flüe, consolidated his Swiss

64. *Joan of Arc, a sketch in the margin of a page from the registry of the* Parlement of Paris. *During the rehabilitation trial (1449–1456), the clerk of the court drew the young lady, burnt by the English in 1431, according to the image that people had of her, with her pennant carrying the name of Jesus and her sword (which actually she never used).*

65. The Trinity and the World, *a painting portraying the vision of Nicolas of Flüe (+1487), from the Church of Sachseln (Central Switzerland). The hermit of Ranft in 1480 asked for a work depicting his 1467 revelation. The six-spoke wheel represents the interior and exterior activities of the Trinity. It is encircled by the symbols of the four evangelists and the mysteries of Christ's life, beginning with the Annunciation and culminating in Christ's death on the Cross—summed up in the Eucharist. In images, it recapitulates the history of salvation.*

66. Raymon Lull, dressed in pilgrim attire, crossed land and sea. Here he climbs up to the image of the Virgin Mary and the Christ Child, who blesses his mission of announcing the Incarnation to the Moslems (German manuscript, 14th century).

65

66

homeland by reconciling the participants of the diet of Stans through his wise and Christian counsel in favor of political moderation. The confederated cantons were indebted to him, for he incarnated a national ideal, not only peacefully but also heroically.[12]

In the fourteenth century a Catalan, Raymond Lull, turned toward Islam to evangelize it. In the fifteenth century, a German, Cardinal Nicolas of Cusa (+1464) showed a remarkably ecumenical spirit in his work at the Council of Florence for the reunion of the Churches of East and West.

As the noblest of her children testify, the Church endeavored to incorporate the challenge of nationalism within the concept of catholicity, just as the people of God had risen up to the challenge of the lay spirit, for a time, with an outpouring of devotion and charity.

One site, more than all others, captures this whole turbulent and difficult period. It is the Sainte-Chapelle, built in Paris by Saint Louis in 1248 to enshrine the crown of thorns brought from the East. It is fittingly called a "chapel," resembling those chapels which will enhance cathedrals in the

fourteenth century. From this time on, a flamboyant style will prevail, harmonizing well with the taste for detail characteristic of the age of nominalism.

What, in fact, is a chapel? It is a place apart—more intimate than the nave—where relics are kept, to be displayed and venerated. At this time, it corresponded to the new taste for the concrete. Usually designed as a place where confraternities could gather and their members might be buried, the chapel attempted to transcend the haunting fears of Christians in the fourteenth and fifteenth centuries: fears of solitude and of death. It is beautiful that, in a Christian age, Saint Louis, a lay person and a national sovereign, should have been the one to build the Sainte-Chapelle. For the age of the palace was about to begin, and with it the Renaissance, which would constitute, in quite another way, a new challenge.

1

1. The complex of the ducal palace of Mantua. At the end of the Middle Ages, civic architecture begins to imitate religious structures and keeps growing till the 15th or 16th century through enlargements and embellishments, as in the case of the Gonzaga family in Mantua. Cloister gardens have become courtyards. There is still a chapel in the ensemble, but it is no longer at the center.

2

2. Pisanello (circa 1395–1450), painted for one of the chambers of the "Old Court" of the Palace at Mantua, a cycle on the Knights of the Round Table and King Arthur. Here, an image from a tournament. A taste for novels that describe the ideal of chivalry of preceding centuries is still very strong during the Renaissance. During his convalescence in 1521, it is that type of literature that Ignatius of Loyola chose to read before becoming a "knight for Christ" after his conversion.

Chapter 5

THE CHURCH AND THE CHALLENGE OF THE RENAISSANCE

The period in the West covering the fourteenth and fifteenth centuries has been called the age of the palace, succeeding that of the cathedral. The substitution is significant, for if the *palazzo* was essentially lay or civil, associated with the urban aristocracy or the bourgeois merchants, it also was the *palazzo pubblico* of the Italian communes, each one independent and a rival of the others. Even the Palace of the Popes of Avignon, begun by Benedict XII (1334–1342) and enlarged chiefly by Clement VI (+1352), was in its appearance administrative rather than ecclesiastical.

The new pockets of prosperity would welcome the Renaissance. Thus Burgundy emerged, with its Flemish estates, and above all Italy, which seems to have invented this "Renaissance." Florence became the center of the revival of art at the moment when the Republic was turning into a tyrannical principality. Its quasi-sovereign was Cosmo the Elder (+1464) of the famous Medici family, which was to rule there from 1434 and to continue, with vacillating changes of fortune, up to the eighteenth century.

The revolution that took place was initially scientific and technological. A symbol for it might be the first mechanical clock, which appeared at the beginning of the fourteenth century, the prototype of all future time-measuring mechanisms that would divide the day into twenty-four hours of sixty minutes each. In a sense, this new invention seemed to depose, or replace, the world of heavenly circles that Dante, with his keen interest in astronomy and astrology, described (*Purgatorio VIII, 2 and Paradiso X*). This revolution was also economic, with the advent of capitalism and the enormous German and Florentine business houses. It was monetary and financial as well, and consequently would soon become geographical so that new sources of supplies and new commercial outlets might be found. Finally, it was accompanied by a new spirit in the intellectual and spiritual domain.

The Spirit of Renewal

With the exception, of course, of saints and mystics, the Church manifested a kind of spiritual decline, torn as she was between lethargy and somnolence on the one hand and excitement and excess on the other. Theological systems became redundant or too complex. They seemed to have no answer to that need for renewal and reform, which Christianity experienced in the midst of national quarrels and rivalries between vested interests.

This renewal first appeared as cultural, artistic, and literary. It is in the shadow of the Avignon papacy, otherwise characterized by the bureaucratization of the Church and by its dependence upon secular powers, that a new poetry would break through, that of Francis Petrarch (1304–1376), a native of Tuscany but already a well-traveled European. Is he the last figure of medieval humanism or the first modern humanist? Although he loved classical Latin and dialogued with pagan authors, he still chose to give pride of place to the contemplative life in his treatise on the solitary life, written when his brother Gerard entered the Carthusian house of Montrieux in Provence in 1342. His Florentine contemporary, Boccacio (1313–1375), even though he too experienced a certain religious evolution, inclined much more clearly to neo-pagan thought, a natural temptation and a challenge for Christianity. We get the feeling that the Renaissance, like Janus, was looking in two directions.

Because of their literary vitality in different fields, these two men who were friends seemed, after the scourge of the Black Death with its train of woes, like precursors of a new spirit that would come to be called humanism. It would give birth to a culture, the Renaissance. Its earliest roots were in mid-fourteenth century Italy and it burgeoned in the Quattrocento to spread finally throughout all of Europe.

What we are talking about is the return of youthful vigor, as after a blood transfusion. Following close upon the obsession with the macabre and the desolation of a brief and imperiled

3. Florence, aerial view. Even though the Palazzo Vecchio and the piazza of the Signoria in the center of the city, where Savonarola and his two companions were burnt in 1498, first catch our attention, the rectangular building in the lower right, called Orsanmichele, exemplifies the complexity of the aspirations of an Italian city during the Renaissance. It is a monument at once communal and commercial, artistic and religious (it contains a miraculous image of the Virgin), under the protection of the Confraternities of the Craftsmen. The best 15th century Florentine sculptors contributed to its exterior decoration.

4. Center of the upper east façade of Orsanmichele. *Luca della Robbia (1400–1482), sculpture showing the Merchants' Tribunal Coat of Arms, terra cotta (1463). Encircled by a crown of luscious fruit, the fleur-de-lis, bearing stalks of grain, surmounts bags of grain prepared for sale and shipment: a symbol of the prosperity of Florentine commerce.*

5. Michelangelo (1475–1564), drawing of a project for the Medici Mausoleum (Paris, Louvre Museum). This artist, whose genius sums up the Italian Renaissance, built for the new sacristy of the Church of St. Lawrence in Florence the tomb of Giulio and of Lorenzo the Magnificent (1449–1492), the most ostentatious of the Medicis. The allegories of the design hardly evoke a typically Christian vision of death and resurrection.

6. Avignon. General view of the Palace of the Popes. Adjacent to the Cathedral, the palace is an example of architecture that is both civil and religious. The 14th-century building has a massive facade. It served as private apartments for the popes as well as for the pontifical administration which flourished widely at that time.

6

7. Miniature illustrating a short story of the third day of Boccacio's Decameron (Parisian manuscript circa 1415, Vatican Library, Pal Lat., 1989). The exterior and interior decorations, the vestments of knights, princess, Popes, and the cardinal are all elegantly stylized.

8. Appolonio di Giovanni, The Triumph of Time, illustration for The Triumphs of Francisco Petrarch, (Florence, Riccardian Library, ms 1129, 15th century). The white-bearded old man who supports himself on two canes is surrounded by four timeless baby cupids. The chariot wheel is an allegory of the passing of time, while the two stags show their age by the profusion of their antlers.

9. *Paolo Ucello (about 1396–1475), The Battle of San Romano, detail (Florence, Galleria of the Uffizi). The painter gives remarkable importance to the heads and breasts of the horses as well as to the lances in the foreground, thus using perspective to bring out of the scuffle an impression of triumphant power.*

11. *Lorenzo Ghiberti (1378–1455),* Presentation of Jesus at the Temple of Jerusalem, *stained glass from the drum of the dome realized by Bernardo di Francesco, 1444 (Florence, Santa Maria dei Fiore). This stained-glass window from the Florence Cathedral is contemporary to Cosimo the Elder, the founder of the Medici dynasty.*

10. *Dome from Santa Maria dei Fiore (Florence), realized by Filippo Brunelleschi (1377–1446). This work combines the lightness of alternating black and white marble with the elegance of its volumes. It creates an equilibrium between the openness expressed by rounded shapes and the closure suggested by the rectangles. Italian Renaissance architecture shows a sophisticated mastery of space.*

life, this was like a reawakening of the vital powers of man and society. People felt alive once more, reborn, as never before in history. Those earlier "Renaissances" of the Middle Ages—in the ninth and then in the twelfth centuries—would be so designated much later by analogy with the Renaissance par excellence, that of modern times, of which contemporaries themselves were conscious.

At the very time when death had been so close and remained so, humanism affirmed that the human person could live. It declared that civilizations were not entirely mortal, because they could be resuscitated, particularly the civilizations of Greece and Rome. Humanism arose in reaction to the preceding period, which now appeared paralyzed or sick, and it contributed now and for a long time to the devaluation of what would soon be called disdainfully the Middle Ages, or intermediary stage between Antiquity and its rebirth or Renaissance. But in this choice of the Greco-Latin civilization, a culture and thought was being favored whose vital center was not Christianity. In adopting the culture of Greece and Rome, Christianity had to accommodate itself to something it had not engendered. However, on the positive side, and in order to remedy to some degree this original sin, the period of the primitive Church would be included in this return to Antiquity, and would be idealized.

We can see arising in both Petrarch and Boccacio the twofold inclination of the Renaissance, its two faces, which meant a new challenge for the Church, calling for constant and delicate discernment. But for the moment, all must conform to the new call to order: Ad Fontes!

The Return to the Sources

To speak of returning to the sources presupposes the recognition of having distanced oneself from them. The Renaissance coincided with a new sense of perspectives, we might even say of perspective itself. It was the beginning of a new kind of history, less focused on divine providence, more preoccupied with distance from the subject and context. In painting, it is precisely from this period that we date the invention of perspective attributed to Paolo Uccello (+1475), the master of the stained-glass windows of the dome of Florence (1442–1445), and also the battle scenes painted according to the technique revived by Melozzo da Forli.

Yet even a century and a half earlier, Giotto (+1337) had had a modern vision of space that set him at odds with Cimabue, as Dante had clearly seen (*Purgatorio XI, 95*). Giotto

9

12. Francesco Colonna, Hypnertomachia Poliphili, *1499. This work of a Dominican friar from Treviso is the first book in the vernacular printed by Aldo Manuce in Venice. It is a strange collection of ideas from classical pagan antiquity cherished by the Renaissance. Here, despite their collapse, the beauty of the Greek or Egyptian ruins remains, and it seems possible to rebuild them.*

12

11

10

replaced the gold in the background of his canvasses with blue, so that his paintings moved from icons to portraits, thus allowing him to individualize his characters. This led to an awareness of the painter, and consequently of the spectator, and of their positions in space and time. We might say that it gave rise to subjectivity in painting. In a certain way, it is the ancient contemplative vision of the whole given in a single stroke which was being abandoned in favor of the outward look and soon the expression of oneself.

This was what happened in the case of Lorenzo Valla (+1457) who inaugurated "primitive humanism." He introduced perspective in the field of knowledge. Thus in 1440 he refused to accept the authenticity of "The Donation of Constantine," which was believed to be the foundational text of the temporal power of the papacy. He also enumerated the stages of the formation of the Latin language in his *Elegantiae* of 1442. Finally and most importantly, he dared to compare the Latin of the Vulgate, faulty at times, with the original text of the New Testament (in his *Collatio* or his *Adnotationes*). He thereby broke with the medieval illusion of being, if not contemporary with all that was received in the way of texts or facts, at least on an equal footing with them. The transformation of historical consciousness in the fifteenth century is suggested by the costumes of personages which, in painting or sculpture, ceased to belong to the artist's period.

We also must recognize that ancient Greek culture had returned fresher and more accessible, thanks to the influx of Greek exiles and refugees. After the conclusion of the Council of Union of Florence (1439), numerous Byzantine humanists remained in the West, for example, the famous Cardinal Bessarion. After 1453, when Constantinople fell to the Turks, many Greeks earned their living by teaching their language to Westerners. In this way, Greeks enabled Westerners to access

13. Piero della Francesca (1406–1492), The Flagellation of Christ, *about 1450 (Urbino, Galleria Nazionale delle Marche). The Passion scene is divided into two spaces using perspective. Background: deliberately antique architecture and clothing; right foreground: a 15th-century environment and costumes, perhaps to accentuate the difference between two time periods nevertheless linked by our salvation through Christ.*

14. Pedro Berruguete (+1503), Federico de Montefeltro and His Son Guidobaldo, *about 1475 (Urbino, Galleria Nazionale delle Marche). The Spanish painter decorated the studio of the Duke of Urbino, designed by Justin of Ghent. The warrior, still wearing part of his armor, abandons his arms to read one of the handsome incunabula. The heir, in royal attire and holding the insignia of power, will have to become a protector of humanistic literature.*

13

the original sources of ancient philosophical systems. They could also now savor the Septuagint, the Greek version of the Jewish Bible, as well as the New Testament and the writings of the Fathers of the Church. Scientific knowledge after the re-discovery of Archimedes, like theological knowledge after the rediscovery of Origen, was transformed. Recourse to the Greek language soon became the touchstone of an authentic humanist.

This return to the sources could not have grown into a current so deep as that of the Renaissance, were it not for a series of factors with multiple effects. Thirst for knowledge and the courage to innovate stimulated new needs which, in their turn, would be met through wealth and inventions.

Factors with Multiple Effects

The Renaissance owed its inception to a combination of economic, technological, and demographic factors. The first factor to have multiple effects was wealth. The Renaissance could not have produced all its fruits without that patronage that went hand in hand with princely or royal concern for magnificence. Thus Italy benefited from her mosaic of petty sovereignties that patronized artists. The progress of graphic technology was itself intimately connected with patronage and commissions.[1] Furthermore, by the act of commissioning a painting, or art in general, the ideal and the reality of the time could be revealed.[2] Kings of the sixteenth century fought over architects and painters. They also patronized humanists, employing them as chaplains, librarians, or private tutors. Popes and bishops

14

15. Chapel of Cardinal James of Portugal (Florence, San Miniato al Monte Church). The tiniest space in the chapel is covered with decorations using all the forms of the arts: a sculptured tomb by Antonio Rossellino, frescos by Alessio Baldovinetti, a painting over the altar by Antonio Pollaiolo (Saint James, the deceased's patron, and two saints). The intent is to create an impression of abundant life at the service of both Church and society. This is conveyed by sumptuous, artistic expression, the symbol of the patron's generosity that is able to encourage the flourishing of the arts even after death.

15

had at their disposal a range of honorary functions, with accompanying duties that left ample leisure for literary pursuits.

The advent of national monarchies with their efforts toward centralization had in great part been stimulated by military factors, such as the technique of making gunpowder or the development of the infantry. They found a nobler justification in the patronage of the fine arts.

At a time when, with few exceptions, monasteries and the old universities were content with medieval learning, sovereigns began to create parallel institutions, such as the new University of Wittenberg in Saxony, founded in 1502, and Alcal in Castille, created two years previously. In other cases, they clearly departed from the traditional centers of learning, as with the creation of a college in Paris (1530) which would become the college of "royal lectors" and later the "Collège de France."

At Louvain, thanks to the endowment of Jerome Busleyden, Erasmus was able to organize the Tri-lingual College in 1517. Wealth and power assured the foundation and spread of a cultural model that could not have supported itself independently.

Next, there entered upon the scene a second, most extraordinary multiplying factor of the Renaissance: the invention of the printing press. Its effect would be to disseminate knowledge far and wide.[3] Like all great inventions, it seems to have been in preparation simultaneously in many places, even outside of China, which claims to be its originator. We can study its development in Prague, and also in the Dutch city of Haarlem. If history has preserved the name of Gutenberg at Mainz, this may be because his argumentative and quibbling temperament has provided us with documents issuing from his various lawsuits. It seems however that the technique of printing was mastered thanks to the association of three men at Mainz around the years 1452–1455: Gutenberg first of all; Fust, his silent partner; and Peter Schöffer, Fust's son-in-law.

The invention of the printing press was a synthesis of various technological advances, all of them indispensable to it: paper, already known for two centuries and also originating in China; manageable or fluid ink; the application of the process of printing; and above all, the creation of movable characters whose typographical signs stood out in relief. The decisive step, therefore, was accomplished by the progress of metallurgy, which provided an alloy of sufficient resistance. Toward the end of the fifteenth century, the printing press had supplanted, if not replaced, the copying of manuscripts, itself improved over time by the development of the *exemplar* or model, which ensured authenticity and avoided the innumerable mistakes of successive recopying.

Engraving was still widely used for pictures and short texts. It is thought that from 1455 to 1501, the date which brings the period of incunabula to a close, six million books were printed, evidently more than all the manuscripts copied in the West during the whole of the Middle Ages. Beginning with the establishment of the printing press, which occasioned a reshaping of education, a good number of people in the West would slowly join the privileged class of readers and writers. At the time the majority of publications were religious in nature and contributed to the evolution of intellectual trends

There was, finally, a third multiplying factor of the Renaissance, contemporaneous with the other two, which was to expand known space. The "crowded world"[4] resulting from the demographic growth would miraculously discover virgin territory, or something close to it. European expansion had its true start at the beginning of the fifteenth century, thanks to the informed and active enthusiasm of the prince of Portugal, Henry the Navigator (+1460). Portugal systematically explored the western shores of the African continent from the capture of Ceuta in 1415 to the sailing around the Cape of Storms, which later became the Cape of Good Hope in 1487.

Spain, occupied for centuries, carried out the *Reconquista* against Islam and succeeded in recapturing the kingdom of Granada in 1492. This was the year when the Catholic sovereigns of Spain granted their protection and financial backing to Christopher Columbus, who was persuaded that he had received a divine mission to discover a western route to the Indies. On October 12, 1492, after more than two months at

16

17

18

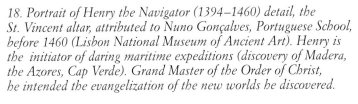

18. Portrait of Henry the Navigator (1394–1460) detail, the St. Vincent altar, attributed to Nuno Gonçalves, Portuguese School, before 1460 (Lisbon National Museum of Ancient Art). Henry is the initiator of daring maritime expeditions (discovery of Madera, the Azores, Cap Verde). Grand Master of the Order of Christ, he intended the evangelization of the new worlds he discovered.

19. The Catholic monarchs, Ferdinand of Aragon and Isabella of Castile, a medallion from the façade of Salamanca University, about 1520. The two sovereigns, encircled by an inscription in Greek and a decoration symbolizing their magnificence, are protectors of the University. Their shared power is shown by the scepter that both are holding with one hand.

20. Government Palace in Tlaxcala (Mexico, east of the capital). Anonymous painting, 16th century. The Spaniard, very properly dressed, takes a posture of command, while the Indian, bent and hardly dressed at all, is probably unloading goods from a boat. The footprints show that this is not his first trip. This could be one of the first representations of the Conquista.

sea, he reached an island of the Bahamas, formerly Lucayes, in the Caribbean Sea. This island became a stepping stone to the conquest of the immense continent that would not even bear his name. The colonization of America, where highly developed but fragile civilizations were to be found, led to forced labor and created for Spain a vast empire. Portugal wanted its own share of the booty and so pursued exploration in the direction of distant Asia. These discoveries gave rise to an influx of precious metals into Europe by means of the *Casa de Contratación* of Seville, which increased European wealth, revitalizing the first multiplying factor of the Renaissance, prosperity.

19

20

21

22

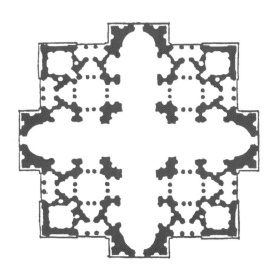

23

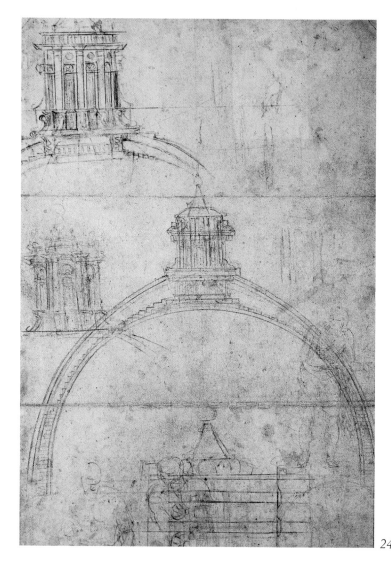

24

21. Fra Angelico. Saint Lawrence's Ordination, *fresco (Chapel of Nicholas V in the Vatican). In 1448, at Pope Nicolas V's request, the Dominican artist painted Saint Lawrence's ordination as a deacon (+258) by pope Sixtus II, who presents him with the paten and chalice, according to the 15th century rite. The decor of the basilica is antique, but the surplices, vestments, and tonsures of the clergy are contemporary, showing in this way the medieval belief that customs, liturgical customs in particular, are immutable in the Church.*

The Church, and especially the papacy, had to situate itself in relation to these great happenings. She continued unrivaled as the most generous of patrons. The humanist Popes of the fifteenth century wanted to make pontifical Rome the capital of the Renaissance. Nicholas V (1447–1455) ordered the construction of a new palace in the Vatican, for which purpose the Constantinian Basilica of St. Peter, on the verge of collapse, was demolished. Pius II Piccolomini (1458–1464) was chiefly a literary man, but it is Sixtus IV (1471–1484) who stands out

22. *Portrait of Pius II (who reigned from 1458 to 1464). Fresco from the Piccolomini Palace, Pienza, Province of Sienna. This humanist Pope is the founder of an ideal city that he wanted to build at his birthplace, but which was never finished.*

23–27. *(23) Bramante's plan (1444–1514) of St. Peter's in Rome. (24) Michelangelo's diagram (1475–1564) for St. Peter's dome (Haarlem, Teylers Museum); (25, 26) Michelangelo: St. Peter's dome; (27) Plan of St. Peter's Basilica and the Vatican Palaces, the* era of Julius II (+1513). *The reconstruction of the medieval basilica at the Vatican, beginning in 1506, became a gigantic project, involving all the greatest artists of the time, and costing a fortune. Money was raised in part by donations offered to gain indulgences, a practice denounced by Luther. The prodigious architecture of the cupola of Michelangelo (138 meters high) meant to affirm the primacy of Peter. It was built over the "Altar of the Confession" which commemorates the place of Peter's martyrdom—considered to be the visible theological center of Christianity.*

25

26

as the veritable protector of the arts throughout his entire pontificate. He had the chapel, which bears his name, built. He and his successors during half a century bequeathed to Rome an inestimable patrimony by commissioning the works of Bramante, Michelangelo, and so many others. The Basilica of St. Peter, begun in 1506, was to require considerable sums exacted from all of the Christian world. The preaching of indulgences and its contestation by Luther would weigh heavily on the balance sheet at the basilica's completion.

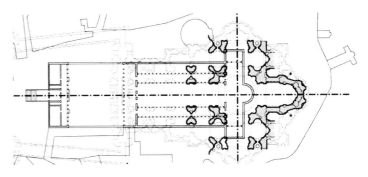

27

28

29

28. Fifth Lateran Council, fresco, attributed to Paolo Guidotti, about 1585 (Vatican Library, south room). Despite mitered bishops and theologians with doctor's caps, this work stresses temporal power. In the center stands Maximilian, the Holy Roman Emperor of the German Empire from 1493 to 1519, with Golden Fleece insignia, accompanied by an armed soldier. In the foreground, "folios" may refer to the Council's decree about printing.

29. Dutch popular print, 17th century. Saint Philip Neri (1515–1595) sells his books to help the poor. He is also in the background conversing with two persons near Chiesa Nuova in Rome.

30. Juan Diego's Vision of the Virgin Mary, Puebla ceramic, Mexico. The Virgin of Guadalupe, in a mantle covered with stars and standing in a mandorla, appears to the young peasant before imprinting her image on his poncho. The inscription Non fecit indicates that this image was "not made by human hands," like certain miraculous icons.

31. Saint Francis with the stigmata, front page of the Vocabulario, a lexicon written in a Mexican language (probably Nahuatl) and Spanish by Franciscan Alonso de Molina, published in Mexico by Antonio de Espinosa, 1471. Requested by Don Martin Henriquez, Viceroy of New Spain, to make possible the teaching of the Gospel. By means of the stigmata ("signs of our redemption"), God had revealed the Gospel through Saint Francis. Franciscans would have a decisive influence in the New World through evangelization.

With Nicholas V having founded the Vatican Library, the Church now had a duty to rejoice in the new invention of the printing press. She did this officially in 1501 with a bull of Alexander VI and then with the declaration of the Fifth Lateran Council in May 1515.[5] This new art, inspired by divine favor, was indeed a cause for rejoicing, but already some concern was expressed about so powerful an instrument. It was good if used "for the glory of God, the progress of the faith and the increase of virtues." However, "the introduction of poison along with remedies" must be avoided with the institution of a preliminary censorship. In fact, systematic censorship would not be set up before the Council of Trent in the mid-sixteenth century.

Finally, the Church could not remain indifferent to discoveries in the New World. With courage and even heroism, missionaries sailed with the navigators. But the concern of the *Conquistadores* for evangelization was accompanied by their greed. We get a sense of this in the "Alexandrine gift," the collection of papal bulls entitled *Inter caetera,* of the Borgia Pope, Alexander VI. The bulls divided the lands of the New World, already discovered or to be discovered in the future, between Spain, the Pope's homeland, and Portugal: "We grant you these territories on condition that you send wise and learned men to instruct the natives in the Catholic faith." Hardly appreciated by other sovereigns, and adjusted by the interested parties themselves, this "gift" was less an act of arbitration than the recognition of an accomplished fact.

We should note that in the new fields opened up by the Renaissance, culture, and the building of a New World, the Church wished to take its part. But was it aware of the dangers and the new challenge offered by this renewal?

31

VOCABVLARIO
EN LENGVA MEXICANA Y CASTELLANA, COM-
puesto por el muy Reuerendo Padre Fray Alonso de Molina, dela
Orden del bienauenturado nuestro Padre sant Francisco.

DIRIGIDO AL MVY EXCELENTESENOR
Don Martin Enriquez, Visorrey della nueua España.

tuum Franciscum:

Signasti domine seruum

Signaste redeptionis nostre.

¶ Indorum nimis te fecit prole parentem.
Qui genus moriens, quos pater alme foues.

Confixus vivis, langues: cum mente revoluis.
Vulnera, cum spe dias, stigmata carne geris.

EN MEXICO,
En Casa de Antonio de Spinosa.
1571

32. *Title page of the Latin translation, made in 1598, of* The Very Brief Account of the Destruction of the Indians, *written by the Dominican Bartolomé de Las Casas (1484–1566), Bishop of Chiapas in 1552. This text, denouncing the poor treatment and even death (but not massacres), inflicted by the Spanish colonists on the Indians at the beginning of the conquest of America, was published in Frankfurt by a Protestant printer. In the 16th century, the number of victims reported by Las Casas was much disputed, as it is today.*

NARRATIO.
REGIONVM
INDICARVM PER
HISPANOS QVOSDAM
deuaſtatarum veriſſima : prius quidem
per Epiſcopum Bartholemxum Caſaum,
natione Hiſpanam Hiſpanice conſcripta.
& Anno 1551. Hiſpali , Hiſpanice, Anno vero hoc
1598 Latine ex
cuſa.

FRANCOFVRTI,
Sumptibus Theodori de Bry, & Io-
annis Saurii typis.
Anno M. D. XCVIII.

33. Giulio Romano, The Stanza of Psyche, *first half of the 16th century (Mantua, Te Palace). Here the Renaissance's pagan tastes are indulged: The story of Psyche loved by Cupid or Eros is depicted in a frankly carnal and sensual manner. The multiplicity of fauna and flora, the nudity of the figures, the frolics of the fauns, nymphs, and centaurs, all create the impression of a world complacent with its pleasures, a mythology that has no need of Christian Revelation.*

35. The Raphael Stanza (Vatican) detail from "The School of Athens." On the left, is Plato, already old, whose pointed finger indicates the contemplation of divine thoughts and who carries the Timaeus; *and on the right, is Aristotle, younger, with his left hand on* The Nicomachaean Ethics, *and whose right hand seems to point to nature and to the reality of the world. These two figures who greatly inspired the Renaissance have mighty countenances.*

33

34. Jean Fouquet (from about 1420 to 1480) Madonna and Child, *1450, the right panel of the Melun Diptych (Antwerp, Royal Museum of the Fine Arts). Despite the discreet presence of angels in the background, the precious jeweled crown, the ermine mantle, and especially the woman's resemblance to Agnes Sorel, the mistress of Charles VII (King of France from about 1422 to 1450), fails to give this admirable portrait of the Virgin the religious dimension of humility and piety required by the topic.*

34

The Temptation to Paganism

From the outset, the Renaissance and its privileged instrument, humanism, manifested an ambivalence and aroused yet again the temptation to paganism. Does not the very word "humanism," coined actually much later, suggest the danger of trusting only in man and having man alone as one's horizon? Man himself seems to take on a new appearance.[6]

At this time, art became pagan, or more exactly, showed a pagan face. It exalted the naked body, both male and female, and feasted on the sensuality of forms. The refinement of colors and materials was a far cry from medieval sobriety and restraint. Without being prudish, it should be pointed out that Raphael used his mistress, *la Fornarina,* as a model for the Blessed Virgin (around 1510),[7] while Jean Fouquet had already represented the fashionable Agnes Sorel, a favorite of Charles VII of France, holding the Infant Jesus to her breast. It is a simple fact that there was a confusion of genres. The wholesale return of the gods and goddesses of antiquity was more innocent, but it indicated that people were turning to something that fell far short of Christianity.

More disturbing still, thought itself became susceptible to paganism. It seemed to be attracted as by a kind of optical illusion to an antiquity full of coherence and wisdom, pagan antiquity as well as Christian antiquity. At this time there was

also the mirage of a primitive or at least pre-Constantinian Church, replete with all the virtues. The neo-Aristotelian school of Padua seems to have been most characteristic of this new pagan spirit.[8] Already in the Middle Ages, the University of Padua had had a reputation for heterodoxy. It was now reaching its high point with Pietro Pomponazzi (1462–1525), who challenged the immortality of the soul (in 1516), challenged miracles, and made a formidable distinction by positing a double order of truths—a doctrine which, in the thirteenth century, had already been attributed to Latin Averroism.

These ideas had a profound influence upon the Renaissance because they satisfied the needs of pure reason along with the rejection of the harmony between reason and faith that had contributed to the splendor of the Middle Ages. Was it by chance that Aristotle was invoked in a debate like the one in Spain around 1550 which lined up the Dominican Las Casas in opposition to the canon of Cordoba, Sepulveda, on the nature of the Indians? Sepulveda, who had followed Pomponazzi's courses, was one of those Aristotelians who thought that the native peoples belonged to the category of "slaves by nature." The missionary, on the other hand, took his stand on the dignity of all human beings, claimed by Pope Paul III for the Indians in America in his bull of 1535, *Sublimis Deus.*

The same line of thought was advanced by Nicholas Machiavelli (1469–1527), the Florentine who fashioned and proposed the model of *The Prince* (1513) for Caesar Borgia. Pursuing the excellent goal of the unity of Italy, the counselor elaborated maxims of pure political realism. The sovereign, counting only on himself for the furtherance of his interests, should prefer to be feared rather than loved, while taking care not to make himself hated. Here, as often happens, it was rather the exceptional destiny of this little book of Machiavelli and its alleged dark side that gave it its importance in the history of ideas—so numerous were its descendants of all kinds.

The man to whom Machiavelli's book was dedicated, Cesare Borgia, bastard son of the future Pope Alexander VI, was typical of the Renaissance soldier of fortune. He also typified the worldly ambitions that popes of the period harbored for their families. Nepotism and favoritism reigned at the papal court which had become truly secularized. Innocent VIII, Alexander VI, Julius II, Leo X, and still others, governed a Rome taken over by paganism. Their scandalous history was known and reported by reliable witnesses, who recounted the papal excesses with greater irony than surprise.[9]

These popes were aware of the need for a reform of a Church become too rich, too carried away by desire. The Church, however, conquered by paganism, seemed indecisive in its conversions, as when Alexander VI learned of the assassination of his favorite son, the Duke of Gandia. He immediately convoked a commission of cardinals to reform the

38 and 39. (38) The reform of the Dominican Order (the order of which Savonarola was a member, 1452–1498), begun by Saint Antoninus (later archbishop of Florence), took its start in the cloister and the cells of San Marco, decorated by Fra Angelico. But the reform under Savanarola also included a humanistic dimension, symbolized by the vast and elegant priory library created by Michelozzo da Forli. (39) A beautiful illustration from an edition of Savonarola's Lenten homilies on Noah's Ark, published in Venice in 1536, at the press of Pietro de'Nicolini and paid for by Francesco and Michele Tramezzino, is proof of the lasting success of his writings. The text is in Latin, but the preface of the book is in Italian. Friar Jerome Savonarola is shown at study in his San Marco cell where books and manuscripts abound.

36

37

36 and 37. (36) Rosso Fiorentino (1495–1540), portrait of Nicolas Machiavelli (1469–1527) (Florence, Uffizi Museum). In this famous portrait of the Florentine humanist, historian, and political philosopher, the intelligence of the eyes and the finesse of the hands are striking symbols of the acuity of the mind. These same qualities are suggested in this 16th-century engraving (37), representing politics through the crown and the scepter as well as through the animals—the lion's appetite for power and the wolf's shrewdness.

Church, but it accomplished nothing. When he was confronted by the Florentine Dominican, Girolamo Savonarola, an authentic reformer, though certainly impassioned and extreme, the duel was without mercy.

Savonarola's inauguration in Florence of "the spiritual reign of Jesus Christ" during the years 1495–1497, in effect but a brief episode, should really be considered in the light of this conflict between the temptation to paganism and the necessity of an evangelical reform. Was not Savonarola proposing that the Church face the challenge of the Renaissance? Of course it is easy to say that the Dominican was totally medieval in his outlook, that he was still imbued with apocalypticism and Joachimism.[10] This could be seen from his enthusiasm for the new Cyrus, whom he saw in Charles VIII, king of France, conqueror of Italy. Here, mention also should be made of his moral rigorism, as when he had paintings and costumes burned on the pyre of vanities.

But it is just as possible to see Savonarola as the defender of Christian art, guaranteeing Catholic honor in the face of the paganism rampant in the society of his day. He clearly opposed Alexander VI when denouncing Roman corruption.[11] "Look here, loathesome Church . . . your luxury has turned you into a shameless woman. You are worse than a beast!" the Dominican stormed from his pulpit.

The engaging personality of the painter Sandro Botticelli (1445–1510) is a good example of the rift between the Christian vocation and the temptation to paganism against which Savonarola inveighed. One senses in all of Botticelli's extraordinary work the tension between pagan exaltation and Christian meditation. It is not simply that he passes from one to the other, evolving from mythological compositions (Spring, Venus, Minerva) to deeply spiritual Virgins. There is at times an amazing combination of the two, as in the "Reredos of St. Barnabas," in which the female saints strongly resemble the goddesses of antiquity. Finally, enthralled no doubt by Savonarola, Botticelli added to his mystical Nativity in 1500 an apocalyptic inscription. The Florentine painter thus appears as a symbol of his times, torn between the vertigo of pagan seduction and the conversion of his art to Christianity.[12]

We can lastly note that in the time of Savonarola the Convent of San Marco, adorned with the frescoes of Fra Angelico and poised to bring about moral reform, first in Florence and then throughout the entire Church, was a center of humanistic studies set once more in their Christian orientation. Even though Marsilio Ficino, the reviver of Plato, had originally taken Savonarola's part and later abandoned him,

40 and 41. (40) *Sandro Botticelli (1444–1510)* The Nativity *(London, National Gallery). In his religious painting, the Florentine artist deploys as much lyric imagination as in his secular painting. Here, Jesus' birth in Bethlehem (Luke 2:8–14) is depicted. In the upper part, the angels, in a heavenly dance, sing glory to God. In the lower part, they give the kiss of peace to the shepherds whom they invite to come and adore the Christ Child. In the very lowest part, some tiny demons seem to have been thrown to the ground. (41) The episode of the Descent from the Cross, painted circa 1495 (Poldi Pezzoli Museum, Milan) is very dramatic. The figures who venerate Christ's body suggest a circular movement, evoking the theological meaning of the event.*

40

38

39

41

43 and 44. (43) The enigmatic book, Utopia, *written in 1516 by Thomas More (1477–1535) at the request of his friend Erasmus, is accompanied by a no less mysterious imaginary map. The capital of Utopia Island, Amaurote, is surrounded by cities that all look quite similar. In the manner of the Gospel, More's style used metaphors, parables, and paradoxes that should not be taken literally, but that evoke the mystery of God's kingdom. (44) The French edition from Paris, published by Angelier in 1550, recognized the enigmatic character of the book by placing a sphinx next to the English humanist, seen in his study.*

42. Pliny, Natural History, *manuscript copied in 1481 by Nicolo Mascarino for John Pico della Mirandola (1463–1494) (Marciana Library, Venice Cod. Lat. VI). This sumptuous illuminated manuscript, a luxury at a time when printing was flourishing, shows the extent of the means used by this young humanist to read the classics from antiquity.*

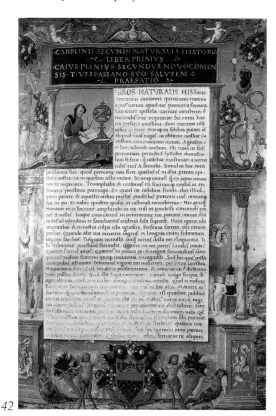

42

43

two of the most typical representatives of Florentine humanism were familiars of San Marco: Angelo Poliziano (+1494), a protegé of the Medicis, and that notable young genius, Pico de la Mirandola (+1494).

Without even mentioning Savonarola's spiritual influence on the Italian mystics of the late sixteenth century, Saint Philip Neri and Saint Catherine de Ricci, we need only consider the immediate posterity of his reform in Italy, men such as the great biblical scholars Sante Pagnini and Zanobio Acciauioli, in order to measure the importance given to an intellectual renewal upon which a true reform of the Church could be built. In fact, by his influence in Spain,[13] and especially through the spread of Pico de la Mirandola's theology—admired throughout Europe in the sixteenth century—we can see in Savonarola the paradoxical forerunner of true Christian humanism.

44

The Christian Renaissance

The greatest humanists, that is to say the professors of the humanities (the *studia humanitatis*), whose vocation was essentially pedagogical, were aware of the danger and the

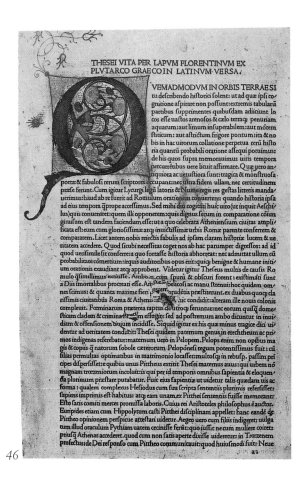

challenge that the renewed temptation to paganism represented for Christian minds. This is why they believed it their duty to propose a profoundly and authentically Christian version of the Renaissance based on the Gospel.

I take as examples only two of the most attractive personalities of the period: the Englishman Thomas More and Erasmus, so tied to one another that they were called "the twins." To be exact, Erasmus ought to be called the first European citizen. Thomas More (+1535) appeals to us because he exemplified the wise folly of the cross lived to the very end. The facetious and profound author of *Utopia* (1516) had a public career brilliant enough to allow him to legitimately enjoy the pleasures of life. Yet he can be seen making a retreat with the Carthusians, or engrossed in family joys and the delights of a scholar. Finally, in fidelity to his conscience, he makes his way calmly and firmly to the scaffold, in order to preserve a certain ideal of Christian loyalty in the service of his country, his king, and the Church.

Erasmus (+1536) was certainly a far more complex personality, with his keen wit, lively sensibility, and egocentricity. For a long time he shied away from affirming his position in regard to Luther (he was dubbed Proteus or Janus—unpredictable as the moon . . .). But the day came when he had to take his stand plainly on the side of the traditional Church, which, despite its abuses and corruption, remained in his mind the best defender of the human being's nobility—his innate freedom, a free will upon which grace could be engrafted. Like Giannozzo Manetti in 1452 and Pico de la Mirandola in 1498, Erasmus in 1525 wanted to exalt human dignity. For Pico, man was a microcosm in the universe, saved and made beautiful by the Incarnation and Redemption of the Son of God made Man.[14]

Erasmus and the Christian humanists, readers of Plutarch and of his "illustrious men," were keenly aware of a certain elite. These they admired while also assigning to them a decisive role, with responsibility to instruct, govern, and lead others

47

48

to the truth. Over and above paradox, of which he made almost catechetical or at least moral use, Erasmus pleaded for a *philosophia Christi.* Christ is the sole Wisdom in this world— but through the paradox of humility, poverty, and the cross. "All things should lead back to Christ," he said, and in his capacity as theologian and scholar, he showed how this could be done. The tools he proposed were: better access to the Bible and to Scripture commentaries, the availability of the greatest Christian writers—above all Augustine and his beloved Origen, and a practical theology based on "good" sense and Gospel values.

To the challenge of paganism, Christian humanism responded by a return to the center: the word of God and the Word of God or the Bible and Christ. Optimists by theological choice so to say, Catholic humanists seemed to fail because the

Protestant Reformation, with its indignant vigor, rejected them and condemned them as accomplices of the paganism which they had in fact helped to curb, to adapt, and even to eliminate.

Humanists were torn between the traditional theologians, who reproached them for no longer being medieval, and the Protestant innovators, who believed them to be atheists, or at the least impious. *Du bist nicht fromm,* "You have no piety," wrote Luther to Erasmus, which must be understood with all the force of the word *impietas* as it was used during this period. This rejection reinforced a certain pessimistic current that also came into play, but a little later on, and which perhaps culminated in the enigmatic tragedy of Shakespeare's *Hamlet* (1601), bringing the sixteenth century to a close.

Stunned momentarily by the clamor, grieving over the failure of its beautiful hope, Christian humanism would

48. *Antonello de Messina,* Saint Jerome in his Study, *about 1465–1475 (National Gallery, London). Jerome is the most appreciated ancient scholar among Christian humanists, who identified with his love for the Sacred Scriptures that he translated and commented upon. Here the learned saint wears the cardinal's cloak, while the cardinal's hat lies on the bench behind him. As a symbol of Jerome's biblical style, the artist emphasizes many little details, drawn with an almost trite precision, for example, the cloth hanging on the left. But the landscape seen at a distance, the birds in flight, and the peacock in the foreground express a poetic touch as well.*

49. *The Christian mystery culminates in Christ's resurrection. It is the foundation of the optimism of Christian humanism. But the resurrection cannot be separated from the sufferings of the Passion and the folly of the cross. In his* Resurrected Christ, *about 1490 (Madrid, Thyssen-Bornemisza Collection), Bartolomeo Bramantino (1465–1530) successfully expressed this twofold reality of the Paschal Mystery. Indeed, Christ stands in a white vestment, but his pallor, the pain in his eyes, and the cross in the background evoke the drama of the Passion and his descent into hell before his Resurrection on the third day.*

50. *Veit Stoss, Rosary Annunciation, 1517–1519 (Nuremberg, St. Lawrence Church). This representation of the angelic salutation (Luke 1:28) repeated in the Rosary is encircled by a crown made of roses, which traditionally was placed on the statue of the Virgin during the recitation of the prayer. The sculpture is also surrounded by an immense Rosary: ten beads for the Hail Mary, one larger bead for the Our Father. The medallions inserted into the crown represent some of the joyous or glorious mysteries. A Trinitarian dimension is also represented: The Father blesses, the resurrected Christ is beneath Him, and the Spirit comes upon Mary in the form of a dove (Luke 1, 35); the hovering angels evoke the heavenly Church.*

51. *The Mirror of the Most Honorable Confraternity of Mary's Rosary, Leipzig, 1515 (Munich, Bavarian State Library). This wood engraving from the Manual of the Confraternity of the Rosary, made by Marcus von Weida, offers a naïve theology of the benefits of the recitation of the Rosary. The Virgin Mary is crowned with roses while the Child Jesus and the angels carry a crown in their hands. The pilgrim Church (Pope and Emperor at the forefront) prays the Rosary, thus allowing souls to be freed from purgatory, the principal benefit of this devotion. The date and location of this illustration, Saxony two years before Luther's preaching against indulgences, make the wide dissemination of a devotion so simplistically explained a questionable matter. However, in Catholicism, devotion to the Rosary, adjusted to the teachings of the Council of Trent, will be revived after the victorious Battle of Lepanto in 1571 and the institution of the feast of the Rosary in 1573.*

51

50

52. *The Master of Messkirch, St. Christopher (Basel, Museum of Fine Arts). The legend of the holy Christ-bearer is widespread in popular spirituality. After his conversion, this giant, who used a tree as a walking stick, took people safely across a dangerous stream. One day when he took a child on his shoulders, the child seemed so heavy that he could hardly carry him over. Asked for the reason why, the child answered by saying that he himself was carrying the world with its sins—an idea shown in this image by the visible shadow of the cross on the globe. Devotion to Saint Christopher is still popular among Christians.*

52

54

53

reappear purified, detached from all its polemical and scornful zeal, to wield at least a partial influence over the Council of Trent and its decisions. The battle against paganism would be truly won when, at the century's end, people would see Francis de Sales winning over with his sweetness a Church less glorious and triumphant than that during the Renaissance, but one where what has been so well named "devout humanism" could be recognized.[15] The Church would be more devout, more virtuous, more alive. In a word, it would be more human, seeming truly "reborn" after its trials and lacerations, even though their traces remain to our own day.

55

Christ and Time: *Reemploying here this title of the famous work written in 1946 by the Protestant theologian, Oscar Cullman (1902–1999), we can see how, through art, Christ's Incarnation gives sense to history and, for the believer, gives it a redeemed dimension.*

56

57

58

55. *Jacopo del Sellaio (1492–1493)*, The Triumph of Time, *end of the 15th century (Fiesole, Bandini Museum). This colorful and glistening composition shows the pagan understanding of time. A winged old man, holding an hourglass, seems to triumph over everything: youth, beauty, and might dominating everything. There are debris and ruins, but also young trees with new leaves, symbolizing perpetual new beginnings.*

56. Reliquary of the Title of the Cross of Christ, *casing from 1492, base from 1827 (Rome, Basilica of the Holy Cross of Jerusalem). This extraordinary relic of the inscription placed on Christ's cross, in Latin, Greek, and Hebrew (John 19:19–22) is a priceless witness that Christ's death is part of an authentic account that took place within human history.*

57. Jesse Tree, *sculpted in a 16th-century retable (Southern France, Ormeau Chapel). The realism of Christ's Incarnation and his place within a genealogy, mentioned by the evangelists (Matthew 1:1–17 and Luke 3: 23–38), are retold by painters and sculptors. Christ's Incarnation—and therefore our salvation—was prepared through the ages by a succession of generations: people with virtues and vices, famous and unknown, whose lineage culminates in the Virgin and her Son.*

58. Apocalypse Tapestry, *14th century (Castle of Angers).* Christ and the Sword. *The book of Revelation ends the Bible and calls attention to the end of time. Here, an illustration of 1:13–16, John's first vision, is of the One, like a Son of Man, who is the Messiah, the eschatological Judge, with the sword of justice in his mouth. Christ, the Master of history, will recapitulate all of time on the Last Day.*

1

1. St. Francis and the Poor Man, Legenda maior
(Rome, Capuchin Historical Institute).
Historically, Church reform occurs through
a deliberate return to evangelical poverty that also
includes care for the outcast. The personality of
Saint Francis, whose humble magnanimity was
recognized by the Protestant tradition, is an
enduring example.

2

2. Painting (1504) by the anonymous master of
Alkmaar (Amsterdam, Rijkmuseum). This work
from the beginning of the 16th century was found
in the Church of St. Lawrence in Alkmaar,
Northern Holland. It depicts daily life and its
pleasures (a young lover romancing his girlfriend
in the background), but also works of charity in
a society that was more and more affluent. We can
observe the distribution of bread to the needy, here
a cripple; notice that the central character looks
like Christ.

Chapter 6

THE CHURCH AND THE CHALLENGE OF THE REFORMATION

Ecclesia semper reformanda! This adage, at once realistic and optimistic, affirms that the Church must always be correcting, converting, and reforming itself. It is easy to understand why some historians, in emphasizing this reform, which was ever sought yet realized only with difficulty, consider the period that extended from the thirteenth to the eighteenth century as one single, overall period. For them, the period of reform begins with the final effects of the Gregorian Reform and concludes with the first falling off of the reforms brought about by the Council of Trent. Their position is a reaction to the short-sighted view that focuses on a fundamental yet too limited phenomenon, the birth of Protestantism. Somewhere in between a history which is too drawn out and an overly restricted periodization lies a more reasonable view, which envisions a single uninterrupted evolution extending from the end of the fifteenth to the middle of the seventeenth century. The adoption of this position, however, calls for a new vocabulary.

When the word "Reformation" was used half a century ago, it was with few objections taken to mean the advent of Protestantism. This event was preceded by a "Pre-Reform," which had paved the way for it and was followed by a Catholic reaction, which was quite naturally called the Counter-Reformation *(Gegenreformation)*. Nowadays this same sequence of events is described in a more complex way.[1] With the rise of the lay spirit, the need for reform had made itself keenly felt in the Church, but the Christian humanism of the Renaissance was unable to respond with a satisfactory and permanent answer. In the fifteenth century, the need was expressed by attempts to renew the religious Orders. At the beginning of the sixteenth century, Evangelism, the attempt to carry over the ideal of Christian humanism into institutions and reality, prepared the way more directly for the two reformations, Protestant and Catholic. Then, after the religious and political upheaval caused by Luther and continued by Calvin, came what must be called the Protestant Reformations in the plural, so much do they differ from each other. Although they were

united in affirming the exclusive primacy of the Bible and faith, they can rightly be seen as antagonists.

The Catholic Reformation was almost slower to define itself than to impose itself. Once launched by the Council of Trent, however, in all the regions not won over to Protestantism, it actually incorporated the efforts of the preceding century for the interior renewal of the institutional Church that had been so poorly handled by political powers and deterred by the effects of internal conflicts.

Thus in the sixteenth century, contemporaneous with the Renaissance just beginning in France and Germany and already coming to a close in Italy, an extraordinary change was at work. It was not only intellectual but also social and political. The different reformations were not so much consequences of this change as forms that it took, and they assumed the character of a challenge as well. At the dawn of the sixteenth century, the entire world—and this included even the most worldly of the popes—was in agreement as to the need for a reform of the Church.

On May 3, 1512, the opening discourse at the Fifth Lateran Council wrung tears from the entire assembly. It was delivered by Giles of Viterbo, Superior General of the Hermits of Saint Augustine, the Order to which Luther belonged. The results were dramatic: "At what moment in the Church's history," the speaker asked, "has our life been more indolent? When has ambition been more shameless, cupidity more pronounced, the excess of sin more brazen? When has not merely such negligence but even such great contempt for sacred things, for the sacraments, for the power of the Church, for holy precepts been so grave? When have our religion and our faith been more ridiculed, even among the common people?"[2]

On the same day Pope Julius II, whom history does not remember for his virtue and humility, proclaimed: "Not only ecclesiastical discipline but lifestyles in general as well have deteriorated among persons of every age and condition."[3] The Council closed in 1517, seven months before the arrival of Luther upon the Christian scene. This last Council before the

4. *Woodcut from the title page of* The Babylonian Captivity of the Church, *Strasburg, Johann Preuss. Dating probably from 1520, it is one of the first portraits of the German reformer. He wears the habit and tonsure of the Hermits of Saint Augustine of the Strict Observance to whom he belonged. His face is hard and his look passionate.*

3. *Lukas Cranach the Elder,* Reformation altarpiece *(1547, Wittenberg, City Church). This painting, dating from the year after Luther's death, tries to sum up his preaching: Christ crucified whom alone he wanted to know (1 Corinthians 2:2); showing Christ's size as surpassing that of the listeners as well as of the preacher. The Reform message presents itself as strictly theological: the good news of salvation.*

Reformation had with great difficulty produced only a few minor reforms, quite incapable of extinguishing the fire that was about to break out. It was hardly "a rough draft" of the Council to come, that of Trent, as the German historian Döllinger has described it.

The real challenge was to be launched by a handful of men, almost intoxicated with the determination to obtain what centuries of good will (but without firm resolve), councils, saints, and Popes had hoped for: the reform of the Church of Christ at its roots. At least, so they thought. But the challenge of the reform to be made (how was it to be made? on what basis?) precipitated the worst division in the history of the Latin Church, with its train of wars, anathemas, intolerance, and troubled consciences. The broken unity of Christians has not since been healed, despite the recent efforts of ecumenism which, incidentally, do not date exclusively from the twentieth century. In every period since that time, efforts have been made to renew dialogue. While a more chronological description of the evolution of Protestantism will be provided in Chapter 15, here I shall simply describe something of the shock caused by the Reformers of the sixteenth century.

The Challenge of Luther

Martin Luther (1483–1546) was an "observant" religious, a Hermit of Saint Augustine, who was part of the reform movement occurring within his own Order. He was both a talented professor of Sacred Scripture at the recently created University of Wittenberg in Saxony, and a spiritual man who was in search of an answer to his personal struggle. There was in his life a somewhat mysterious period between 1513 and 1517. This he described, in a celebrated bit of theological literature written almost thirty years later, as a sort of epiphany or illumination. Like many conversion stories, the text has acquired in the course of maturation an extreme density.[4]

Luther was meditating on the text of the Letter to the Romans, Chapter 1, verses 16 and 17: "For I am not ashamed of the Gospel: It is the power of God for salvation to everyone

who has faith, to the Jew first and also to the Greek. For in it the righteousness of God is revealed through faith for faith; as it is written, 'He who through faith is righteous shall live.'"

Luther assures us that he then passed, suddenly as it were, from the concept of a God who judges and is impossible to satisfy because of human inability to carry out His law, to that of a God who gives righteousness, and "in His mercy, justifies through faith." He thus rejected an active, formal justification,

5

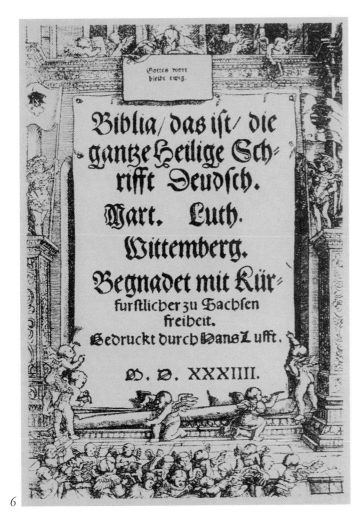

6

6. *Frontispiece for Martin Luther's translation of the Bible, Wittenberg, 1534. The privilege of printing the Bible in German, a powerful propaganda tool for Lutheranism, was granted by the Prince Elector of Saxony. The motto in the upper part of this title page reads, "God's Word lasts forever" (1 Peter 1:25).*

in order to gain access to a passive justification, one received gratuitously and without merit. God no longer sees the individual as a sinner, for sinner he remains regardless of what he may do, but rather as righteous, imputing to him the only merits which can find grace in His eyes, his own in Christ Jesus.

Beyond the peace of soul felt by Luther in the tower of his monastery in Wittenberg, what other great change had taken place? It was not, as Protestant historians have long thought, an almost total innovation through a new reading of the Gospel, for in fact the Fathers of the Church and medieval theologians also had seen the justice of God as His mercy. Rather, on the basis of a dazzling intuition, a new architectural axis of theology was put in place.

The challenge of the Lutheran Reformation was to take this theological truth as the sole basis of theology, to give it pride of place, to hypostasize it, to select and organize all else in relation to this spiritual intuition. For Luther, everything rested on the certitude of salvation through faith "because of Christ," which was, according to him, the teaching of the Letter to the Romans. He once remarked that the entire Gospel could be summed up in this one text as it contained everything.

We are saved by faith alone, by grace alone, and since this is found in Scripture, by Scripture alone. The challenge for Luther lay not in what he affirmed but in what his affirmation denied: faith *without* works; grace *without* free will; Scripture *without* tradition. This point is crucial, for not only did Luther intend to base himself on *Scripture alone* but also to judge all tradition in the light of biblical revelation as he interpreted it.

Catholic historians have perceived two great moments in the hardening of Luther's position. Contrary to what has long been thought, the 95 theses against indulgences, whether they were posted on October 31, 1517, or not, are no longer considered pivotal. Despite their harsh tone, despite the attack on the communion of saints, whose feast was to be celebrated on the following day, All Saints Day, the theses were perhaps no more than an appeal for theological discussion, a *disputatio* of the medieval type, by a professor full of ideas making use of his doctoral privilege. Rather, it is the year 1519 in Leipzig that is now considered significant. That was when Luther's adversary, John Eck of Ingoldstadt, pushed him into denying the infallibility of the Councils, which implied the break with Tradition, henceforth seen as merely human words, and with the Church, which could err even in matters of faith. The formal beginning of this rupture was expressed in the "reform writings" of the year 1520.

Under the eloquent title of *The Babylonian Captivity of the Church,* Luther set out to destroy the sacramental structure of

7. Hans Memling, Triptych of the Last Judgment (about 1467–1471), detail from right panel (Gdansk, National Museum). An obsession at the end of the 15th century, eternal damnation is represented very realistically here. The damned, races and ages all mixed together, are plunged into hell, pushed by a horned demon. They hold to each other as if to symbolize that they mutually led each other into evil.

8. Christian emblems and mottos (Lyon, John Marcorelle, 1571). The art of emblems, symbolic characters accompanied by a short poem and sometimes a motto, flourishes in the 16th century, in particular at the hands of the Italian Andreas Alciato (1492–1550). Here, the shame caused by his original sin is represented through Adam, who thinks he can hide after the fault as he also hides his nudity. But God's call, "Adam, where are you?" (Genesis 3:9) already expresses God's offer of mercy to all humanity.

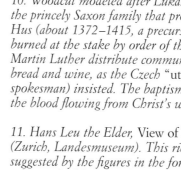

9. John Wycliff (about 1330–1384) gives to Oxford University a new interpretation of the Sacred Scripture that he holds in his hands. (Popular engraving from the 15th century.)

10

10. Woodcut modeled after Lukas Cranach. Represented here is the princely Saxon family that protected the Lutheran reform. John Hus (about 1372–1415, a precursor of the Reformation's ideas and burned at the stake by order of the Council of Constance) and Martin Luther distribute communion under the two species of bread and wine, as the Czech "utraquists" (for whom Hus was spokesman) insisted. The baptismal fountain draws its efficacy from the blood flowing from Christ's wounds.

11. Hans Leu the Elder, View of Zurich, painted 1492–1496 (Zurich, Landesmuseum). This rich merchant city, its wealth suggested by the figures in the foreground, possessed impressive religious buildings, such as the Fraumünster or Grossmünster, where twenty-five years later Zwingli's preaching will launch the Swiss Reformation.

13 and 14. John Oecolampadius (1482–1531) is Basel's reformer, and Martin Bucer (1492–1551) Strasbourg's. Both were influenced by Luther at first, but eventually separated themselves and affirmed more radical positions. These engravings are taken from Icones, by Theodore de Bèze, successor to Calvin in Geneva, where this collection of portraits of the Protestant reformers and their successors was published in 1581. These images popularized Protestant reformers and created an idea of Protestant unity that was in fact lacking.

12. Huldrych Zwingli (1484–1531), contemporary engraving by René Boyvin. The Zurich reformer wrote his own set of theses, developed independently, without direct influence from Luther.

HVLDRICVS·ZVINGLIVS·
ANNO ÆTATIS·44·
·B·

14

the Roman Church by retaining only two sacraments, Baptism and the Eucharist. In the *Address to the Christian Nobility of the German Nation,* written in the vernacular in order to wield greater influence, he intended to demolish the three walls raised by Rome to enslave, as he saw it, Christianity: the distinction between clergy and laity, for which full recognition of the universal priesthood of believers should be substituted; the clergy's monopoly on the interpretation of Scripture, to be replaced by a proclamation of the clarity and limpidity of the Word of God for every believer; and finally, the claim that only the Pope can convoke a Council, a claim of which he must be dispossessed so that Roman tyranny might be opposed.

Then followed the great Lutheran affirmations, often expressed in dialectical terms. Luther provided multiple examples which he loved to find in Saint Paul or Saint Augustine: "Man gives nothing, he receives all." This was indeed his absolute position in the crucial debate over the freedom or enslavement of the will. It was Erasmus who revived the debate, clearly perceiving that this issue was at the heart of the challenge, of the radical opposition to the humanist as well as Catholic ideal.

Between 1524 and 1526, these two great adversaries confronted each other. In Luther's view, man did not have free will with which to cooperate in his salvation because his will was corrupted by sin. To affirm such freedom was at the same time to deny its existence, since it was a question of an attribute of God, which man in pride wished to assume.[5] For the humanist Erasmus, on the contrary, God was so generous that He shared His own freedom with us, making us collaborators in our own salvation. It was at this level that the challenge of

the Lutheran Reformation could be taken up again by the Council of Trent and by the Catholic Reformation.

From 1520 on, Germany in the broad sense, and other countries well beyond, were set ablaze by Luther's words. Such a conflagration demonstrates the depth of the Christian expectation of renewal in the Church. John Hus in Bohemia and Wycliffe in England, in spite of their heresies, had legitimate complaints which Savonarola in his own way had also incarnated.

It was not long before other reformers rose up: Zwingli in Zurich, Bucer in Strasburg, Oecolampadius in Basel. Each one, without accepting everything from Luther, for they were very often more radical than he, recognized himself in the prophet of Wittenberg. In 1529, some German princes formed a party at the imperial Diet and *protested* the prohibitions against celebrating the new cult. They thereby, in fact, gave the name "Protestant" to this movement, which would now form new Churches. The new communities began to form institutional structures and then, the following year, confessions of faith (Augsburg, Tetrapolitan . . .). Even though the Reformers had originally wished only to forward the great plan of purifying the Church, they precipitated its rending by their attack on dogma.[6]

As Lucien Febvre put it, Luther did not reproach the Church of his time with "corrupt living"—he was not naive enough for that—but with "corrupt belief."[7] This sense is conveyed by the pen or in the conversation of the Reformer in his Table Talk. But neither the muddleheaded genius of Luther—hyperbolic, Erasmus called it—nor that of Bucer, more nuanced but more versatile, would have sufficed to implant Protestantism firmly had not a man appeared in French-speaking countries who believed in structure and in a new Christian order.

15. John Calvin (1509–1564), a portrait engraved by René Boyvin, two years before the Geneva reformer's death. His ascetic face is often associated with the austerity he imposed on the city of Lake Leman, constituted as a "City-Church" in 1541, after a first unsuccessful attempt in 1536.

16. The old city of Geneva is shown here at the time that Theodore de Bèze (1519–1605) succeeded Calvin as the spiritual guide of the city. During the Savoyard invasion of 1602, the townsmen repulsed the attack of the Duke of Savoy, a Catholic, who considered himself the legitimate sovereign there. (See lower left of the engraving.) In the center is St. Peter's Cathedral. (From the workshop of the engraver Hochenberg, Cologne, beginning of 17th century).

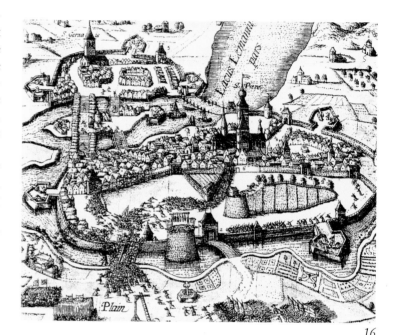

15

16

17

The Challenge of Calvin

John Calvin (1509–1564) was a Frenchman, a lawyer, a humanist in the strict sense of the word, that is a connoisseur of ancient languages, and a layman. He converted to what was called "the new faith" in the years 1533–1535, almost fifteen years after the eruption of Luther. He belongs therefore to another generation, that of sons, of consolidators. Being more Latin by nature and temperament, he would provide the Reformation with different options, more intellectual and institutional. His two great legacies were precisely a body of dogma and a Church.

Calvinist dogma is inscribed in his great book, *The Institutes of the Christian Religion,* whose principal object can be deduced from the old French word, to institute, meaning to teach. The first edition was dated 1536, the last 1560. Calvin never stopped perfecting and adding to his work. Over the course of editing, fundamental themes came to the fore. Predestination was given more and more prominence. The aging Calvin, against all reasoning, never ceased to ponder the inscrutable, impenetrable divine plan destining individuals in advance to salvation or damnation. He centered his thought, we could say his mystique, on the divine sovereignty and its mystery. Yet his theology was also Christocentric, ceaselessly recalling the role of the great Mediator.

Calvin proposed a very precise organization of the Church with his concept of ministries, as discovered by his master Bucer in the New Testament. There were to be pastors, deacons, doctors, and elders. He thus excluded the traditional ecclesiastical hierarchy founded on the Sacrament of Holy Orders, which he rejected. Using the model of the four ministries, he tried, in the midst of tempests and high seas, to build a reformed Christian framework in Geneva, the city seemingly assigned to him by Providence and recently liberated from the yoke of Savoy. In opposition to the anarchies of those claiming to be purely spiritual and the calculations of politicians, Calvin created in Geneva a Christian order, austere, puritanical before the fact, and extreme in its morality, discipline, and liturgy. Like Zwingli, he rejected medieval and Roman "superstitions"—images and ornaments. From 1536 until his death in 1564, this Frenchman succeeded in consolidating a Protestant theocracy in Genevan territory.

Like every great founder, Calvin knew to choose a firm and accredited successor. His choice fell on Theodore of Bèze (1519–1605) who preserved the heritage. He was a far cry from the subtle and conciliating Melancthon (1497–1560) who, after

17. Title page of Calvin's treatise on Predestination and God's Providence, *Geneva, the press of John Crespin and Conrad Badius, 1550. Inspired by a selective reading of Saint Augustine, Calvin developed his theology of double predestination for eternal happiness or damnation. His teaching became more and more radical, creating opposition even in Geneva, but his ideas had a great influence on the Puritans.*

18. The Paschal Lamb, *a Christian emblem published in* Icones *by Theodore de Bèze, Geneva, published by John of Laon 1581. The verses that accompany this traditional symbol of early Christianity condemn pagan myths, like the one about the Golden Fleece (perhaps an attack on the House of Austria, which instituted an Order of that name), in order to affirm the* Christocentrism *of the one Lamb of God, the Savior, who is the only treasure of the Church.*

18

19

19. The seating plan for the ceremony of the opening of the English Parliament in April 1523, in the presence of King Henry VIII (Windsor Castle, Royal Collection). In the 16th century, the English Parliament will become simply a chamber of endorsement for the king's whims in religious matters. In 1523, Henry VIII looked like the champion of the Catholic faith, which he defended against Luther by a treaty published under the king's name. In recognition, two years later he received from the Pope the title of Defender of the Faith. At that time, Thomas More was Speaker of the House of Commons. Ten years later, the same king's new religious ideas would also be approved by the parliament.

having replaced Luther—the admirer of his own disciple—had failed to maintain the unity of German Lutheran Protestantism

From the outset, Protestantism appeared to be diverse, divided, and beset with opposition, despite truces negotiated at great cost and rapidly broken. It consisted of a broad range of positions, from the major and national Protestantisms of the Scandinavian type to apocalyptic movements in which the visible Church was practically denied and the sacraments suppressed. The most dramatic example of this radical reform is the violent fire that descended upon the city of Münster in the year 1520. People thought that the new Jerusalem had come down from heaven in an apocalyptic atmosphere that could only end in tragedy. There was a whole range of what might be called "left wing" forms of Protestantism, characterized by the rejection of infant baptism, or anabaptism

The various Protestant movements were divided according to their concepts of the Eucharist, ranging from symbolism to a belief in the Real Presence, the latter differing from Catholicism in the manner of explanation. They also varied according to their ecclesiologies, ranging from the maintenance of the episcopal structure to the Presbyterian model in which the pastor issued from the community. The Anglican Church, precipitated into existence by the tyrannical will of its founder, Henry VIII, has oscillated throughout its history between the two traditions, Catholic and Reformed, ending finally by finding for itself the role of *via media.*

In the face of such turmoil, what response could the Roman Church make?

The response of traditional Catholic theologians contemporary with Luther and Calvin no longer seemed adequate. Having become repetitive and attached to stereotyped expressions, scholasticism, or rather the scholastics of the time, no longer possessed the medieval vigor which would have produced a convincing doctrinal response. The modern response, that of humanism, was confronted by its own limitations. Because of its exaggerated taste for nuances and compromise, it was too intellectual, as it were, too subtle to stand up against the brutal shocks of the Protestant Reformation.

What is most astounding is that, in the midst of these trials and upheavals, it would be from a cross-fertilization of humanism and the scholastic tradition that the response to the Protestant challenge would in fact issue: the Catholic Reformation.

The Catholic Reformation

It was not enough merely to have the energy to resist. This energy was often lacking to Catholics subject to the pressures

21

20

20. Saint Clare, after her death, welcomed by Christ, the Virgin Mary, St. John the Baptist, Saint Catherine, and other saints. *Detail from an altarpiece in the Poor Clares' Monastery in Nuremberg, 14th century (Nuremberg, Germanic National Museum). This convent became famous for its resistance to the Protestant Reformation and for the tenacity of its abbess, Caritas Pirckheimer (1467–1633) during the persecution that followed.*

of an influential minority, and, it would seem, little prepared to meet the challenge. There were some heroic, or simply courageous acts. We should note the resolute politics of a city like Fribourg in Switzerland, quickly opting for the Roman Church, escorting all undesirable preachers to the border, and encouraging those who taught orthodox doctrine. We can also think of the famous Pilgrimage of Grace in York, which took place in 1537 in opposition to the brutal measures of Henry VIII. To take a different type of example, there was the remarkable stance of the Abbess of the Poor Clares of Nuremberg, Charitas Pirckheimer, who single-handedly succeeded in saving her monastery from accepting the Reformation and in getting her brother Willibald to return to the Church.

Yet there had to be more than these isolated cases; a reform of the Roman Church had to come. What were people waiting for?

A Rough Sketch of Reform

During the first half of the sixteenth century, the Church had more or less designed a rough sketch of a Catholic reform, or had

22, 23 and 24. (22) *Holbein the Younger,* Henry VIII *(1491–1547),*
King of England, about 1534–1536; (23) *Lukas Cranach the Elder,*
The Emperor Charles V *(1500–1558) (both from Madrid,*
Thyssen-Bornemisza Collection); (24) *Jean Clouet,* Francis I
(1494–1547), King of France, about 1520–1525 (Paris, Louvre).
The political fate and religious destiny of 16th-century Europe
depended largely on these three young, brilliant sovereigns, separated
by their military rivalries and political ambitions. Henry VIII
removed England from the Roman Church; Charles V attempted
to save the German Empire from Protestantism, but he failed in
part, thus leading to his abdication in 1555, while François I,
although sensitive to the evangelical renewal at the beginning
of his reign, chose to maintain the Catholic faith in France.

dreamed about it, but had not actually set it in motion. There
were several reasons for this. One was the papacy's fear of conciliarism, which it believed had evolved from the rise of the lay
spirit and of which it had been the victim. For their part, the
local Churches felt that only a Council could succeed in making
changes in depth. A second reason lay in the international politics
in which the Papal States were a player. Popes were involved in
the conflicts over European hegemony between the three young
kings avid for power: Henry VIII, Francis I, and Charles V.

Yet a lengthy and exacting work was about to begin. It
doubtless called for patience, a thing difficult to maintain in
a period of crisis. But it could benefit from all the previous

25. *Murillo (1618–1682), Saint Felix of Cantalice (about 1515–1587) receives the Child Jesus from Mary's hands (about 1675, Seville, Provincial Museum). This painting shows one of the most popular figures among the first Capuchins. Completely illiterate, he expressed a simple devotion to the Baby Jesus and his Mother, a devotion understandable by ordinary Catholics. The Capuchins, a reform branch of the Franciscans in the 16th century, promoted a renewal of piety both at home and in mission lands.*

26. *Project for a mission village by the Capuchins of Cumana (in today's Venezuela), end of 17th century. The Franciscans were among the first missionaries to organize "Reductions" to protect the converted Indians from the excesses of colonization by gathering them together into villages. The Jesuits will replicate this system on a large scale.*

27. *The Sorrowful Virgin, sculpture from Quito (Ecuador), presently in the Capuchin Monastery in Santiago, Chile. The evangelization of Latin America reflects Spanish spirituality in its often dramatic tendencies. Here, the Lady of Sorrows, in a gesture of offering seems to carry the swords that pierced her (Luke 2:35) and bears a crown that resembles the crown of thorns that Christ wore during his Passion.*

25

27

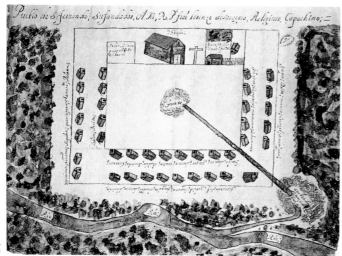

26

28

efforts of reform exemplified, for instance, by religious Orders since the second half of the fifteenth century. Some of these had reformed themselves, thanks to the movement issuing from the *devotio moderna,* by means of internal congregations or by the repossession of an abbey. New Orders were founded: the Theatines in 1524, the Capuchins in 1528—but with troubled beginnings—and most notably, the Society of Jesus in 1534. The desire of Ignatius of Loyola and his companions to leave for Jerusalem would be transformed into availability for every type of apostolic and missionary enterprise. These Orders became powerful instruments of the Catholic Reformation.

Finally, there were also local successes centered around certain bishops of whom Gian Matteo Giberti (+1543) of Verona was the model. It was all these initiatives and a sense of urgency lest entire countries should become Protestant that at last led to the convocation of the Council of Trent.

28. Giambettino Cignaroli (1706–1770). The Virgin and the Child Appear to Saint Cajetan of Thiene (1480–1547) (Vicenza, St. Cajetan). Similar to the treatment of Murillo (see fig. 25), the painter here recalls the vision received by this priest on Christmas 1517 at St. Mary Major, Rome. This vision led him to become co-founder of the Theatines in order to promote the reform of the clergy, thus anticipating the program of the Council of Trent.

30. A depiction of one of the Guarani Indian "Reductions" (the village of the Virgin Mary of Candelaria). The plan for these protected villages was uniform. They were built around a central plaza with a tall column surmounted by a statue of the Virgin Mary, and two small shrines.

30

29

29. Anonymous painting, before the middle of 17th century (Rome, outer sacristy of the Church of the Gesù). This scene doubtless took place in 1540, when Paul III (1468–1549) approved the new Society of Jesus. Saint Ignatius, surrounded by the first Jesuits, gives to the Farnese Pope a small book—either the Spiritual Exercices *he composed and practiced with his companions, or the* Formula Instituti, *first draft of the Jesuit Constitutions. The Cardinal-Nephew is pictured in the background.*

THE CHURCH AND THE CHALLENGE OF THE REFORMATION

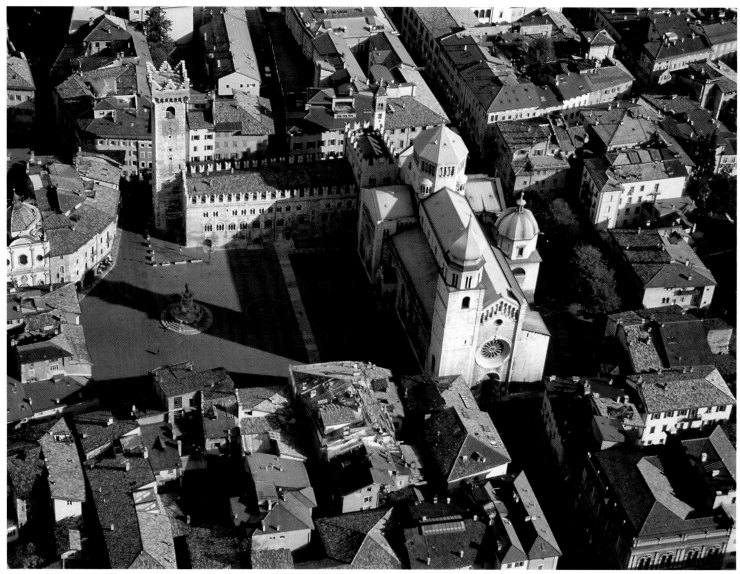

31

31. *Trent, cathedral and town square. The choice of this city, halfway between Germany and Italy in both its history and its culture, was a compromise between the Emperor and the Pope. Between 1545 and 1563, it received the Council Fathers and the sovereigns' representatives, who proceeded to redefine Catholic doctrine and discipline and so assure a thorough reform of the Roman Church.*

32, 33, 34, and 35. *In the Duomo of Milan, where Charles Borromeo (1538–1584) was archbishop, the paintings exalt various aspects of the reforms instituted by this saint. He visits the plague victims at the time of the great epidemic of 1576 (32) (G.B.Crespi, 1602–1604); (33) He makes one of his famous pastoral visits in the mountains, during which he preaches to the whole population (G. Landriani, called the Little Duke); (34) He reaches out to the poor, distributing the riches produced by his sale of the principality of Oria (Giovan Battista known as il Cenaro, about 1602–1604); (35) He welcomes the Jesuits, the Theatines, and the Barnabites into his diocese, to be religious artisans of the Catholic Reform (Crespi, 1602–1604).*

A Program of Reform

Incredible as it seemed, when thirty conciliar Fathers met at Trent on December 13, 1545, they were embarking on a work that would have a considerable impact on history. It would be done in three great periods (1545–47, 1551–52, and particularly 1562–63) with interruptions which, each time, could have seemed definitive since they were due basically to political considerations. But from session to session, this Council provided a program for a pastoral reform after having reaffirmed the Catholic faith. Actually, it did not want to choose between the redefinition of dogma and pastoral initiatives that came up alternately during the debates. Refuting Protestant theses during its first two periods, the Council became more clearly reformative in 1562.

Here again, however, the Council depended on previous or contemporary work, from the *Consilium de emendanda Ecclesia* elaborated in 1537 by a commission of cardinals including such eminent and prudent men as Contarini and Reginald Pole, to the *Liber Reformationis* which the German Emperor submitted

34

35

to the conciliar Fathers during the last months of their meeting at Trent.

The theological, dogmatic, and highly sensitive work of the first two periods was immense, forming a framework of which we are still heirs. The decrees on Scripture and Tradition, on justification, original sin, the one which reaffirmed the Sacrifice of the Mass, and those on the theology of the sacraments and of merit, although discussed at length could not say everything, as the sometimes difficult work of interpretation would later show. Nevertheless the results accomplished were great and often more nuanced than is admitted.

Cardinal Morone had the immense merit of bringing to a finish so lengthy and exacting an enterprise by means of his talents as a diplomat and a theologian. Under the inspiration of Bartholomew of the Martyrs, the archbishop of Braga in Portugal, and with the impetus given by Cardinal Charles Borromeo, nephew of Pope Pius IV, the Council ended with a daring and complete program. The obligation of residency for bishops was reaffirmed, as was the holding of local synods. For the formation of priests, the creation of seminaries was determined, and for that of the faithful, the elaboration of

a catechism. An institution such as the Index of forbidden books pertains more to the sphere of a Counter Reform, that is, one in direct opposition to Protestant influence. But the pastoral program of the Council of Trent can in fact be centered around the idea of a preaching renewed in all its forms and confided to the diocesan bishop whose first duty it was. It thus responded to the Protestant challenge with a free preaching of the pure Word of God.

A Reform Applied

In contrast to preceding attempts at reform, there was still the need for an actual application of the directives of the Council. This began concretely with the production of a better text of the Vulgate, a catechism for the use of parish priests, as well as a new Missal, and a revised Breviary. The Catholic Reformation was providing itself with concrete instruments for daily use.

Of greatest significance, however, was the action of great bishops. The most effective of these was Charles Borromeo (1538–1584), who became one of the models of the Catholic

36. Saint Francis de Sales (1567–1622) Bishop of Geneva residing in Annecy, gave to Saint Jane de Chantal (1572–1641) the Rule of the Visitation on June 6, 1610, extending permission to the nuns to help the poor outside their cloister, a rule that had to be modified when the Council of Trent prescribed a re-enforcement of cloistered life for nuns. Painting by Noël Hulle (1711–1781).

36

37

37. Andrea Sacchi (1598–1661), painting of a Roman church decorated for the first centenary of the Society of Jesus in 1639 (Rome, Barberini Palace, National Gallery of Antique Arts). After difficulties at the beginning, caused mostly by Pope Paul IV (1555–1559) and by the death of Ignatius of Loyola in 1556, the Society of Jesus flourished. At the beginning of the 17th century, there were 8,500 members in 23 provinces. Its founder was canonized in 1622.

Reformation, traveling about his immense diocese of Milan on pastoral visitations, "celebrating" Synods, and creating seminaries. He was an authorized interpreter of the Council, having been present for its considerations and acts. In the same spirit a generation later, Francis de Sales (1567–1622), the bishop of Geneva in exile at Annecy, provided the laity with their own spirituality by introducing them to "the devout life." Spain too was an important center of reform in depth.

It has been said that the Ignatian spirit penetrated Catholicism by way of Jesuit colleges, the Exercises of Saint Ignatius, and Marian congregations,[8] three means of giving the laity the spirit of active individualism which is so effective. It is certain that the Society of Jesus played a primordial role in the response to the Protestant challenge, with Laynez, for

38

38. *The Roman College, façade. Inaugurated on February 22, 1551, this institution quickly became the most attended and most famous of the Jesuit colleges. Saint Ignatius provided it with a printing press. The students, young candidates for the Society as well as other students, were first taught Arts (philosophy and Liberal arts) and then Theology, following the model of the University of Paris. In 1584, Gregory XIII gave it a university charter, and in his honor, it became known as the Gregorian University.*

39. *Bartolomeo Ammannati, Coat of Arms of the Society of Jesus (Rome, Gesù Church, façade). This emblem is an abbreviation of the word Jesus, since in the Greek word* Jesous, *the letter "E" becomes "H" in capital letters. But other interpretations were given such as* Jesus hominun salvator *(Jesus, Savior of Men) or* In hoc signo vinces *("By this sign, you will conquer") referring to Constantine's victory in 312, or still,* In hac cruce salus *("In this cross is salvation").*

39

41

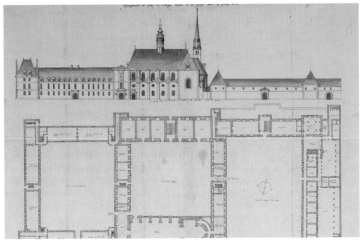

40

42

40, 41, 42. *(40) Stephen Martellange (1569–1641), project for La Flèche College in Sarthe (France). This college, founded in 1603 by King Henry IV, was entrusted to the Jesuits. Descartes was among its first students and he attended it till 1614. (41) Courtyard from Evora University (Portugal), an elite Jesuit university in the 17th century, known particularly for its Biblical commentators. (42) The Jesuit College in Kutna Hora in the present-day Czech Republic, and St. Barbara Church. Built between 1667–1700 by the* Italian architect Domenico Orsi in an F shape (in honor of the Emperor Ferdinand II), this imposing structure symbolizes the influence that the Jesuits had in the Catholic re-conquest of Bohemia. These Jesuit institutions of higher education trained the elites of Catholic Europe and, especially through the Marian congregations that they came to promote, assured spiritual and moral support to Catholic society.

43, 44, and 45. (43) Antoine Wiericx. The Miracle of Segovia (Brussels, Royal Library, Print Collection). John of the Cross (1542–1591) enters into intimate dialogue with Jesus, whose cross and crown are radiant. Christ asks the Carmelite reformer what reward he wants for his works. His reply: "Only the privilege to suffer for you." On the front of the altar one can see the Carmelite coat of arms, also in visible in (45) a work (published in Lyon in 1639) from Padre Marco Antonio Alegre de Casanate, Spanish Carmelite. This text relies on the tradition that the Carmelite Order, actually started in Palestine, had been founded by the prophet Elijah and his disciple Elisha. (44) Finally, the same Coat of Arms is also found on this unusual Diploma for a Doctor in Theology from Quito University, 1759, that appears to be granted by Saint Teresa of Avila (1515–1582). The long-held image of Teresa as a theologian was ratified by Paul VI when he declared the Carmelite Reformer a "Doctor of the Church" in 1970. A symbol of the divine love that pierced the heart of the saint can be seen next to her. It will be reworked by Bernini (fig. 53 p. 139).

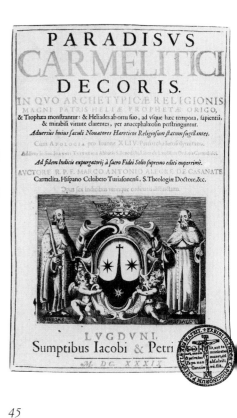

43

44

45

example, the successor of Ignatius as head of the new Order, who was so active at the Council of Trent, or Peter Canisius in German-speaking lands.

We must not forget the importance of the renewal of contemplative life, hidden though it was. Not without reason was Teresa of Avila (+1582) called "the Reforming Mother," for in 1562, before the conclusion of the Council of Trent, she "reformed" Carmel with John of the Cross (+1591). An interior certitude shines forth in the paintings of El Greco (+1614), impossible to account for or to understand without reference to mysticism,[9] the precursor of an art wholly oriented to the confession of faith.

The Catholic Reformation was actually a reaffirmation of traditional faith, framed in a response that did not call structures into question but tried to reanimate them by the choice of the holiest and most competent persons. In the end,

46, 47, and 48. Domenicos Theotocopoulos, called El Greco (1541–1614), from Crete, succeeded in integrating the style of icon painting into Spanish religious art, thus giving it a spiritual intensity lost during the Renaissance. (46) This painting from the sacristy of Toledo Cathedral, the city where he then lived, was made in the years 1603–1607, and it depicts Peter's denial and his bitter repentance (Mark 14:72), even though it also shows him as head of the Apostles, as expressed by the keys hanging from his arm. (48) This illustration of Pentecost (Acts 2:1–4), from about 1600 (Madrid, Prado Museum), is truly a mystic poem in images. El Greco follows the icon tradition of including the Virgin Mary, who is in the center, since she is the figure of the Church, born on that day. (47) Even the later portrait of Fray Hortensio de Paravicino (1580–1633) (1612, Boston, Museum of Fine Arts), a Trinitarian whose cross can be seen under his black mantle, reveals a gaze of spiritual intensity mixed with anxiety, giving a note of modernity to this painting.

48

49. *Saint Isidore the Farmer, polychrome wooden statue of the 17th century (Cuenca, Ecuador; Bertha Cisneros de Cueva Collection). The patron saint of Madrid who lived at the beginning of the 12th century, called the Worker (Labrador),* is dressed here in rich *clothes like a gentleman, perhaps to portray the nobility of his virtues. His canonization served as a mark of recognition for the city that became the capital of the* Spains *in 1561. Lope de Vega (1562–1635) highly praised this saint and even organized poetic jousts in his honor that took place in Madrid in 1622.*

50 and 51. (50) *Anonymous Flemish painter,* Saint Ignatius, *about 1600 (Brussels, Jesuit Provincial House).* (51) *Andres Reinoso,* Saint Francis Xavier resurrecting an Indian, *about 1619 (Lisbon, Church of St. Roch). The first two Jesuits, both Basques, who met in Paris and were canonized together in 1622, shared the two main tasks of the Catholic Reform. The reform inside the Church was begun and pursued in Rome by Ignatius of Loyola, undisputed captain of the Society; but, as soon as 1540, foreign missions were undertaken by Francis Xavier, sent to India by Ignatius at the request of King John III of Portugal.*

52. The Patronage of St. Philip Neri, *Memorias historicas, Mexico, printed by Maria de Rivera, 1736. In the 18th century, the Oratorians in Mexico sought to celebrate the charm, humor, and passionate mysticism of their holy founder Philip Neri (1515–1595), who had gathered into community Roman priests, whose exemplary lives are here blessed by angels.*

50

49

51

it brought about the full-flowering of gifts in the service of the Church through holiness of life.

One of the most telling symbols of this joyous and optimistic reform could be seen in the ceremony of March 16, 1622, the year of the death of Francis de Sales when crowds thronged St. Peter's in Rome for five canonizations. Isidore of Madrid, a saint of the Middle Ages, seemed to represent medieval tradition and continuity. Then followed four saints of the sixteenth century—already—all indefatigable artisans of the Catholic renewal: Ignatius of Loyola (+1556), founder of the Society of Jesus;. Francis Xavier (1562), one of the first Jesuits and missionary to distant lands; Philip Neri (+1595),

who through the Oratory of Rome had renewed priestly life; and finally Teresa of Avila who symbolized the renewal of contemplative life. The dramatic and fervent liturgy allowed for the people to intervene with applause while the music and trumpets burst forth with resounding Mediterranean joy, reminding those gathered that all the persons being canonized were either Italians or Spaniards.[10] The Church seemed to join earth to heaven in the Basilica of St. Peter, which had just been completed in 1614 and would be consecrated in 1626. This was not a demonstration of triumphalism but rather a reminder that the challenge of the Reformation had been met and conquered by holiness alone.

52

53

53. *Bernini (1598–1680) created the Cornaro Chapel in Our Lady of Victory Church in Rome between 1644 and 1657, the site of a divine drama that utilizes all the resources of the Baroque to express God's power and grandeur. These are the attributes that Saint Teresa experiences in her ecstasies (or her* transverberation, *according to the technical term used to describe this type of sculpture).*

54. The Bark of Faith and Love, *a scene-drawing from 1710. The Catholic Reform takes on the global, cosmic, and glorious dimensions of Christian salvation in architecture, painting, and sculpture as well as in music. A century later, the allegory becomes triumphant, as in this painting where caves and theatrical decor illustrate the trials of the boat of faith whose pilot is love (commonly depicted by a sort of Cupid), blown about by the Four Winds through the tempests of life and of history.*

54

1

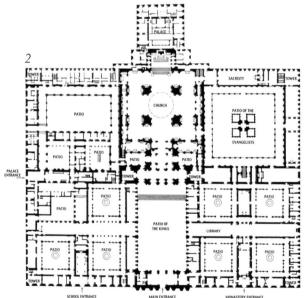

3

2

1 and 2. At one and the same time monastery, sanctuary, palace, and pantheon of the royal dynasty, the Escorial was erected on an undeveloped site, northwest of Madrid. At the request of King Philip II (1527–1598), the architect Juan Battista de Toledo started the construction in 1563, and Juan Battista de Herrera completed it in 1584, in memory of the Battle of Saint Quentin, won on August 10, 1557, the Feast of Saint Lawrence. To fulfill a vow made to this saint, the instrument of his martyrdom, the grill, was used as a basic shape for the plan of this ensemble of buildings and it became the sculpted emblem repeated everywhere. Simplicity, austerity, and grandeur characterize the architecture. In the center, the church is surrounded by multiple patios of varied sizes, more like cloisters than courtyards. This granite building expresses the theological-political designs of Philip II, who wanted to govern not only Spain but all of Spanish America.

3. Titian (about 1490–1576) was protected by Philip II of Spain for more than 20 years. This allegory of the Battle of Lepanto (Madrid, Prado Museum), painted between 1572–1575 at the end of a long career, exalts the protection of God and of the Virgin Mary over the victory of October 7, 1571. It was a victory of Christians over the Turks (seen on the left), whose humiliating position—in chains, with banners, turban, and shield on the ground—contrasts with the attitude of Don Juan of Austria, who carries a child holding the palm of victory. On the right, the painter's signature can be seen on a column. The Battle of Lepanto was glorified by many great artists of the time (Tintoretto, Veronese) and by poets such as Juan Ruffo in his Austriade, or Fernando de Herrera, who brings out its providential significance.

Chapter 7

THE CHURCH AND THE CHALLENGE OF ABSOLUTISM

In the face of confessional differences and wars of religion, the order we see in Europe in the sixteenth and seventeenth centuries could not have been established except by the affirmation of the following principle: *cuius regio, eius religio,* or, every person must follow the religion of his prince. The formula was actually coined a few years after its first application at the Peace of Augsburg (1555), which divided Lutheran Europe from Catholic Europe.[1] At the end of the Thirty Years' War, a confrontation in which all Europe was involved, similar rights would be accorded in Calvinist countries.

When the Jews, expelled from all Western countries in the mid-fifteenth century and later from Spain in 1492, had practically speaking no place of refuge but the Papal States, the Christendom which in the Middle Ages had incorporated Jewish and Muslim minorities found itself diminished. It was not by chance that, left to itself, it became divided so passionately along religious lines. As a result, the nation-states would see to it that the exclusivity of belief would be respected. One law, one faith, one king: This was the program of unity chosen in the seventeenth century. It is easy to see that faith here is hemmed in by a juridical edifice and an institution which, even though wishing to be rooted in the sacred, remains essentially secular.

The enigmatic personality of Philip II (+1598), king of Spain since 1556, was one of the first incarnations of absolutism. He represented the defense of Catholicism, which he wished to see triumph in England, first through his marriage with Mary Tudor until her death in 1558, and then by force of arms with the disaster of the Armada in 1588. His policy in the Low Countries met with fierce resistance. In Spain, however, he inaugurated an effective government designed to safeguard the Catholic faith and based on a complicated administration. The architecture of his Palace, the Escorial, built like an immense grill, (the instrument of the torture of Saint Laurence), is symbolic of this political and religious order. Romanticism would make it the setting of the stifling of liberty, as we see it depicted in Schiller's *Don Carlos,* reproduced by Verdi in his opera.

So characteristic and remarkable a desire for uniformity and symmetry can also be observed in classical architecture. However, this order met with much opposition before being firmly established. There were several phases in the seventeenth century. The first half of the century was filled with upheavals and even revolutions, mirrored in literature, for example, where we find affectation as an excessive reaction to the attempts at authoritarian simplification. Traces of this can be found in France in the history of language, so closely connected to power and ideas. Malherbe arrived upon the scene in 1628 and in 1634 Cardinal Richelieu founded *l'Académie française* (1634), charged with unifying and purifying the French language. During the personal reign of Louis XIV, after the death of Mazarin in 1661, the European model of an absolute monarchy was organized. We find its symbol in the classical arrangement of the gardens of Le Nôtre at Versailles, completed by the transformation of the palace (1668–1686).[2] This was in many ways the apogee of absolutism, with domesticated nobles bustling about. Then came "the crisis of the European conscience." The first signs of it appeared in the year 1670, but according to its historian Paul Hazard, it extended from 1680 to 1715, which was also the date of Louis XIV's death.

The dominant characteristic of the period was the attempt to achieve monarchic and state absolutism, and then, the reality of its existence. This constituted a challenge for the Church insofar as by nature and perhaps in reaction to the tumult and troubles of the preceding century it was attracted to absolutism. With its desire for order and hierarchy, the Church's institutional and intellectual complicity with this type of thought and political order is not difficult to understand.

All of this led, therefore, to a muted and ill-defined conflict, hard to identify but real, in that the consequences of absolutism would prove harmful to the rights of the Church.

4, 5, and 6. (4) Versailles, 1669 plan, reproduction from an engraving of Blondel, 1752. Initial work on the transformation of Louis XIII's hunting pavilion began in 1661 when Louis XIV, after Mazarin's death, began his reign. This was also the year of the fall of the king's finance minister, Fouquet, creator of an ambitious castle at Vaux-le-Vicomte. Versailles would be its triumphant rival. The plan, with its radiating crossroads, reveals a symbolism of the sun, this star that "produces life, joy and action" to use the Sun King's words, which allude to his programs and reign. The combination of rationality and symbolism echoes Descartes' ambition to explain theology rationally. (5) Flore Basin, an evocation of spring, shows the ambition of the French garden to domesticate nature. The countryside is changed into an urban decoration. (6) In Versailles' gardens, designed by Le Nôtre between 1661 and 1668, visitors or courtiers (themselves the object of the king's own theoretical study between 1689 and 1704) must be led from periphery to center, the splendid site of absolute power.

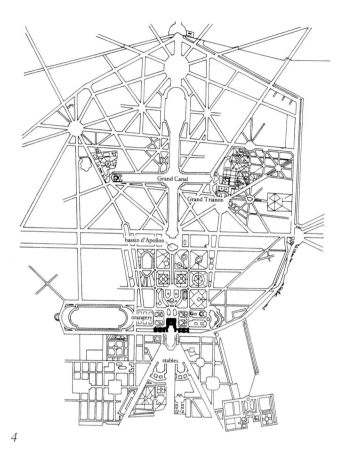

4

6

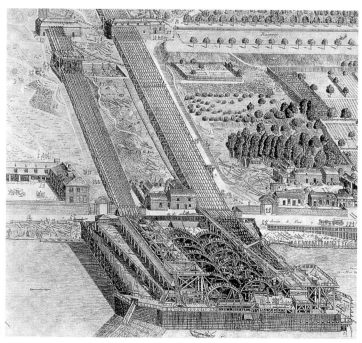

5

7

8

7 and 8. If monarchical power was already well established in the 16th century, it is nonetheless Louis XIV who gives it a liturgical dimension in his every day court ritual. Art collaborates in giving a personal dimension to absolutism. Bernini (1598–1680) executed in 1665 this bust found in the Chateau of Versailles, the same year that he also realized the equestrian statue of Louis XIV. (7) The baroque visage has become a mask, and the wig accentuates its artificiality. Charles Andre Van Loo (1684–1745) painted Louis XV in majesty (8), deploying the insignias of power: the ermine mantle, the crown and scepter worn on coronation day, quasi-sacraments of monarchy, also the war helmet. Finally, we also notice his hand resting imperiously on the staff decorated with fleurs-de-lis, the insignia of supreme military power.

10

10. Claude Lefebvre, Portrait of Jean-Baptiste Colbert (1619–1683) (Chateau of Versailles). Louis XIV's minister strengthens the role of the State through controlling the production of goods and by protectionism over French products. This portrait shows how absolute monarchy gives to those who serve it loyally the right to acquire some of the signs of power: nobility, honors, such as the Order of Chivalry, whose cloak Colbert wears, and moreover personal wealth. The sculpture of Antaios carrying earth that gives him strength, seen on the right, is not there by chance.

9. First edition frontispiece (London 1651) of the Leviathan *by Thomas Hobbes (1588–1679). The social contract obliges men to renounce their natural rights and to rely on an absolute state for protection. The state is personalized here by a monarch holding both the sword of temporal power and the crosier of spiritual power in order to take charge (between the cannon and the lightning) of both martial and legislative activities.*

9

The Absolutism of the State

Since the fourteenth and fifteenth centuries, we can discern the gradual development of the State. Its international dimensions had been studied by a long line of thinkers, from the Spanish Dominican Vitoria (+1546) to the Dutch Protestant Grotius (+1645), founder of the peoples' law, the *ius gentium*. To be sure, these thinkers grounded themselves in natural law. However, in the end they served to accentuate the sovereignty of each national entity. The sovereignty of the State, that is, the monopoly of public power allocated to a central apparatus, found expression in Jean Bodin's *Six Books of the Republic* (1576). The result was a philosophy of power similar to that of the Englishman Thomas Hobbes who demonstrated in his *Leviathan* (1651) that the State was the best defender of individual interests and liberated men from the fear of initial chaos. At the center of this evolution was a little known but important thinker, William Barclay of Aberdeen. In his *De*

11

12

13

11. The Battle of White Mountain *in a German engraving from that period. This first battle of the Thirty Years' War was a Catholic victory over the Protestant troops of the Bohemian States on November 8, 1620. It marked a decisive step in the confessional realignment of Europe in the 17th century. An important victory in military history, it also became a symbol of the Protestant-Catholic confrontation, energized by the mystical apocalyptic spirit of the Carmelite Dominic of Jesus and Mary (1559–1630), who turned it into a modern crusade for Catholics.*

12. *An orator from the nobility, recognizable by the sword he wears at his side, tries in 1648 (first year of the troubles of La Fronde) to convince the Parisians to rebel against Cardinal Mazarin's politics (Engraving, Paris, Bibliothèque Nationale). On the left bank of the Seine, across from the Louvre, seat of royal power, and the Île de la Cite, agitation is stirred up by the aristocracy and by Parlement aimed at limiting the king's reach toward absolutism.*

regno et regali potestate of 1600, he defended the divine right of kings while denying all temporal authority to the Pope.

Thus, in the seventeenth century the State became the key reference point for realities which were in fact independent of it. The State became confused with the nation, with the homeland, with the crown, or with government. It went so far as to absorb the economy through mercantilism, or the monopoly of manufactured goods (Colbertism).

It is not surprising, therefore, to witness so much resistance, rebellion, and turmoil with the advent of an absolutist order in the first half of the century. Political/confessional conflicts followed one upon the other: the Thirty Years' War (1618–1648) which ended by dividing all of Europe, the Revolution of Oliver Cromwell (1645) which resulted in the assassination of Charles I in 1649 in the name of a republican Presbyterianism, local rebellions in 1640 and 1641 against Castilian domination in Catalonia, in Portugal, and Andalusia. Finally, there was a last attempt of the feudal lords and intermediary groups to retain some power in the face of the mounting absolutist monarchy. The Fronde, a kind of civil war between elite factions in France from 1648 to 1653, marked the end of the political apprenticeship of the young Louis XIV.

Once these conflicts had been resolved or put on the back burner, absolutism reigned in Europe, but not without grave consequences for the Church, which was confronted with an institution which by definition admitted of no rivals.

The Ecclesiological Consequences of Absolutism

Having assimilated or subjugated every kind of political or social power, it was quite logical that the State should seek to be equally coextensive with the Church. This was the case in the sixteenth century with the Protestant principalities and with Anglicanism, for which Richard Hooker (+1600) provided a theory that allied theology with political philosophy. The specter of a national Church arose also in France when the monarchy revived Gallican "rights" in relation to the Holy See. The State sought to control and dominate the Church, particularly by means of episcopal nominations, leaving it only with what we now consider tasks of public service: social assistance and education

In Catholic Europe, France was for the moment the only country to openly present its claims in ecclesiology.

14. Bartolomé Esteban Murillo, Saint James of Alcala and the Poor, *1682 (Madrid, San Fernando Royal Academy). In the 17th and 18th centuries, as the Church creates home missions to evangelize the countryside, she also takes charge of social services. Here, needy people and beggars of all ages wait for the distribution of soup for the poor that starts after a prayer said by Saint James of Alcala (1400–1463). This Franciscan friar is seen as a symbol of the Mendicant Orders' dedication to the poor.*

15

13. *Thomas Rowlandson (1756–1827),* The Great Hall of the Bank of England *in London, watercolor. (Paris, Library of the Decorative Arts). The first state bank, founded in London in 1694, is in charge of the financial affairs of the government and becomes the Mint, producing money guaranteed by the State. Not only does it assume one of the essential attributes of sovereignty, but it also provides a powerful financial and economic lever for the State.*

15. *St. Lawrence Church, Almancil, Algarve (Portugal). In this isolated church on a hillside in the extreme south of Portugal, flourishes the typical art of* azulejos, *varnished earthenware squares of Arab origin, introduced in Portugal after 1584. The inside of the church is completely covered by them. Here they show St. Lawrence, a deacon of the early Church, whose ministry was to distribute alms to the poor. One can read on the legend, "The Church gives its treasures to the poor," a fragment from Psalm 111:9 (Vulgate version).*

Gallicanism

The doctrine according to which the Church of France enjoyed a certain autonomy in regard to Rome, on the basis of an ecclesiology more in conformity with Tradition than that of pontifical predominance, had very ancient roots. It was overtly supported by the University of Paris in the fourteenth century, leading to the triumph of its logical consequence: the primacy of the Council over the Pope which was proclaimed at Constance in 1415. A century later, Gallicanism was put into practice in the Concordat that Francis I imposed upon the Holy See in 1516, and which would govern relations between the French monarchy and Rome up to the Revolution. The first instance is an example of theological Gallicanism, the second of political Gallicanism.

Alarmed by the threat of a Gallican schism similar to that which Henry VIII had unleashed with Anglicanism in the sixteenth century, the papacy was extremely cautious in its relations with the French Church and especially with the Bourbon absolute monarchs who manifested their independence. Thus the decrees of the Council of Trent were accepted in France in practice, but not the ecclesiology behind them which seemed contrary to "Gallican rights."

In the seventeenth century, theological Gallicanism received new expression with broad repercussions when Edmond Richer (+1631) published a pamphlet (*Libellus*) "on ecclesiastical and political power" in 1611. This theologian extended legislative power in the Church to priests as well as to bishops. Although the government of the Church remained monarchical, the magisterium, that is the authority of defining and teaching the faith, pertained to all who had received the sacrament of Holy Orders. This view was diametrically opposed to ultramontanism, which concentrated the magisterium in the person of the Pope and also ran counter to the traditional Gallicanism of the Episcopalian type. The more democratic "Richerism," allying itself with Jansenism, seemed dangerous to both king and bishops.

Now Louis XIV had wanted to extend Gallican practice as far as possible. Taking his cue from Richelieu (+1642), who had vainly set his heart on the title of "Patriarch of the West" or at least "Patriarch of the Gauls," and also from Mazarin, the king adopted an aggressive political stance in regard to the Pope from the beginning of his personal reign. Not only did he provoke the Pope by various incidents at his embassy in Rome. Under the pretext of the acquired privilege of collecting the revenues of vacant sees (the *"Régale"*) and of making

16

17

18

16. *Philippe of Champaigne.* Portrait of Cardinal Richelieu, 1635 *(Paris, Louvre). The majestic bearing of this great man of the French State (1585–1642) suggests his political intelligence. He was dedicated to the restoration of royal authority, which made him the architect of absolutism. He also was the reforming pastor of his diocese of Luçon, a theologian, and a patron of writers, a passion that incited him to create the French Academy in 1635.*

18. *Pierre-Imbert Drevet (1697–1739), engraving from a portrait by Hyacinthe Rigaud (1659–1743). Bossuet, Bishop of Meaux, defended a "political Christianity." Despite his often justified reputation for intransigence, he tried to find compromises compatible with Catholicism. Although he supported the revocation of the Edict of Toleration for Protestants in France, he did not hesitate to dialogue with the Lutheran Leibniz. Confronting the ecclesiology of Rome, his Gallicanism remained moderate. He was a powerful personality and an ardent servant of both Church and state.*

17. Robert Nanteuil (1630–1678). *Cardinal Mazarin, engraving, 1653. Promoted to government power in France through Richelieu's patronage while he was Nuncio in Paris in 1635, Giulio Mazarini (1602–1661), a lay cardinal, had to deal with the nobility's resistance (La Fronde). Victorious in the confrontation, he prepared the way for the personal and absolute reign of the young Louis XIV.*

appointments to the benefices during the interim, he sought to exercise his rights to the full. But Pope Innocent XI, a strong personality, resisted Louis and refused to canonically institute the bishops named by the king in virtue of the Concordat.

Louis XIV was sure of the support of the Parisian theologians who had already in 1626 condemned an "ultramontane" book of the Jesuit Santarelli on the deposition of kings by the

Pope. But most importantly, the king had on his side all of the French bishops, with the exception of two who in any case were Jansenists. The conflict reached its climax at the Assembly of the Clergy of France, convoked in October 1681. It adopted a declaration known as "the four articles," inspired by Bossuet (1682). In addition to acknowledging the privileges of the Church of France, a Gallican ecclesiology was developed recognizing the divine origin, direct and immediate, of monarchical power and rejecting the pontifical doctrine which claimed the primacy of the spiritual power over the temporal. The king had this declaration inscribed among the laws of the kingdom. Since it was unacceptable to Rome, a rupture could well be feared.

The consistent policy of the Gallican kings, however, was never to go beyond the point of schism. Being "the eldest Daughter of the Church," France must remain faithful to communion with Rome. This is why the move toward appeasement began upon the death of Innocent XI (1689). In 1692, Innocent XII, who was more conciliatory, agreed to provide for thirty episcopal sees and in the following year Louis XIV reversed his position, if not on the teaching in the declaration of 1682, at least on its application. We have to remember that danger was threatening from the Turks, who were literally at the gates of Vienna (1683). It was no longer the time for disunity.

Finally, Louis XIV needed the apostolic authority in order to uproot the recent appearance of Jansenism. Yet the bull *Unigenitus,* while condemning the Jansenist, Quesnel, reaffirmed the primacy of the Pope and so could have but a precarious victory in France. It would be the occasion for a revival of Gallicanism among the nobility in the legal profession (jurists) and among the bourgeoisie, which had been paving the way for it throughout the eighteenth century.

19

21

20

19. Peter Paul Rubens, Saint Ignatius Presenting to Pope Julius II the Students of the German College, *preparatory sketch for an engraving, about1603 (Edinburg, National Galleries of Scotland). Founded in 1552, the college's mission was the formation, in Rome, of future priests from Germany or from other regions of Central Europe. But it also educated young adults from rich families. This college will play an important role in the re-Catholicizing of the Empire by educating priests and lay elites.*

20. Frontispiece from De gemitu columbae sive de bono lacrimarum *(Cologne, 1634). Engraved portrait of Robert Bellarmine (1542–1621). This Jesuit, who entered the Society of Jesus in 1560, is one of the most influential personalities of the Roman Church at the beginning of the 17th century. A famous scholar, he was one of the experts who revised the Vulgate, a well-known author of controversies, which are the public lectures that he gave in Rome and one of the examiners of Galileo. He also took a position on the disputed question of the Pope's general power over temporal matters. Contrary to the theocratic conception current in Rome, he believed, at least theoretically, that papal power over temporal affairs ought to be only indirect.*

21. Laurent de la Hyre (1606–1656), oil on copper (Rennes, Fine Arts Museum). The meeting of Abraham and Melchisedech, a traditional theme in iconography (see the medieval representation from Reims Cathedral, fig. 3 p. 68), is pictured here with Abraham dressed in a musketeer's attire. Melchisedech wears the high priest's robes. The offering is already Eucharistic: the bread and the cup of wine.

Pontifical Ecclesiology

The various ecclesiastical responses that Rome formulated in the course of her confrontations with Gallicanism, and later with royal absolutism, were based on the vision of Robert Bellarmine (1562–1621), especially in his refutation of William Barclay. The Jesuit cardinal reaffirmed, with moderation, the rights of the Pope in temporal matters in line with the medieval tradition. He praised the benefits of a *respublica christiana* that would be truly subject to the Pope in spiritual matters, with the two powers functioning in harmony.[3] Above all, he provided a definition of the Church in which he introduced the idea of the Pope as head of the body in his role of vicar of Christ, its supreme Head. The Gallicans reproached him for ascribing limitless importance to an element that had only to do with the earthly mode of the Church's existence.

It is true that Bellarmine emphasized the visible aspect of the Church, in its pontifical and monarchical dimensions, even though this was tempered by aristocracy and by election. Catholic fidelity was closely bound to a concept of the Church as a *society* rather than primarily as a *mystery*. At the same time the idea of pontifical infallibility was developing and in August 1682, Pope Innocent XI even thought of defining it in response to the Four Articles of Gallicanism. This would have been an absolute way of responding to the challenge of absolutism.

22. *Nicolas Van Veerendel (1640–1690),* Vanity *(Caen, Fine Arts Museum). The painting of the 17th century is fond of the genre of "vanities," still life intending to recall the brevity of life (Psalm 38:6). Here, the painter from Antwerp proposes a poetic composition around two skulls adorned with flowers, themselves ephemeral (Psalm 89:4–6). In the foreground, we can see what seems to be a bubble, remembrance of the "Homo bulla," an adage that runs through pagan and Christian antiquity: Human existence is nothing but a soap bubble that lives for a minute and then bursts.*

We can understand how these two absolutisms, opposed in matters political and ecclesiastical, could have joined forces when confronted with a common enemy. Jansenism, by its very excess, would contribute to the consolidation of the different absolutisms, but only for a limited time.

22

Jansenist Movements
or the Theological Reactions to Absolutism

Jansenism was both a religious and in the broad sense "political" phenomenon of vast complexity. It is more precise to say that there were Jansenisms in the plural as the term may be applied to different generations, from the end of the sixteenth century to the middle of the eighteenth. It refers to movements in France but also in Lorraine and the Low Countries, that is at the frontiers of the Catholic world. From a theological point of view as well, it was a teaching with various nuances, playing upon the distinctions and subtle relationships between freedom and grace, which already in the fifth century had brought into opposition Saint Augustine, the preacher of grace, and the monk Pelagius who stressed freedom and nature. The Council of Trent, countering the extreme Augustinianism of Luther and Calvin in the mid-sixteenth century, had asserted a balance between the role of divine grace necessary for salvation and given in Christ, and the cooperation that man's will should bring to it, but had not clarified the modalities of their ordering.

It is true that in theological thought there had always been on the one hand a more pessimistic view, wherein man was seen as corrupted by original sin even in his freedom and was redeemed only by sheer grace, and on the other hand a more optimistic, "humanistic" view, professing confidence in the healing of man's freedom (free will), making him capable of collaborating actively in his own salvation through the acquisition of merits.

The debate opened with the claims of theologians from Louvain, Michael Baïus (+1589) and John Hessels (+1566). Basing his arguments on extracts from Saint Augustine's anti-Pelagian writings, Baïus disputed the state of innocence before the fall, which he did not consider to be a supernatural gift. The implication was that the grace of redemption was also not a supernatural gift. It seems that "Baianism" was a prefiguring of Jansenism.

However, it was the work of the Spanish Jesuit, Molina (+1600) which opened the controversy whence Jansenism was born as a reaction. In his *Harmony of Free Will with the Gifts of Grace* (1588), Molina minimized the effects of original sin.

23. *G. Edelinck (1649–1707),* Blaise Pascal, *engraving, 1691. The inscription encircling the portrait recalls the brief life of this philosopher-scholar: 1623–1662. First recognized for his scientific treatises, after a sort of ecstasy on November 23, 1654, he turned to religion, to Jansenism, as had his family in the 1640s. He brilliantly defended its theology of grace against the Jesuits in* Provincial Letters, *(1656). His major project* Apology for the Christian Religion, *remained unfinished, but his* Pensées, *gathered in 1670, remain.*

23

26. Phèdre, *Racine, staged by J.M. Villegier (Theater de l'Est parisien, 1992). Inspired by Euripides and Seneca, this drama, written by Racine in 1677, is characterized by the ancients' notion of fate—a transposition of predestination, a notion defended by Jansenist theology, in which Racine had been raised. Without using costumes from antiquity, but rather setting the drama in Racine's own era, the representation here shows a scene between the heroine and her nurse Enone, whose perfidious advice will give to Phèdre's love for her young stepson a sense of destiny and a tragic ending. The failure of this work interrupted Racine's career. Twelve years later, he turned to biblical subjects.*

24   27

24. *Pieter Boel (about 1622–1674).* Allegory of the Vanities of the World. *(Lille, Fine Arts Museum). Vanity in a morbid sense is supplanted here by a meditation on vanities in the plural. The accumulation of objects of symbolic power is a reminder of all that man will have to leave behind at the hour of death, whose presence is represented by a tomb and ruined building. Military glory (equestrian figurine), royal power (crown), ecclesiastical dignities (bishop's miter), Arab might (turban), and the earth itself (globe in the center of the painting)—all will disappear with the coming of death.*

25. *Charles Le Brun (1619–1690),* Portrait of Jean Racine (1639–1699), *drawing. It is not Corneille's rival, nor the gentleman at court who is shown here, but rather the pious author of Christian tragedies and spiritual canticles shown at the end of his life.*

27. *Philip of Champaigne,* Saint Cyran *(Grenoble Museum). Portrait of Jean Duvergier de Hauranne (1581–1643), abbot of St. Cyran in Poitou, friend of Cornelius Jansen, with whom he shared the same theological ideas. From 1630 on, St. Cyran exerts an influence on the religious women of Port-Royal, the monastery that will become a symbol of Jansenistic resistance and for whom Philip of Champaigne will become the official painter (see fig. 28, 29). But the artist was from another generation, and therefore this 1673 portrait was not executed from a "live model."*

25

26

Receiving sufficient grace from God, man was capable of *making it efficacious* by his acceptance. The faculty of theology of Louvain, traditionally Augustinian, then furnished the response, which is the crux of the various Jansenisms: salvation could only come from a totally gratuitous divine favor which was *immediately efficacious* for the predestined. This salvation could in no way be the result of any human effort, which was as incapable of obtaining this grace by itself as of resisting it. To affirm the contrary was, for these theologians, the proof itself of the monstrous pride of man.

The movement drew its name from the Dutch theologian Jansen or Jansenius (1585–1638), named bishop of Ypres three years before his death, whose posthumous work, *Augustinus* (1640), was a voluminous refutation of Molinism. The diffusion of this treatise in French circles was assured by Jansen's friend Jean Duvergier de Hauranne (1581–1643), abbot of St. Cyran in Poitou and always designated by the name of this monastery. Saint Cyran had been imprisoned for five years by Richelieu for opposing the alliance which the cardinal-minister had concluded with the German Protestant princes, supposedly for reasons of state. In France, Jansenism possessed from the start a political dimension of opposition to absolutist monarchy.

The theological conflict broke out only later, although the *Augustinus* had already been condemned at Louvain as a result of pressure from the Jesuits, while "the Jansenism of Jansen" became that of Port-Royal. The members of the Arnauld family, both male and female, set themselves up as the spokespersons of French Jansenism. Antoine Arnauld (1612–1694), known as Arnauld the Great, reopened with his "apologies for Jansen" all the polemics which became a political affair of state in the middle of the seventeenth century.

It must be admitted that the Jansenist party was rich in remarkable personalities. The best known was the scholar and thinker Blaise Pascal. His *Provincial Letters* was a brilliantly ironic and dialectical defense of Jansenists against the Jesuits. Then there was the most talented of the playwrights of the French classical theater, Jean Racine. Very often, the background

28, 29. (28) Philip of Champaigne (1602–1674). Mother Agnes and Sister Catherine de Sainte-Suzanne *(Paris, Louvre) and (29) Pieter van Schuppen,* Mother Marie Angelique Arnauld, *engraving, 1662 (after Champaigne). The history of Port-Royal, the citadel of Jansenism, and its fight against the Jesuits for a more Augustinian theology, are intimately tied to the Arnauld family, bourgeoisie, and jurists. Antoine Arnauld (1560–1619) had twenty children, most of whom played a key role in the Jansenist movement. It all began with Mother Angelique (1591–1661), who started a reform in the Cistercian monastery of Port Royal des Champs in 1602. Then she was assisted by her sister Agnes (1593–1671), abbess of Port Royal in Paris. Champaigne, official painter for the Queen Marie de Medici, Henry IV's widow, frequented the Jansenist circle about 1643 and successfully expressed in his large-scale works the austerity of these barren monastic cells and of the faces of these consecrated nuns.*

29

28

30

of his tragedies can only be understood in reference to Jansenism. We also could cite the artist Philip de Champaigne, who did portraits of the protagonists of the movement.

The Jansenists had at their disposal two Cistercian monasteries: Port-Royal in Paris itself, and Port-Royal-of-the-Fields in the valley of Chevreuse, where the sisters of Arnauld the Great reigned. The *solitaires,* men of great talent, had come together there and had even organized a system of education, the Little Schools. Some bishops, among them Henry Arnauld, supported what was becoming a party within the Church and even within the state, especially among lawyers and *parlementaires.*

This party was formed on the occasion of the condemnation in 1653 of five propositions taken from *Augustinus.* Arnauld distinguished the law from the fact: by law these propositions, such as for example the one that denied that Jesus Christ died for all men, were condemnable. However, *in fact* they were not to be found in Jansen's treatise. Port-Royal took refuge in this position and in 1664 refused to sign the formula repudiating the propositions.

Anxious to resolve the situation, Pope Clement IX recognized the distinction between law and fact and inaugurated

31. *Carlo Maratta (1625–1713),* Clement IX (1600–1669) *(Vatican Museum). Pope Clement IX (born Rospigliosi) had been the principal architect of the pontificate of his predecessor, Alexander VII. While he was concerned to unify Europe's Christian rulers, he managed, during his short pontificate (1667–1669), at least temporarily, to appease the conflicts provoked by Jansenism through the "Clementine Peace," also called "the Peace of the Church" (1668).*

30 and 32. (30) Nicolas Bocquet, engraving, the Abbey of Port-Royal-des-Champs *(1702) based on a painting by one of the Boullougne brothers. In the foreground, we can see the church flanked by a cloister and the nuns' dormitories, reflecting the Cistercian plan. In the background, we can distinguish the quarters of the "gentlemen of Port-Royal," these "solitaries" who lived there to study and meditate. After the dispersion of the last religious in 1709 (32), the buildings were demolished, under a royal order in 1711, two years before the bull* Unigenitus *that officially condemned Jansenism.*

the "peace of the Church" which lasted for some thirty years (1669–1700). Port-Royal continued to develop, but the mistrust of Jansenism did not cease to grow with Louis XIV and his entourage. The court at Versailles was persuaded that Arnauld's party had been sympathetic to the Fronde, the civil war that had attempted to weaken the monarchy. Thus Mazarin and many others with him thought that Jansenism, with its pessimistic, Augustinian, and individualistic outlook, closely resembled Calvinism with its republican nature, or at least its democratic tendency. Since in 1685 Louis XIV had revoked the Edict of Nantes instituted by Henry IV to grant freedom to his Protestant subjects, it made sense to eliminate the Jansenists as well even though they held other dogmatic positions far afield from those of Calvin.

The Jansenists would themselves soon provide occasion for an all-out fight, but these belonged to another generation. This new Jansenism put forth by Barcos (+1678), a nephew of Saint-Cyran, and especially by Pasquier Quesnel (+1719), who found refuge in the Low Countries where Arnauld had died, basically stressed predestination. Yet it also embraced the parliamentary Gallicanism which had democratic tendencies. The suspicions of the monarch of Versailles were indeed being confirmed.

At the urging of Louis XIV, Pope Clement XI, first in 1709 and then again in 1713 with the bull *Unigenitus,* directed the official teaching on grace toward Molinism and above all reaffirmed the preeminence of the Holy See over Christian princes. Thenceforth Jansenism was to founder in spectacular and even hysterical manifestations, with convulsions and miraculous cures, but also to fulfill its schismatic and sectarian destiny. A Jansenist Church was established in Holland, electing in 1723 an Archbishop of Utrecht and having him consecrated by a French prelate.

Thus were condemned the pessimistic theses of Jansenism, together with its dogmatic positions and even some of its practices, such as that of recommending very infrequent Eucharistic Communion. Dogmatic Jansenism would never revive, but its rigid morality would perdure within Catholicism. It approached Puritanism and concurred with the latter's overall vision. The nineteenth century and even the twentieth would still retain this heritage of Jansenistic morality with its obsession with hell.

The Unity of the Nation and of the Faith

Ecclesiastical and theological conflicts led the absolutist powers to reaffirm ceaselessly the necessary unity of both faith and nation. Let us take two examples, convergent in their very opposition.

In 1673, the English monarchy, which had been reestablished in 1660, required that every State official belong to the Anglican Church and recognize the supremacy of the king over the Church. This discrimination in regard to Catholics and Puritans, which lasted until 1829, obliged the Duke of York to resign from his position as Grand Admiral of the Fleet because he had become a Catholic in 1670. Upon becoming king of England in 1685, James II would also find it difficult to remain on the throne.

The second example is that of the Revocation of the Edict of Nantes in 1685. When Henry IV, after his abjuration of Protestantism, had granted, in 1598, guarantees of worship and military strongholds to his former coreligionists, he was clearly breaking with the general sentiments of the times. Richelieu, the great servant of the monarchy, later undertook to suppress the political privileges of this "state within a State." The political and literary activity of Bossuet prepared the way for religious unification. Through preaching, through persuasion at times mixed with bribery, and also through violence, conversions multiplied, so that Louis XIV became persuaded that France was "wholly Catholic" as Bayle would ironically say. Monarchical absolutism delighted in the French version of the principle, *cuius regio, eius religio.*

In 1685, the papacy failed to manifest the gratitude expected by the king. The *Te Deum* organized by the French ambassador in Rome was sung quite half-heartedly.[4] To be

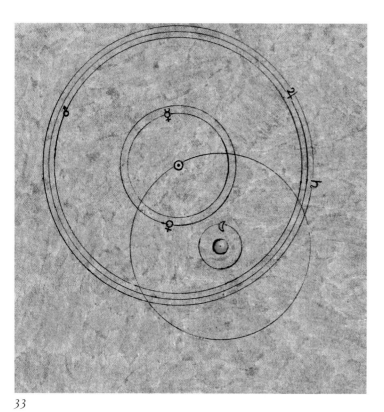

33

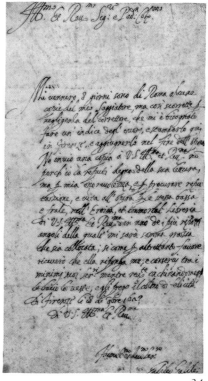

34

33 and 34. The Galileo affair (1564–1642) integrates a great many factors—scientific, diplomatic, personal, but mostly theological. Calling himself a good Catholic, the reason for his obedience at the end, the scholar and astronomer nevertheless believed in the autonomy of science in relation to scriptural teachings and adhered to the Copernican system (drawn here by Sandro Corsi) (33) that seems to contradict Scripture. Paradoxically, Galileo had good relations with Cardinal Bellarmine and with Cardinal Barberini, the future Pope Urban VIII who would condemn him, and with Cardinal Federico Borromeo (1564–1631), Saint Charles' cousin and successor, whose reform in Lombardy he continued. Here (34) is a handwritten letter from Galileo to Cardinal Federico (1623) kept in the Ambrosian Library that the cardinal founded in Milan in 1602.

sure, the papacy had not been in agreement with the Edict of Nantes, but no more could it accept its revocation under the accompanying conditions, in an atmosphere of forced conversions and communions, with, as Saint-Simon was to pitilessly remark sixty years later, "the King basking in the thousands of sacrileges." The Church sensed the limits of an enslavement to absolutist thought and practice.

Responses to the Challenges of Absolutism

Caught in the meshes of an absolutism lording it over Christianity, the Church could only answer on its own grounds. It reaffirmed its conception of the Church in opposition to Gallicanism and its theology of salvation in opposition to Jansenism. We would do well to interpret the disastrous "Galileo affair" within the context of a rejection of absolutism in thought.

Galileo (+1642), a pious man and a faithful Catholic, was confronted by the Roman authorities because of the firmness of his Copernican convictions and above all the audacity of his hermeneutics. These authorities were less than convinced by the arguments of Copernican cosmology and suggested that they should only be used as hypotheses. In his letter to the Grand Duchess Cristina of Lorraine, written in 1615,[5] Galileo proposed abandoning the literal interpretation of the Bible which taught "not how the heavens go, but how one goes to heaven." He was condemned in 1633 for a number of reasons, some of them mysterious as to whether of a political or personal nature. Galileo paid for his claim: to establish the truth as a scholar. Indeed, he appeared to be heralding a new kind of absolutism, that of thought. The paradox is that the purely scientific reasons he advanced for adopting the Copernican system have since been judged erroneous while the Church has now belatedly but completely affirmed his prophetic views on the interpretation of Scripture.

In the seventeenth century, the Church responded on its own grounds, those of theology and most notably of Christian action. The activity and devotion of the Catholic Reformation, bearing its most beautiful fruits in the seventeenth century, are reflected in the arts. In Peter Paul Rubens (+1640), a Franciscan Tertiary of Antwerp, Claudel clearly perceived an inspiration that was at once realistic and spiritual: "And who better than Rubens has glorified the Flesh and the Blood, the very flesh and blood that a God willed to put on, the instrument of our redemption?"[6] On the other hand, Rembrandt

(+1669), his Protestant contemporary, used the play of light piercing the shadows—as did the Catholic artist, Georges de La Tour (+1652). Perhaps the classical artist who best characterized the Catholic effort to impregnate all culture with theology was Nicholas Poussin (+1665),[7] who found his inspiration in Rome. The series on the *Seven Sacraments,* undertaken in 1638, shows a keen knowledge of liturgical practices in the primitive Church. Painting also reflected the morality of the times, expressed in the representation of "vanities," which evoke with elegance and pessimism the fleeting character of human life.

At a time when classical Christianity was oscillating between the heroic, aristocratic morality of a Corneille or a Descartes, the fatalistic and pessimistic morality of a Racine wholly occupied in showing heroes ruined by passions, and the bourgeois morality of a Molière, portrayed and caricatured in Molière's *Tartuffe,* causing great scandal,[8] the Church proposed models whose inspiration was drawn from the Gospel. We must remember that the seventeenth century, particularly in France, was an era of saints.

To counter absolutism in thought, the Church produced schools of mysticism which were solid, serene, and balanced,

37. Rembrant (1606–1669), Return of the Prodigal Son, about 1668 (St. Petersburg, Hermitage Museum). In this illustration of the Gospel parable about the mercy the Father grants to those who return to him (Luke 15:11–32), the Dutch painter aims the light on the father's face and especially on his hands that reclaim and protect his son, in tattered clothes, who came to seek mercy. From the "light/darkness" motif of this work, painted at the end of the artist's life, rises the dimension of mystery. Even though the artist had some difficulties with the Reformed Church to which he belonged, due to his financial bankruptcy and the scandal of his concubinage, his grasp of religious mystery continually deepened.

37

35 and 36. Peter Paul Rubens (1577–1640). Triumph of the Church *(Madrid, Padro Museum) and* Circumcision *(Vienna, Fine Arts Academy, painting gallery). This prolific artist, whose genius is expressed in all genres from mythology to battle scenes and portraits, is also a great religious painter who successfully provided an enthusiastic visual transcription of the Catholic Reform. A characteristically baroque movement animates these biblical scenes. For example, in the* Circumcision *of Jesus the figures in the lower part are all bowing while the angels, in a burst of light, lean down to contemplate the scene. This same movement animates the* Triumph of the Church: *A woman with tiara held over her head holds the Eucharist in a monstrance and sits in a chariot pulled by horses guided by the Virtues. The wheels run over heresy. An angel perched on the horse's back carries Saint Peter's keys under a parasol called a "conopea" in liturgical vocabulary—the insignia for a Basilica that clearly indicates that this is the exaltation of the Roman Church.*

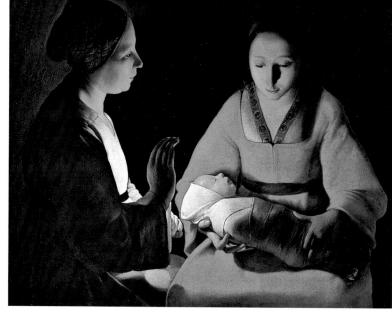

THE CHURCH AND THE CHALLENGE OF ABSOLUTISM   154

41. Andrea Pozzo (1642–1709) Saint Ignatius in Glory, *(St. Ignatius, fresco of the central nave ceiling, 1691–1694). This* trompe-l'œil *ceiling is the masterpiece of this artist who became a Jesuit in 1665. He successfully created a spiral sensation of height for the eyes, due to an ascending circular movement framed by imaginative architectural elements. The vertigo often felt by spectators invites them to meditate on the unfathomable intensity with which the earth reaches out toward heaven.*

38. Georges de la Tour (1593–1652) The New Born, 1645–1648 *(Rennes, Museum of Fine Arts). In his religious vein, for he also liked to paint very secular topics, this French painter, whose piety seems to be inspired by Franciscan spirituality, exploits the play of light, showing almost every time its source: here a candle, however hidden from the spectator's view by the servant's hand. This light is concentrated on the child's head, becomes feebler on the two women's faces, and does not penetrate any further, allowing a harmonious play of contrasts. This scene, part of ordinary daily life, suggests a Madonna and Child and also implies a theology of the incarnation of the spiritual.*

39 and 40. Nicolas Poussin (1594–1665), The Adoration of the Shepherds, *around 1637 (London, National Gallery) and* The Sacrament of Matrimony, *1647–1648 (Edinburg, National Gallery). Poussin illustrates Greek mythology as well as biblical or evangelical themes, but he also paints allegories such as* The Four Seasons *or even dogmatic themes such as* The Sacraments of the Church, *done at the end of his life. Whatever the subjects, we always find antique decor, a love of (sometimes distant) landscapes, and a symmetrical arrangement that by no means prevents movement and expression. We can see how much dynamism there is in the classical arts and, in the case of a sacramental representation, how the dogmatic reality takes on the dimensions of history and tradition and how it can welcome the depths of Christian life and make it fruitful.*

42 and 44. (42) Portrait of Jean Baptiste Poquelin *known as* Molière (1622–1673), *about 1660 (Moscow, Pushkin Museum) and* (44) *engraving showing René Descartes (1596–1650) (Paris, Bibliothèque Nationale). Is Descartes, the philosopher and mathematician, the solitary who wandered all through Northern Europe (where he died), so different, in spite of the generation that separates them, from Molière, the actor and author, enemy of hypocrisy, and astute observer of human nature, who died while performing his last play? We find in them both that search for truth in ideas, passions, and behavior, which constitutes the approach to morality of the classical age.*

43. *Abraham Bosse (1602–1676) Paris,* 17th Century Styles in Dress, *engraving about 1635 (Paris, Library of the City of Paris). The enormous production of this painter is a mine of information on the French society of his time. Fashion was very important, even a tyrannical aspect of life at the royal court. By imposing a style of dress, Louis XIV made it a means of control for the nobility of Versailles. Molière's* Bourgeois Gentleman, *in the play of 1670, let his tailor, a seller of expensive goods, dictate the obligatory and costly fashion of good taste.*

45, 46. *Simon Vouet (1590–1649) (or after Vouet),* Saint Vincent de Paul (1576–1660) (Paris, Lazarist House). *The advisor of Queen Anne of Austria (who owned this portrait), the saintly founder of the Daughters of Charity (1633) and of the Congregation of the Mission, called Lazarists (also in 1633), is depicted here at the end of his life. In humble attire, his ardent and kindly eyes and even his prominent nose give him a sympathetic look. (46) We can recognize his physical appearance in the painting of 1732 by Jean Restout (1692–1768), showing Saint Francis de Sales dressed in episcopal vestments installing Vincent de Paul as superior of The Visitation in 1622, and presenting to him Jeanne de Chantal (1572–1641) and the first Visitation nuns, whose relatively old faces indicate late vocations. They were often widows.*

42

43 · Paris. Costumes du XVIIᵉ siècle.

44

beginning with Francis de Sales in France. These offset the excesses of quietism. But the Church also produced schools, such as the Jesuits, that provided the basis for a Christian life through the *Exercises* of Saint Ignatius, the Marian congregations,[9] and, for priests, the Society of Saint-Sulpice.

To counter ecclesiological absolutism, the Church of the seventeenth century proposed an evangelizing and missionary vision, dynamic and even triumphant. We see this in the creation, or renewal, of the Congregation *De Propaganda Fide* in 1622 whose first secretary, Ingoli, had a broad-minded respect for various cultures.[10] This was the beginning of an unprecedented expansion of foreign missions, stemming from the discoveries of the sixteenth century. The apostolic thrust manifested itself also in "interior missions" in which the Rosary, devotion to the Sacred Heart, and recourse to the sacrament of Penance were preached. Rural areas were thus re-evangelized.

To counter the absolutism of the rich and powerful, the Church proposed a simple ideal of charity. The best known example of this was Vincent de Paul, a committed anti-Jansenist, counselor of the Regent, chaplain of the galleys, and founder of the Sisters of Charity who cared for the poor. He was a fine symbol of the response of the Beatitudes, a language which the Enlightenment would no longer wish to hear.

1576. St. VINCENT de PAUL, fondateur et 1er Général. 1660.

45

47, 48. (47) Saint Louise de Marillac (1591–1660), engraving of G. Du Change (Paris, Bibliothèque Nationale). The widow of Antoine Le Gras, she created with Vincent de Paul the Daughters of Charity. One of the first sisters, bringing broth to the sick, is represented in the other engraving (48). She might be Marguerite Noiseau, who had taught herself to read while watching her cows, and whom Vincent de Paul had sent to Louise de Marillac. She died in 1633 from the plague contracted while nursing a poor woman; an example of the dedication so often found in the Christian 17th century.

46

47

48

1. *Jan van der Heyden (1637–1712),* Roomful of Rarities, *1712 (Budapest, Szepmuveszti Museum). The painter finds inspiration in his own library, showing a cabinet full of curiosities, attesting to the interest in nature and culture of all kinds typical of the 18th century. On the right, the Bible is opened to Ecclesiastes 1:1 ("Vanity of vanities . . ."); next to it is an atlas of the world by Blauew (*Theatrum mundi *1663–1667), globes of the world, Japanese swords and lances, a Chinese porcelain, a rug from Smyrna, the painting of Dido's death by Pietro Testa, and finally on the mantlepiece, an armadillo, the small shelled mammal from South America, preserved.*

Chapter 8

THE CHURCH AND THE CHALLENGE OF THE ENLIGHTENMENT

"Hierarchy, discipline, the order which authority sought to insure, and dogmas which firmly regulated life: this is what men of the seventeenth century loved. Constraints, authority, dogma: this is what their immediate successors of the eighteenth century detested. The former were Christians, the latter anti-Christians. The former believed in divine law, the latter in natural law." Thus wrote Paul Hazard in *The Crisis of the European Conscience,* one of those books which itself has shaped the history of ideas. Discovering this crisis in the years 1680 to 1715, he went on to add, "The majority of Frenchmen had thought as Bossuet did; then suddenly the French were thinking like Voltaire. It was a revolution."[1]

The Church and Intellectual Shifts

It was Bossuet's destiny to represent the ideal of his century, the seventeenth, but also to witness its ending with its rifts and conflicts. One could cleverly have made him out to be the upholder of a threatened classical order, or to be more exact, an order that had been broken, shattered by the baroque, as defined by Heinrich Wölfflin at the beginning of his book, *Renaissance and Baroque* (1888): "a style which marked the *dissolution* of the Renaissance or its *degeneration* . . . In Italy this degeneration lay in the passage from a rigorous art to 'a free and picturesque art' of a precise form." Without going into the twenty-two types of baroque art distinguished by Eugenio d'Ors, who sees here a permanent cultural phenomenon and "the multiple and morbid blossoming of the ego," we need only recall the origin of the word *barrueco* in Spanish, which designates a pearl with irregularities and flaws. Even though it may be very beautiful it is without value. This absence of style which becomes dynamism of form conceals what in the history of art translates into the intellectual stakes of the passage from the classical age to the baroque, a culture of transition.[2]

From 1679 to 1702, Bossuet and Leibniz, with different concerns and above all with different motives, carried on an ecumenical correspondence. They entertained the distant hope of ecclesial unity, but two modes of thinking and being were confronting one another. Bossuet thought in terms of the unity of the Church, the state, and the faith, according to a vision constructed from demarcations, boundaries, clarifications, and definitions very close to the clear and distinct ideas of Descartes and his static mechanics. For the Lutheran philosopher Leibniz (1646–1716), a brilliant amateur in all disciplines from mathematics and physics to linguistics and theology, the ideal of thought was dynamic, the form always open and in process of unification through deepening. The future was synthetic. The Church should accept the *chiaroscuro* revealed in painting, the gradations, the flights, the plays of light.[3]

Let us take the idea of variations. For Bossuet, this was a sure proof of error, of going astray, a sign of metaphysical and dogmatic inconsistency for which he would have liked to carry on a work of doctrinal clarification with the Protestantism he knew so well. In 1688 he wrote a *History of the Variations in the Protestant Churches.* Protestants, on the other hand, and Leibniz preeminently, considered these variations, these successive approximations, as signs of the vitality of faith. Restlessness was indispensable to Christianity and to its progress. The "positive" infallibility which Bossuet attributed to the Church of Rome and which implied the existence of an active magisterium was nothing but "negative" for Leibniz. The Churches were not teaching error as far as salvation was concerned, but neither could they pride themselves on possessing one metaphysical truth.

What Leibniz proposed to Bossuet at all levels, including that of the dogma of the Eucharist so scholastically defined in Catholicism, was the primacy of charity, which was precisely life, dynamism, progress. With charity, one kept to the essential: It brought reconciliation, unification; it was the synthetic

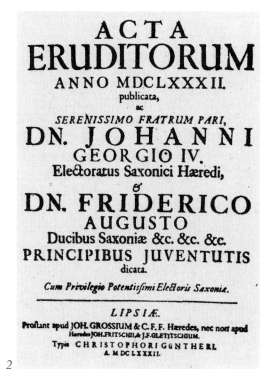

future of Christianity. Love of God and fellow human beings was above all else and could penetrate to the most obscure perceptions of the soul. Leibniz in this sense was more baroque than Protestant. His ecumenical dream moreover was coupled with the utopia of universal peace which inspired the Protestant philosophers of the period, ranging from his own *Treatise on Sovereignty* of 1676 to the project for perpetual peace which Kant elaborated in 1795. This utopian dynamism was in stark contrast to the Revocation of the Edict of Nantes, which claimed to effect uniformity in denying differences. Bossuet supported it, less from the angle of religious unification than from that of maintaining the unity of the kingdom.

These intellectual revolutions, however, were penetrating Catholicism insidiously. The classicists experienced them as so many deviations and each time we find Bossuet in the vanguard of the battle. The first example is the Quietism of both Madame Guyon (+1717) and Fenelon, stemming from the Spanish theologian Molinos (1628–1717) whose *Spiritual Guide* (1675) saw twenty editions in six years, counting its Italian and French translations. In this search for "the pure love of God," expressed in disinterested charity and ending in "holy indifference" even in regard to one's own salvation—

its psychological transposition—there was a profound anti-intellectualism. Madame Guyon wished to bypass the metaphysics underlying dogma so as to retain only the annihilation of the creature. Whatever might be the orthodoxy of the Quietists, we can easily see the *baroque* modality of a tendency already known in medieval Christianity or among the Alumbrados of sixteenth century Spain—a reaction to an order conceived as too external. Quietists were condemned at Rome and at Paris. They had wanted to make love preeminent, to the detriment of hope, and their taste for the mystical privilege of passivity contrasted with the active freedom of the Christian which Bossuet would defend. If Bossuet could perceive in his great adversary, Fenelon, an underhanded attack on the very heart of Christian mysticism, he must have reacted all the more strongly on seeing the precursor of modern exegesis, Richard Simon (1630–1712), attack the very source of the faith, Sacred Scripture. In his *Critical History of the Old Testament* (1678), which because of Bossuet's vigilance could only appear in tolerant Holland, and then in his works on the New Testament (1689–1693), the ex-Oratorian was "a critic of the Bible" and "nothing more." His originality consisted in isolating his reading of Scripture from the apologetic

4. *Jean Hainzelman (from Paris),* Portrait of Miguel de Molinos, *an engraving made from life during his September 3, 1687, abjuration of his Quietist theses in the Church of the Minerva in Rome.*

5. *Elisabeth-Sophie Chéron (1648-1711)* Jeanne-Marie de la Motte, Dame Guyon *(Moscow, Pushkin Museum). This portrait, which conveys the subject's austerity, must have been painted in the first years of the 18th century.*

4

5

concerns of Bossuet or the counter-apologetics of Spinoza, whose *Tractatus theologico-politicus* of 1670 was judged subversive by Jews and Christians. Christians would confuse the two enterprises of Simon and Spinoza.

Now Simon never claimed anything other than the right to be "critical," a new word which was not well received, as he admitted,[4] but which conveyed the right to express oneself in the technical terms "of the art one was treating of." Renewing the theology of biblical inspiration and the study of the exegetes who preceded him, Simon in no wise denied the Tradition he postulated. When Bossuet affirmed the obscurity of Sacred Scripture it was in order to justify in opposition to Protestantism the need for a Church as teacher of scriptural interpretation. Simon was in full agreement, but added also the need for exegetical criticism.

If Richard Simon was persecuted, it was not only because he took a certain pleasure in criticism but also because his stance was confused with a profound tendency of his time which saw the increase of unbelief in direct proportion to the emergence of the triumphalism of the Enlightenment.

6. *Jean-Baptiste Lemoyne,* François de Salignac de la Mothe-Fénelon, *bust in marble.*

6

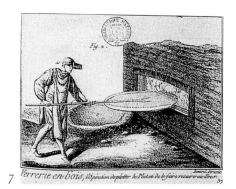

7. *Engraving from the* Encyclopedia *of Diderot and d'Alembert: here a description of glassworks, showing re-firing techniques. The* Encyclopedia *shows a great interest in the arts, in technology, and in the first industrial production, with detailed explanations and the help of numerous charts and descriptive illustrations.*

8. *Meindert Hobbema (1638–1709),* Trees at the Edge of the Water, *around 1660, oil on wood (Madrid, Thyssen-Bornemisza Collection). This artist, who lived in Amsterdam, was a student of Jacob van Ruisdael (1628–1682), whose engraving he reproduces here. His representation of nature is more wild (see the dead branches here), than French or even English landscape painters.*

The Enlightenment and the Increase of Unbelief

While in the sixteenth century unbelief, to say nothing of atheism, had still been considered an intolerable scandal, such things could henceforth emerge from their underground existence and be flaunted in public. In the eighteenth century unbelief was clearly on the rise. Yet in order to analyze the phenomenon we need to make a careful distinction between the intellectual elite on the one hand and the masses on the other.

In the widespread challenging of ideas at the beginning of the eighteenth century, a certain number of philosophers stood aloof from established Christianity. If atheists, or at least materialists like Diderot who directed the Encyclopedia, were still rare, deists such as Voltaire and Rousseau exerted an enormous influence. Even more than "the great Architect of the universe," it was a divinity found in the depths of nature which awakened religious feeling in the human heart.

Generations rediscovered themselves in *Emile (Profession de foi du vicaire Savoyard)* (1762) of Jean Jacques Rousseau. In spite of his headlong negation of original sin, Rousseau gave an affective content to natural religion. An author of secondary merit such as Bernadin of Saint-Pierre, who wrote the successful novel *Paul and Virginia* (1787), was typical of this sentimental religion of nature in which "God is known through his works" when he is not confused with them.

In France an anonymous text appeared in 1803, entitled *The Life of the Legislator of Christians without Lacunae and without Miracles.* Jesus continued to be accepted but His divinity was placed in parentheses. As for Spinoza a century earlier and those who followed, miracles were unendurable to reason. Religion had to be separated from the supernatural, reasonable, enlightened, and exempt from all "superstition," the enemy. It was superstition that Voltaire stigmatized when he cried out, *"Ecrasez l'infâme!"*

Heretofore in countries such as Italy, France, Spain, and Austria, the Catholic Reform had produced beautiful fruit owing to the in-depth activity of the "interior missions." Carried on systematically, these missions endeavored to reawaken the people and to uproot the remnants of an attraction to magic and superstition in beliefs and behavior. Although by contemporary standards of taste the preaching was too focused on fear of damnation or on moral conduct in sexual matters, it nonetheless provided the masses with the fundamental principles of Catholic doctrine and morality.

But when objections were raised by the elite, the rural and often illiterate popular masses were also affected. Almost everywhere a lowering of public morality could be noted: an

8

9

9. *Jean-Antoine Houdon (1741–1828), Bust of Jean-Jacques Rousseau, 1779, terra cotta, (Paris, Museum of the Arts décoratifs). Houdon became famous through his busts of the great personalities of his time such as Voltaire, Diderot, Washington, and Franklin, successfully capturing, as in this case, the psychology of his subject.*

10. *The banquet offered by King Frederick of Prussia for Voltaire at the Sans Souci Castle. Voltaire lived there from 1750 to 1753. (Copy of the painting by Adolph von Menzel (1815–1905) that was burned in 1945). The French philosophers, guests in the courts of "enlightened despots," attempted to teach their principles of good government; thus, in 1773, Diderot visited Catherine II in St. Petersburg.*

11. The Salon of Madame Geoffrin (1699–1777). Every Wednesday, in her mansion on the Rue Saint-Honoré in Paris, she hosted the members of the "Republic of Letters," French or foreigners. In this painting by Gabriel Lemonnier (1743–1824) (Louveciennes, Malmaison Museum), guests listen to the reading of one of Voltaire's works. On the right, next to the hostess, is the Prince de Conti. Other such salons existed, as for instance Madame Necker's, the wife of the noted financier and that of Madame Helvetius, the wife of the philosopher.

12. Jean Huber (1721–1790), a self-taught artist in Geneva, shows an intimate meal with Voltaire, with whom he associated for twenty years.

13. Print from William Hogarth (1697–1764), drawn about 1752. With satirical verve, this painter and engraver depicted London's underworld, showing the link between alcohol (the "royal gin" seen on the tavern sign) and the misery that forces poor people to pawn their most essential utensils (on the left), rather than hanging themselves in despair (upper right).

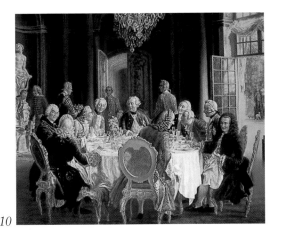

increase of theft, crime, and high numbers of illegitimate births. According to the expression of a priest of the time, the determining role of money and love of wealth transformed Christians whose private lives had once been admirable into honest pagans. It is true that there were differences from one region to another. The influence of the interior missions could have been decisive in preventing this slow de-christianization.

The decline in religious education, due among other things to the expulsion of the Jesuits beginning in 1760 and the mediocrity of the teaching in seminaries, and polarized as it was by moralism, affected the entire Christian population. Poorly formed clerics transmitted a simplistic faith. The Catholic Reform slackened and the Church, harassed by the "philosophers," was on the defensive, oscillating between silence and a complicity with "the spirit of the times." Such was the title of a book by Wessenberg, vicar general of Mainz and outstanding artisan of secularization in Germany, which appeared in 1801.

In response to the challenge of the Enlightenment, a significant portion of clergy merely opposed an attitude of connivance, trying to take into account what was legitimate and true in the attacks of the philosophers on "religion." Of these attacks, the most obvious, apart from an anti-clericalism that was at times excusable, was the obsession with the problem of evil which had manifested itself from the time of the Protestant Bayle[5] to the metaphysical scandal occasioned in Voltaire and his philosopher friends by the Lisbon earthquake of 1755. What has been called the Catholic *Aufklärung* or Enlightenment arose in reaction to the Catholic Reform, that is, to the pontifical ecclesiology underlying it and symbolized, for example, by the ideal and practice of the Society of Jesus. But many also rose up against a liturgy which they faulted for its superabundance of the sacred seemingly needing to overflow

14

15

16

14, 15, and 16. Examples of baroque art in three Catholic countries.
(14) Sansevero Chapel, Naples. It was renovated at the beginning of
the 17th century for the deceased members of the princely Sansevero
family, but transformed, according to the baroque ideal, between
1749 and 1771, at the initiative of Prince Raymond di Sangro
(1710–1771), the grand master of Free Masonry in Naples. All the
plastic arts are included: architecture, paintings, trompe-l'oeil and
sculpture (altar and statuary) treated with opulent majesty.
(15) Steinhausen Church (Baden Wurtenberg) was built between
1723 and 1733 by Dominikus Zimmermann (1685–1766) and
decorated by his brother Jean-Baptiste. This pilgrimage church, which
conveys the style of a "salon," gives an impression of joy and light
through its ingenious and elegant forms. (16) Finally, in Toledo, this
ornate light source of the cathedral, conceived by Narciso Tomè in
1721–1732, allows light to filter directly from the apse wall, creating
a dramatic and surprising effect, characteristic of the rococo, which
will be called "churrigaresque," named after a famous family of
artists, creators of the Spanish baroque.

17

18 *19*

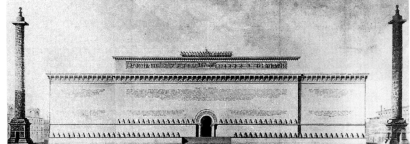

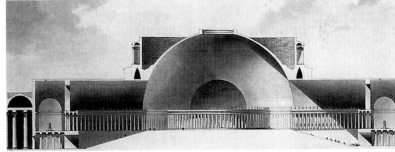

17. The Salt Works of Arc-et-Senans, begun in 1775 by Claude-Nicolas Ledoux (1736–1806). In this industrial plan, he realized the utopian ideas that he developed theoretically in 1804 in his Architecture Considered according to the Aspect of Art, Culture, and Legislation. *The concentric plan spreads like rays from the central factory in order to give form and elegance to the industrial work. In hopes of creating a happier life, he gave attention to social space, as testified by the never realized project for a common room and even a pantheon.*

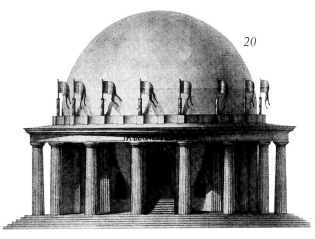

20

18, 19, and 20. Etienne Louis Boullée (1728–1799), (18) Palace for the National Assembly (1790) and (19) Museum and Temple to Fame (section and interior view), 1793 (Paris, Bibliothèque Nationale). In these plans, the architect proposed an esthetic adapted to the republican ideal through a return to antiquity and by the use of rational geometric forms. (The metric system was imposed by the French Revolution.) (20) We see the same concerns in this Temple to Equality, designed by J.-J. Lequeu in 1794, favoring a spherical form that symbolizes neither hierarchy nor inequality.

21 and 22. (21) *Anonymous,* Maria-Teresa of Habsburg, *Austrian empress, 1740 (Prague, Archbishop's Palace).* (22) *School of Martin van Meytens,* Coronation of the Emperor Joseph II *in 1764 (Vienna, Kunsthistorisches Museum). The imperial monarchy of Vienna represents the Catholic model of the "enlightened despot." Joseph II wanted to impose his rationalist and utilitarian views on the Church: Josephism is named after him. The ostentatious pomp of his coronation moved the center of interest from the sacred to the profane. The Church is put at the service of secular power which, covered with glory, knows best what is just and good for the people.*

23. *The Enlightenment scorned monastic life, considered it idle, and worked to make it "useful." However it was not as decadent as people thought. The Carthusian Monastery of Valbonne (Gard, France), completed in the 18th century, had a rectangular cloister with a perimeter of 350 meters, twenty-four cells and diverse chapels.*

into a "baroque" style of architecture, at least in southern Germany, Austria, and Italy.

The "Adaptations" of the Catholic Enlightenment

Febronianism

The fact that the Pope was the temporal sovereign of the Papal States, and thus a potential ally or adversary, certainly deepened the mistrust with which pontifical power was viewed in the eighteenth century. The hostility of Clement XI (+1721) toward Germanic emperors as well as toward the princes of Savoy and their political stance in Spain and Italy led to the challenging of this temporal power of the Popes. It was denounced as harmful to religion and to the very welfare of the Church.

But the mistrust of monarchs and of their national episcopates went back much further. Its roots were medieval. Even though it was recognized that the Catholic Reform of the Council of Trent had been led and set in motion under the religious impulse of Rome, many reservations remained regarding its claims to jurisdiction over the entire Church. These were expressed in the theory and practice of Gallicanism in France, which had not been vanquished but had found a foothold once more at the time of the Enlightenment philosophy, particularly in a Germanic setting.

The ecclesiastical vision on which the politics of the Germanic emperors was based was called "Febronianism," after a theologian of Luxemburg who became coadjutor bishop of Trier, Nicolas von Hontheim (1701–1790). Under the pseudonym "Febronius," the bishop published in 1763 a work in Latin on the authority of the sovereign pontiff, which was then translated into French, Spanish, Italian, and Portuguese. His object was to highlight the rights which, flowing from the nature of the Church, ought to belong to the national episcopates and thus to thwart the interventions of the Roman Curia and the activity of the nuncios.

Febronianism was in effect a kind of absolutist episcopalism. It maintained that the bishops were the heads of the Church and that the bishop of Rome, although he had historic primacy, had no power outside his own diocese. Febronius emphasized in a coherent way the role of a Council, a gathering of all the bishops and the ultimate judge of pontifical pronouncements. He also addressed an appeal to princes whom he saw as responsible for religious affairs in their own countries.

21

A few years later in 1786, four archbishops of Germanic regions, three of whom were electors of the Empire, protested the designation of a nuncio to Munich and drew up a document which was a practical application of Febronianism. This text, known as "the Punctuation of Ems," claimed the right to exercise fully powers hitherto granted by the Pope and emphatically refused to recognize the exemption of religious Orders under the direction of Rome. This claim underlay a large part of the religious policy of the nation-states in the eighteenth century.

Josephinism

Supported by Febronian thought while remaining independent of this ecclesiology, the Austrian Hapsburg rulers of the

22

23

Holy Roman Empire adopted a religious policy in the spirit of the Enlightenment. It is currently called "Josephinism" after the Emperor Joseph II. He ruled alone from 1780 to 1790 after having been associated since 1765 with the government of his mother, Maria-Theresa, who had been a little more moderate in these matters. His religious policy spread out from Austria and his brother Leopold, archduke of Tuscany, was even more zealously its partisan.

Inspired by the "Voltarian" chancellor, von Kaunitz, "Josephinism" was basically concerned with the secularization of religious Orders and, of course, of their domains. While his mother had fixed the minimum age for definitive commitment to religious life at twenty-four (instead of sixteen, as provided by canon law), Joseph II in 1781 directly attacked contemplative congregations, which were judged "idle." The Carthusians, Carmelites, and Camaldolese were purely and simply suppressed while the Benedictines and Premonstratensians might continue in existence if they engaged in activities deemed "useful to society." Teaching, hospital work, or pastoral duties, particularly in parishes, enjoyed the imperial favor because secular diocesan priests were not "exempt." "Secularized" properties were turned over to a "general fund for religion," to be used for the building of new churches and the support of parish priests. Thus in a short time an impressive number of new parishes were founded.

When Pope Pius VI went to Vienna in 1782 to try to prevent these measures, he was coldly but courteously received by the government, which granted no concessions. The people, however, warmly acclaimed him. Yet, Joseph II continued his policy, purifying worship, struggling against superstition, and founding general seminaries in his desire to form an "enlightened" clergy. In doing this, he subsumed under the administration of the state what would appear to be the innermost life of the Church.

Going still further, the grand duke of Tuscany, in summoning the synod of Pistoia in 1786 undertook to legislate a simplification of the liturgy. The tendency of the Enlightenment to wish to rationalize the symbolic and to consider worship from a pedagogical perspective can be clearly seen here. Thus, homilies and teaching were stressed at the expense of rites and symbolism. These regulations, moreover, were not inspired merely by a wish to shorten the liturgy. In fact, they sought to better highlight the Eucharist, sometimes lost in the sea of multiple devotions and to introduce a certain sobriety where superabundance had become excessive.

24

Attacks on Religious Life: Suppression or Reform?

A similar evolution regarding religious life can be noted in France. In order to reform certain abbeys or Orders that had fallen into a state of laxity in discipline, if not morals, as well as a state of financial neglect, a "Commission of Regulars" was established. Its principal architect was the archbishop of Toulouse, Loménie de Brienne, a perfect exponent of the "Enlightenment." In order to insure a rectification judged necessary by the French bishops, the Commission proposed a certain number of measures which ended in the suppression of the privilege of exemption, the abolition pure and simple of certain Orders which no longer had recruits or had an insufficient number, and the abolition of houses or priories that were too small. In addition, the age for solemn vows was raised.

Within this general context, the suppression of the Jesuits is easier to understand. The Society of Jesus was too powerful, too widespread, too much engaged in large, contested missions such as Paraguay or China, and above all too attached to the Pope, not to have enemies almost everywhere. In the extraordinary affair of the "Reductions" in Latin America, where entire communities of Indians, regrouped in Christian republics under the direction of the Jesuits had been able to maintain themselves for a century and a half (1610–1768), the opposition came from colonial interests.

The affair of the "Chinese rites," for its part, revealed the spirit of the times. The stakes were modern, and the whole affair paradoxical.[6] Having succeeded in penetrating into China, the Italian Jesuits obtained recognition of the possibility of adapting Catholic rites to the various customs of the people. Thus ran the so-called privilege granted by Paul V in 1615 giving permission to celebrate the liturgy in Chinese. Once this step had been taken, the Jesuits did not hesitate to integrate rites which they considered "purely civil," such as ceremonies in honor of Confucius or of ancestors. The scandal broke at the end of the seventeenth century and held Europe's attention throughout the first half of the eighteenth century.

Paradoxically, this early form of inculturation was defended by the philosophers, particularly Voltaire, who loved to exalt Confucius as "the sound interpreter of Reason alone . . . who spoke only as a sage and never as a prophet." Yet it was definitively forbidden by Pope Benedict XIV in 1742 in order to defend the faith against all infiltration of the superstitions denounced by the Enlightenment. Similarly, he regulated the role played by miracles in the canonization process (1738) and the role of religious art (1745).[7]

Attacked from all sides, the Jesuits were expelled from Portugal in 1759 at the instigation of Pombal, from France in 1764, and from Spain in 1767. Under considerable political pressure, Pope Clement XIV (1769–1774) resolved to suppress

24. *A never finished church in* Reduction of Jésus *(Paraguay). The missionary projects of the Jesuit Reductions were of great size; their churches could receive thousands of people. From the point of view of urban planning, the Reductions (identical in form everywhere) surpassed in size all the cities in the vicinity, except Buenos Aires and Cordoba.*

25. *Guiseppe Castiglione (1688–1766).* Spring Serenity, *scroll, (Beijing, Museum of the Palace of the Forbidden City). At the court of the Quings, this professional baroque painter from Lombardy, a Jesuit known by the name of Lang Shining, learned to adapt himself to the Chinese culture during the 51 years he served the emperors. From his experience resulted a very delicate art, respecting the oriental codes, but maintaining western concern for detail and precision (see fig. 31 p. 237).*

25

26. *Matteo Ricci de Macerata (Li Mateou) and "Doctor Paul" (Xu Guangqi) (1562-1633) a Chinese scholar who converted in 1603 and played an important role in the imperial court (Athanasius Kircher,* China monumentis illustrata . . . *Amsterdam, 1667). The two men wear the habit of the Confucian sage, according to the carefully thought-out decision of Ricci starting in 1592. Kircher (1601–1680), a linguist, a mathematician, and curious about all the sciences, was also one of the best theoreticians of baroque music.*

26

the Society in the Brief *Dominus ac Redemptor* of 21 July, 1773, giving as his principal reason the peace of the Church. Only the Orthodox Empress of Russia, Catherine II, and the Protestant Frederick II of Prussia took a kind of malicious pleasure in retaining "their" Jesuits, whose scientific talents they appreciated. The expulsion and then the suppression of the Jesuits was a blow to education almost everywhere in Europe, for they were the experts in this field.

If the hostility against the Jesuits was primarily political in nature, attacks on monastic life or on the liturgy clearly indicate the mistrust of the Enlightenment for the contemplative life of the Church or at the least its incomprehension of this mystery. Moreover, the strongest attacks came from within the Church: in Germanic countries from the Benedictines Tautenstrauch (+1785), Dalberg (+1817), and Wessenberg (+1860). Kant would have been perfectly understood by the followers of this Catholic *Aufklärung,* with its desire to confine religion "within the limits of pure reason."

At the intellectual level there was no true response to the challenge of the Enlightenment, which seemed to have surprised the Church in a position of weakness. This was all the more manifest in that the Enlightened found allies in a clergy that seemed "bedazzled" by them. Certainly preaching retained its influence. In the country of the *Aufklärung* the Augustinian Abraham of Santa Clara (1648–1709), with his burlesque and truculent manner, knew an enormous success

27

28

before being posthumously disavowed by a more dignified and conventional style of preaching.[8]

However, authentic appeals to the Catholic conscience were not made in vain, especially in Italy where many illustrious men succeeded in evangelizing and in preaching a very Christocentric spirituality. Among these were John Baptist Rossi (+1764) in Rome, Saint Leonard of Port-Maurice (+1751) in Florence and again in Rome, Saint Paul of the Cross (+1776), founder of the Passionists at Orbetello, Saint Gerard Majella (+1755) in Naples, and above all Saint Alphonsus Liguori (+1787), founder of the Redemptorists. When the Roman urchins ran through the streets on 16 April 1783 crying out "The saint is dead" it was indeed the popular conscience recognizing in the eccentric and dirty pilgrim, Saint Benedict Labre, an authentic witness to Christ. Marginal and ritualistic, Benedict could be said to represent the absolute antithesis of sanctity for the Enlightened.[9]

Devotion to the Sacred Heart, biblically and theologically very rich, also represented, from the time of the visions of the Visitandine nun Margaret Mary (1673–1675), a reaction to an approach to faith that was too abstract and conceptual. We need to recognize here a desired return to devotion to the

29

30

31

27. In the Abbey of Tyniec, founded in 1044, not far from Cracow (Poland), the Benedictines from the Polish Congregation rebuild their premises in the first half of the 17th century in the baroque style. This pulpit, audaciously designed as a ship moving through open space to proclaim God's word, uses the symbolism of the Church as a boat tossed on the ocean of the world that remains stable due to Christ's presence within it.

28. Portrait of Benedict Joseph Labre that successfully depicts his austere and humble appearance in modest and simple clothing and with the rosary worn around his neck, a detail attested in all the representations of him.

29 and 30. (29) 18th century Monstrance (Santiago, Chili, National Historical Museum) and (30) Holy-Water Font with the Sacred Heart emblem (Naples, St. Mary the Egyptian in Pizzifalcone, consecrated in 1717). The two major Catholic devotions, the Eucharist (not only at Mass, but also for Adoration of the Blessed Sacrament) and the Sacred Heart of Jesus, were two ways for the Roman Church to emphasize the mystery of the Incarnation.

31. St. Alexis Church (Rome, on the Aventine), 1700. This was an era when mistrust of legends and superstitions was growing and when Pope Benedict XIV created new regulations for the cult of the saints. Here baroque piety (at the hands of the architect Andrea Bergondi) exalted and glorified a part of the stairway where Alexis had lived in humiliation for seventeen years, and where he died without even being recognized by his own family.

human nature of Christ, touched and heard by the apostles, as if to give an incarnational response to deism. The wholly simple and solidly "Christocentric" devotion to the Virgin Mary of Saint John Eudes and Saint Louis Mary Grignion de Montfort (+1716) also met with immense success.

Against this background of a tug-of-war between a certain philosophical or political elite, to which many bishops belonged or with which they were at least in league, and a strong religious spirit among the masses which was genuine even though mixed with some remains of paganism or superstitious practices, the political regime of the French Revolution came down on the side of Enlightenment ideas and drew out the conclusions in the realm of religion. A large portion of Europe would eventually come under its sway.

The French Revolution of 1789 was not anti-religious in the beginning. It simply represented with determination the generally prevalent Gallican convictions. But with the fall of the monarchy, it turned against Catholicism which proved to be feeding the flames of resistance especially in the west of France. From the end of 1793 until April 1794 (Year II of the Republic), the different regimes that succeeded one another organized a systematic dechristianization. Places named after

32

33

saints were changed, the calendar was reformed, the traditional week was replaced by the ten-day week, religious garb and processions were forbidden, and so forth.

These negative measures were accompanied by a "transfer of sacredness" by the Enlightened. They moved from the feast of the Goddess Reason, which was more aggressively opposed to religion, to the worship of the supreme Being under the influence of Robespierre, who thus canonized deist beliefs in 1794. Under the Directory, "the ophilanthropy" of a syncretistic type and the civilly based ten-day system quickly succumbed to ridicule. It does not seem that the Revolution, victorious in much of Europe, was bent upon exporting its anti-religious politics to the territories it occupied.

Furthermore, this anti-Christianity stirred up reactions where politics and religion were inseparably associated, especially in the cult of the Sacred Heart, a symbol of the royalist cause. Preceded in Germany by Novalis, Chateaubriand, beginning in 1802, proclaimed the rediscovery of "the genius of Christianity." The Restoration would inaugurate a return of popular piety for the nineteenth century, even though insidious or systematic dechristianization would leave indelible traces. Once again the long-range challenge of the Enlightenment was directed at the heart of a believing people.

If we seek a symbol of the disruption and tensions of Catholics in the eighteenth century, we might choose the music of Mozart who died in 1791. His Christian faith, limpid and childlike, is revealed in his correspondence, but outdoes itself in the genius of music. But what contrasts in his work! There is the Coronation Mass (1782), some of whose melodies anticipate the *Marriage of Figaro* (1786) in this assumption of secularism, of the created which is the soul of baroque. There is the attraction of the Free Masonry to which he adhered in 1784 with its "philosophical" ideal through an initiation, as in *The Magic Flute.* But in the same year, 1791, that of his death, there is that most profound cry of the *Requiem* where all heaviness rises up toward grace. In this evolution, can we not perceive the trajectory of Christianity in the eighteenth century, a religious century that is little appreciated?

32. Homage to the Supreme Being, *anonymous engraving, end of 18th century (Paris, Bibliothèque Nationale). This ancient-looking temple (see fig. 20 p.165) is surmounted by a Father God and the caryatids, supporting the temple on each side of the portal, seem to be images of Justice and Charity. The philosophical cults did not rule out references to the Christian heritage.*

33. *This propaganda illustration of the Revolution intended for the countryside, for the "good folks in the cottages," is an engraving by Legrand after Debucourt. Using revolutionary symbols, it shows the people's joy at the proclamation of the Decree of Floreal 18th, year two of the Republic (May 7, 1794). As mentioned in the text in the center of the engraving, the Convention, according to Robespierre's report, established the worship of the Supreme Being and recognized the immortality of the soul.*

34, 35, and 36. (34) *Joseph-Siffred Duplessis (1725–1802),* Mozart at the Harpsichord *(Paris, Louvre). From 1762, when he was six years old and for about ten years more, Mozart was brought as a child prodigy to all the courts of Europe—Versailles, London, etc. (35) An autographed manuscript of his eucharistic hymn* Ave Verum Corpus, *composed in June 1791, six months before his death (Vienna, National Library). This composition was written only shortly before* The Magic Flute, *whose comic character of Papageno is seen here (36) in a costume designed by Jean-Denis Malclès (Hamburg Opera, 1968), and before his* Requiem. *All of them show the same graceful inspiration, whether devoted to sheer entertainment, Masonic symbolism, or Catholic piety.*

34

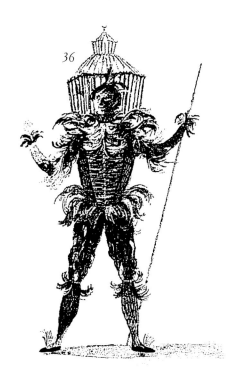

36

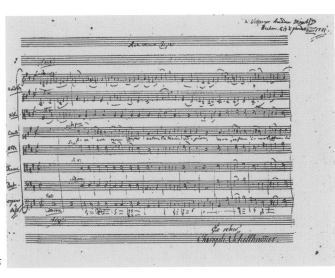

35

1

2

1 and 2. The Seal of the Republic, representing bundled sheaves and a Phrygian cap on top, circa 1792, and an etching showing the three orders of the Nation forging the New Constitution together, circa 1790 (Paris, Bibliothèque Nationale). Destroying a thousand-year-old social and political order, called the Old Regime from now on, the Revolution desired unity: "one and indivisible" claims the Republic motto—a unity expressed in the gathering together of the sheaves. It tried to show that in 1789 changes were brought about by the common will of the clergy, the nobility, and the third estate. In ancient Rome, the cap from Phrygia in Asia Minor was a symbol of liberty, for it covered the head of the freed slave. It will be Marianne's headdress, the personification of the Republic.

3

3. Eugene Delacroix, Pietà, 1844 (Paris, Louvre). The relationship between romantic art and religion is far from simple. Delacroix, who did not hide his lack of faith and who was mostly inspired by pagan or patriotic themes, received an official commission in 1840 for a chapel to the Virgin. In May 1844, he finished this completely unconventional Pietà, in which the figures in red form a sort of halo around the Virgin (with arms outstretched as if on the cross) and the dead Christ. The painting was highly criticized; however, Baudelaire considered it a masterpiece in its capacity to inspire profound feelings of sadness.

4. Frontispiece and title page of The Genius of Christianity (here in a 6th edition of 1809). After his conversion to the family religion of his childhood, Chateaubriand published a speech in defense of Christianity in 1802, the year of the ratification of the Concordat between the French government and the Holy See. His apologetics is adapted to ideas of his time. The illustration exalts the civilizing mission of the Church; the subtitle notes her esthetic role. Furthermore, Montesquieu's citation, aptly chosen, gives to the Christian religion a role in earthly happiness, this "new idea in Europe," as Saint-Just had claimed for the Revolution.

4

GÉNIE
DU CHRISTIANISME,
OU
BEAUTÉS DE LA RELIGION CHRÉTIENNE,

PAR FRANÇOIS-AUGUSTE CHATEAUBRIAND.

Chose admirable ! la religion chrétienne, qui ne semble avoir d'objet que la félicité de l'autre vie, fait encore notre bonheur dans celle-ci.
MONTESQUIEU, Esp. des Lois, liv. 24, c. 3.

SIXIÈME ÉDITION.

TOME PREMIER.

A LYON,

De l'Imprimerie de BALLANCHE père et fils, aux halles de la Grenette.

M. D. CCC. IX.

Chapter 9

THE CHURCH AND THE CHALLENGE OF THE REVOLUTIONS

The eighteenth century had been the century of intellectual changes but by the end of the period these had begun to be incarnated politically as well. The plan of the nineteenth, despite the restorations, would be to consolidate political revolution and to overcome the consequences of social transformation. Moreover, given the economic and geographical background, we are really talking about the coming to be of a new world.

When Talyrand remarked at one point in his tortuous career, "He who has never known the old regime does not know the sweetness of life," the revolutionary Saint Just countered with his famous "Happiness is a new idea in Europe." They were not talking about the same thing nor to the same audience, but behind the maxim of the Jacobin lay the ideology that would hold sway in the twentieth century. The French revolution sought to impose its ideas for the good of the people in opposition to the "tyrants." The death of King Louis XVI on 21 January 1793 had a political significance far more clearly recognized than that of the execution of Charles I in England. An honest man had been condemned so that an idea might be put to death.

The Church had made its own this regime issuing from feudalism. It gave the regime legitimacy through its union with the state, anointing it and living in symbiosis with society as symbolized by the maintenance of civil registers by Catholic clergy. This old regime which allowed of many exceptions, many compromises ("severe in principle, soft in practice," as Tocqueville defined it) had finished by paralyzing, indeed enslaving Catholicism in the eighteenth century, at least among the higher clergy. The Revolution of 1789, followed by anti-clericalism and religious persecution, changed everything.

Political Revolutions

At the end of the eighteenth century and throughout the nineteenth, European states were shaken by a series of political revolutions. The meeting of the Estates General at Versailles in 1789 represented an outdated but traditional institution. We might say that it was the "lower clergy," composed in large part of parish priests, heroes of Gallican Richerism, who had caused the scales to tip toward the French Revolution. In fact, when this lower clergy joined the Third Estate on 23 June 1789 for the verification of powers, the foundations of the old regime were quietly shaken. It was decided to take no more account of the immemorial division of the three orders, three functions, which had become mythical. Voting was to be by individual ballots. This was the recognition of the individual as a unique political subject, reasonable and free—a theory advanced and exalted by the philosophy of the Enlightenment. The priest Barbotin wrote: "Parish priests are blessed on all sides: it is said that they have saved France."[1]

This is all to say that the political and constitutional revolution that took place was not anti-religious at its inception.[2] The clergy consented to the abolition of its privileges. The sale of Church goods, undertaken in order to recoup a State on the verge of bankruptcy, was not at the time considered pillage. Even the Civil Constitution of the Clergy, voted in on 12 July 1790 in the purest tradition of Gallicanism, manifested no intent to persecute. It simply looked forward to an administrative reorganization of the French Church. The political mistake consisted in applying the new democratic principles unilaterally without prior agreement with the Holy See. Neither the ecclesiastical structure of the Church in France nor its communion with Rome were taken into account.[3] Furthermore, in a desire for national unity, loyalty to a new political order that appeared totally foreign to the Church's tradition was imposed by oath.

The other point of divergence was the short-sighted application of the ideas of the Enlightenment to religious life. Contempt for the contemplative life and the somewhat insulting liberation offered to members of religious Orders in the name of human rights were to engender misunderstandings and resistance.

5. Jacques-Louis David (1748–1825). The Coronation of Napoleon I, detail (Paris, Louvre). In this gigantic painting, the new emperor, who crowned himself as a symbol of his autonomy, occupies the center. Pope Pius VII, whose fine features are well rendered, is moved off center near the main altar on the right of the painting. The halberds held by the guards in the foreground are competing with the crosier seen in back.

The division of the Church in France into two parties, constitutional and refractory, the terrible religious persecution, and the campaigns of dechristianization that opened with full force after the fall of the monarchy in August of 1792, created cleavages and resentment which have not yet altogether disappeared in French society. These traumas began with the War of the Vendée, a resistance movement that was both political and religious opposing the Republic.

As soon as civil war quieted down under the Directory, the papacy made prudent efforts at compromise with the successive regimes. Bonaparte, then still the First Consul and personally a deist and above all a fatalist, wanted to reconcile the nation and the Church as he announced to the clergy of Milan in 1800. The following year he succeeded in persuading Pope Pius VII to sign a Concordat, worked out after numerous and exhausting negotiations. This agreement met with some resistance in France and the Belgian regions, crystallizing in the schismatic "Little Churches." Yet it allowed the reconstruction of a State Church dependent upon a Minister of Religion. Seventy-seven "organic Articles" were imposed unilaterally by the French government in the purest Gallican tradition, even insisting on the necessity of accepting the ecclesiastical charter of the absolute monarchy or the "Four Articles" of 1682! Pius VII agreed to assist at the coronation of Napoleon. His only reward was exile and trials when he opposed French ambition in Italy after the reunion of the Papal States with the French Empire in 1809.

At the time of the Restoration, Cardinal Consalvi, Pius VII's Secretary of State, negotiated with great skill at the Congress of Vienna which created a new European order. The Pope refused to excommunicate Napoleon on his return from the island of Elba as the sovereigns requested. He also refused to participate in the Holy Alliance which, under the aegis of the mystical tsar Alexander I, aimed at bringing about a pact of solidarity and the union of thrones and altars. Instead, the Holy See preferred to negotiate concordats with each government. In France, it had to be content with renewing the Concordat of 1801 with the restored monarchy. In Italy, the Pope was constrained to accept Josephinism in the regions governed by Austria (Lombardy and Venice) or occupied by it (Parma and Tuscany). In 1817, the Holy See concluded a concordat with Bavaria and in 1818 with the Kingdom of Naples.

Each time it was a matter of compromise, but the collaboration between Church and State was at least defined. Rome went on to show a certain audacity in signing concordats with non-Catholic powers (Russia in 1818; Prussia in 1821; the Low

6. *Josef Zutz,* The Congress of Vienna, *print (Vienna, Historical Museum of the City of Vienna). Under the gaze of the statue of Justice, the sovereigns and diplomats, designated by numbers referring to the caption, establish the frontiers of a Europe that will last more or less until 1870. A clergyman (Consalvi?) can be seen in the second row center.*

Der große Wiener Friedens-Congress zur Wiederherstellung von Freiheit und Recht in Europa

5

7. *Simon Bolivar becomes a mythical figure for Latin America. Cuba gives his name to a famous brand of cigars.*

7

8

8. *Francesco Hayez (1791–1882),* Camille Benso, Count of Cavour *(Milan, Brera Museum).*

Countries in 1827). This alliance with regimes judged legitimate allows us to understand the Church's reticence in regard to national revolutions now that it finally seemed to have resigned itself to the vicissitudes of political revolutions.

National Revolutions

The nineteenth century witnessed the emancipation of nations according to a principle which we can see has become popular in the twentieth century. The Church's attitude varied widely according to the context and circumstances of the advent of the new State and the claims of nationality, particularly when made during political revolutions as in 1830 and 1848. Let us consider a few examples.

When the countries of South America gained their independence from Portugal and Spain around the 1820s through the personality of Bolivar, the papacy seemed to hesitate. Bolivar was the incarnation of the philosophy and prejudices of the Enlightenment, but he was also a statesman concerned for civil peace and a realistic judge of Catholicism's place in the South American continent. In this instance, the Church appeared divided between its concern for legitimacy and for the obvious good of the populations that needed pastors. Though initially reluctant to confide the patronato to these new secular and anticlerical governments, the Church eventually ratified the changes out of a sense of pastoral realism and collaborated with the new States, especially under the pressure of Cardinal Cappellari, the future Pope Gregory XVI.

The rise of the kingdom of Belgium in 1830 caused the Holy See much concern at first. Rome was astounded to see a political and national revolution incited by Belgian Catholics, particularly the Flemish, and supported by their clergy, demonstrating that a partnership between the Church and "liberalism" was possible. Yet in Rome, such a thing was viewed as "monstrous." Thanks to the role played by Sterckx, the new Archbishop of Malines, the Church in Belgium succeeded in reassuring the Holy See as well as in bringing about harmony and collaboration between "the free Church and the free State," as Montalembert put it.

This formula was taken up again by Cavour. Obviously, the Italian problem posed the greatest difficulties. In Italy there was an ill-defined combination of secularism and anticlericalism or at least criticism of the Church's life on the one hand, and national claims on the other, lumped together under the confusing and at the time explosive term "liberalism" by

9 and 10. (9) Michele Benedetti, Metternich, *engraving. (10)* Pius IX, *drawing made during the first years of his pontificate. In 1846, when Cardinal Mastai Ferretti was elected Pope, he was considered a liberal and a hopeful force for Italian unity, while the Austrian Chancelor was the symbol of everything reactionary.*

11. P. Barabino, Proclamation of the Roman Republic *(on February 8, 1849), lithograph (Milan, Bertarelli collection). The declaration stated precisely that "the Roman Pontiff will have the necessary guarantees for an independent use of his spiritual power." But, taking refuge in Gaeta, Pius IX made a solemn protest to the diplomatic corps.*

9

10

11

12

the so-called "clericals." For the liberal party, the chief obstacle was the temporal power of the Pope in the Papal States. Initially seen to be a key component of a united Italy, the papacy would come to be banished from the new Italian state.

It was at center-stage when Cardinal Mastai became Pope Pius IX, who was at first considered a liberal—the worst imaginable catastrophe according to Metternich, that pillar of European order. Gioberti and the neo-Guelf movement, as well as Rosmini, imagined the Pope as the president of an Italian Confederation. But the Roman revolution of 1848, beginning with the assassination of Count Rossi, the Pope's Prime Minister, shifted all perspectives and revealed a papacy more conservative than anyone had hoped or feared.

When the dynasty of Savoy was enthroned to embody the new kingdom of Italy, the Papal States appeared as the ultimate obstacle to the unity of the peninsula. The new kingdom indulged in nibbling away at pontifical possessions culminating with the entrance of the Italian armies into Rome in 1870. Two months earlier, the Roman Church at the first Vatican Council had defined the dogmatic infallibility of the Vicar of Christ. The Pope, now seeing himself a prisoner in the Vatican, could not bring himself to give up what belonged not to him but to the universal Church, and struggled with all of his strength against the politics of the "liberal" Italian state.

The Holy See was also intimidated by the demands of Polish Catholics in 1831. In a very tactless brief of 9 June 1832, Gregory XVI reminded the bishops of Poland that they owed obedience to legitimate political authorities against "those who were spreading new ideas." Despite secret negotiations and subsequent denials, the harm was done in the view of European public opinion, even after an indignant discourse given by the Pope in July 1842 in which he declared he had been deceived.

Actually, the Holy See's primary intention was to consider the good of the faithful. In the absence of a government requiring careful handling, the Church was a bit bolder in regard to England. The Catholic hierarchy was reestablished there in 1850 in the wake of the immense Irish immigration. Similar action was taken in Holland in order to provide an ecclesial structure for the strong Catholic minorities. But it must be admitted that this demand for the liberty of the Church was not without its pitfalls and that, if there was misunderstanding between Catholicism and society, it was indeed reciprocal. The War of the Sonderbund in Switzerland, the problem posed in many places by the presence and action of the Jesuits, and the Kulturkampf of the second half of the

12. *Jeff Katz,* The Potato Famine, *1846–1847. A picture of the misery brought about by the disease that destroyed the potato crops, almost the only food for the large population of the poor. It caused the death of one and a half million people as well as their emigration to England and the United States under often terrible conditions.*

13. *Paulin Guérin,* Father Felicité de Lamennais *(Château of Versailles). This portrait, which shows him writing his work of 1825,* On Religion Considered in its Relation with the Political and Civil Order, *focuses on his intellectual character.*

14. *Louis Janmot (1814–1892),* Père Lacordaire *(in 1847) (Paris, Saulchoir Library). This portrait of the French Dominican who was widely honored as a spellbinding orator, and who restored religious life in France, is the work of a Catholic painter. It shows a certain academism. The romantic landscape behind him depicts the Alps, where Lacordaire established a novitiate for the French Dominicans in the medieval monastery at Chalais (Isère).*

13

14

century, all attest to it. Doubtless the protagonists were not fully aware that their conflict was carried on against the backdrop of an intellectual revolution that was for the most part beyond their grasp.

Intellectual Revolutions

After the changes effected by the Enlightenment and clumsily taken up again by the revolutionaries in celebrating the Goddess of Reason and the supreme Being, Catholic thinkers were eager to oppose these deviations. Yet they also wanted to take an active part in the new world that was emerging. Such was the sad case of Félicité de Lamennais (1782–1854), poorly understood despite the recent access to sources.[4] Beginning in 1815, his influence on the French clergy and also on the clergy of young nations like Belgium and Poland was considerable and therefore redoubtable. His perspective from his earliest works until his condemnation was essentially apologetic, desirous to defend a Christianity confronted with thinking that was hostile to it. This also was the ideal that inspired the group of remarkable men who surrounded him at the time of *L'Avenir* (1830–1831): Lacordaire, Montalembert, Gerbet . . . At first they enjoyed the favor of the Holy See because of their ultramontanism, which contrasted strongly with the prevailing climate of Gallicanism and Josephinism.

Why, in the end, was Lamennais condemned in 1834 in spite of the real fondness shown him by Gregory XVI? Metternich's maniacal hostility cannot explain everything. In fact, it seems that at bottom the debate was about the nature of political sovereignty.[5] Was God directly as it were "the supreme leader of society" through the mediation of a legitimate sovereign by divine right or was it in fact the people who gave the entire political and philosophical system its foundation?

While the Holy See remained fixated on the political ideal of the old regime, Lamennais was proposing to baptize democracy, not that of 1789 with its theory of national sovereignty but that of 1793 which located the source of power in an abstract and mythical people. All this he did while claiming to be basing himself on the Gospel. When Rome refused to accept his updated theocracy, Lamennais drifted toward a purely secular and lay humanitarianism. Liberal Catholics, that is to say Lamennais' disciples who abandoned him after 1834, would demand a separation of Church and state that did justice to their contemporary world and to the autonomy of the temporal sphere.

15. *Honoré Daumier (1808–1879),* Ecce Homo, *around 1850–1852, oil on canvas (Essen, Museum Folkwang). Daumier, the famous caricaturist of political and social life, began in 1848 to take on mythological and biblical themes. This episode from John 19:5 is treated here in a Chinese shadow style, which gives it force and originality.*

16. *Trinity College, Oxford. The English university city was the site of a religious renewal within Anglicanism, rejecting the deism and rationalism of the 18th century. If many followed the Oxford Movement's leader, John Henry Newman, in his conversion to the Roman Church in 1845, others, with Pusey (1800–1882), stayed loyal to the Church of England to which the colleges belonged and whose* Book of Common Prayer *they followed.*

15

Thinking alien to Catholicism came to characterize certain minds through a seduction which at times appealed to a diffuse religious sentiment, at other times to the most rationalistic historical critique foreshadowing the great theological confrontations of the twentieth century. Basically we are speaking here of the founders of German liberal Protestantism. Pastor Friedrich Schleiermacher (1768–1834) was attracted by a mystical intuition of union with the infinite which he separated from dogmatic affirmations. The ideas of David Friedrich Strauss (1808–1874) were more radical. His *Leben Jesu* or *Life of Jesus* (1835) denied all historical foundation for the supernatural elements of the Gospels. In 1865, he made a clear distinction between "the Christ of faith" and "the Jesus of history." We come upon his influence once again in Ernest Renan (1823–1892), who did not hesitate to admit that the study of German and Hebrew, which he taught for a long time, had radically changed his perception of Christ. His *Life*

of Jesus (1863) presents Christ as "a gentle Galilean preacher," a man whose mission was to reveal God to man.

It was in this atmosphere of demythologization at all levels, an atmosphere in which either Reason or the People were given a sacred character, that we can understand that unusual document of the Holy See, the *Syllabus of Errors* (1864), a catalogue of eighty theses previously condemned by Pius IX. This small appendix to the encyclical *Quanta cura* was felt to be an unqualified challenge to all modern ideas. The Holy See's intention was to guard the faithful from the seduction of what was vaguely referred to as "liberalism and socialism." But it was a very negative way to counter error.

Pius IX could not but grieve over the liberalism demanded by anti-clerical governments which, judged by appearances, had only mistrust and derision for the inner life of the Church. It took the tenacity of liberal Catholics, too democratic for Catholics and too Catholic for secular parties, to gain recogni-

17. *St. Peter's Abbey in Solesmes (Sarthe). A native of the region, Abbot Prosper Gueranger here re-established Benedictine monastic life that had been suppressed by the French Revolution. He made it a liturgical center by fostering Gregorian chant and ecclesiastical studies. The abbey church and abbot's house (at right) are medieval, but the reconstruction of the monastery is in a Romanesque style and also suggests the massive solidity of the Papal Palace in Avignon (see fig. 51, p. 87).*

tion for a point of view that took into account the gains of the revolution of 1789.

Some Catholic thinkers, relatively unknown at the time, felt it would be wise to return to theological Tradition. Johann Adam Möhler (1796–1838), a professor at Tübingen, rediscovered in the first place the mystery of the Church as it had been manifested by symbolism and the sacraments. The restorers of monastic life in the nineteenth century, out of an instinctive and reasoned respect for Tradition, intuitively brought this concept to bear in abbey life. Among these were men like Dom Guéranger at Solesmes with his restoration of Gregorian chant to a place of honor.

Newman, like Möhler, discovered the most profound response to the intellectual revolution in a return to the Fathers of the Church. Having entered the Catholic Church after a long spiritual journey, Newman perceived all the dimensions of catholicity. For the minds of his time, he wrote

the *Grammar of Assent,* explained Tradition as a development, almost an unfolding of doctrine, and finally accepted the subjectivity of religious experience in a way that makes him so modern.

But we should mention here the great text of Vatican Council I, *Dei Filius,* a dogmatic constitution that recalls the classic middle way between the excesses of reason and sheer recourse to faith. Responding to the quarrels of the beginning of the century, the Council, which remained unfinished, could offer no response to the problems that modernism would pose and which express so clearly the intellectual revolution of the nineteenth century in a new world.

This world was indeed considerably changed by scientific discoveries and technological advances.

RELIGIOUS THEMES IN PAINTING
BETWEEN ROMANTICISM AND REALISM

18 and 19. *Caspar David Friedrich (1774–1840).* Abbey in an Oak Forest, *1809–1810 (Berlin, Charlottenburg Castle) and* Cross in the Mountain, *1808, painted for the chapel of Count von Thun-Hoheinstein at Teschen (Dresden, State Art Collection), oil on canvas. Friedrich is the emblematic painter of German Romanticism, creating a symbolic and religious interpretation of nature. The monastic ruin and the cross inserted into a wintry or mountainous landscape, brightened by rays from the sun, are two good examples.*

18

19   20

20. *Delacroix,* Christ on the Cross, *around 1847 (Rotterdam, Boymans van Beuningen Museum). Several times this French artist tried his hand at religious painting (see fig. 3 p. 174). By the strength of his genius, he gives to the drama of Golgotha a gloomy and mysterious power and a feeling of great tension.*

21. *Gustave Courbet (1819–1877),* Burial at Ornans, *1849, oil on canvas (Paris, Louvre). This event from the daily life of his birthplace in the Doubs was presented by Courbet to the 1850–1851 Salon. It is one of the paintings that marks Courbet's passage, under the influence of socialist ideas, toward a realism that excluded romantic pathos. Here a religious event is depicted with almost sociological and ethnological detachment, successfully showing its communitarian dimension.*

21

22

22. *Jean-Francois Millet (1814–1875),* The Angelus, *1858 (Paris, Louvre). This is one of the best known paintings of the 19th century. It is larger than the detail reproduced here, inserting two peasants in a flat landscape of cultivated fields in the vicinity of Barbizon. This work served as symbol of the values of work and piety in a rural civilization threatened by industrialization and urbanization.*

23. Lighting a German town by arc-light, from a publication that appeared in Leipzig in 1873.

24. Claude Monet (1840–1926), St. Lazare Station, *Paris, 1877 (Cambridge, Massachusetts, Fogg Art Museum, Maurice Wertheim Collection). Monet created a series of paintings on this railroad station. This one accentuates the smoke and vapor effects which already in the 19th century are polluting the air of large European cities.*

24

23

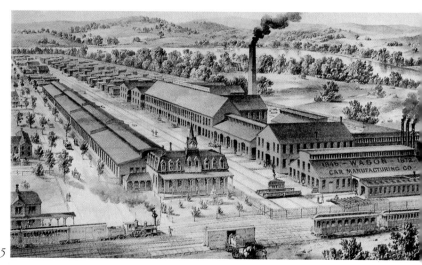

25

25. The Wilson Manufacturing Company of Springfield (Massachusetts) produces cars for the American railroad companies. In this colored engraving from the end of the 19th century, the factory is harmoniously integrated into the bucolic landscape in order to glorify train construction as a symbol of technical progress.

The Industrial Revolution

Beginning first in England and later elsewhere, the industrial revolution extended progressively through Europe and then to North America. Its symbols were the railroad and electricity; its motto, progress; its social or quasi-religious expressions, Saint Simon's socialism and positivism. Its immediate results, however, were destitution and the birth of a working class born of the rural exodus toward machinery and the large cities. It cannot be said that the Church "lost the working class" in the first half of the century. The phenomenon of a decisive distancing from Christianity came later.

26. Drawings describing the activities of the "sect" led by Prosper Barthélemy Enfantin, who called himself "Father Enfantin" (1796–1864). The sect was established at Menilmontant, a suburb of Paris at the time. Between 1830 and 1832, Enfantin started up again the newspaper called Le Globe *and distributed it free. An anticlerical, he claimed to be the Messiah of a new religion. The followers of "The Religion of Saint Simon" depicted here devoted themselves to activities considered typically feminine, since woman's liberation was a part of their program.*

29. The Slums, the neighborhoods of poor worker in London, an engraving by Gustave Doré (1832–1883) made after the great illustrator stayed in the English capital in 1872.

Le Père Enfantin, Chef de la Religion Saint Simoniène.

Saint-Simonien, récurant la Batterie de Cuisine.

Saint Simonien Linger.

Saint Simonien revenant du Marché.

Saint Simonien décrotant et civant les Souliers et les Bottes.

Saint Simonien faisant la lésive ?.

26

27. T. Touillon, Auguste Comte (1798–1857), lithograph (Paris, Bibliothèque Nationale), the founder of "scientific sociology." Influenced by his platonic love affair with Clotilde de Vaux between 1844 and 1846, "scientific sociology" was later transformed into a Positivist religion based on human perfectibility through scientific progress. Its motto was "Love as foundation, order as foundation and progress as the goal."

28. Camille Pissaro (1830–1903), Le Boulevard Montparnasse, 1897 (St. Petersburg, Hermitage Museum). Urban Paris was transformed by Haussmann (1809–1891), Prefect, 1853–1869. Large avenues and boulevards were intended to facilitate traffic, as well as intervention of police in case of barricades. Impressionist Pissaro shows the dense carriage and pedestrian traffic of the late 19th century.

27

28

30. American membership certificate for a union of metalworkers, 1851. Drawing by James Sharples, worker/trade unionist, suggests the ideal of a worker aristocracy based on merit and good work. Worth and wisdom reward workers and engineers, an angel (with the dove of the Holy Spirit overhead) distributes heavenly crowns, and the cornucopia is concretized in images of the industrial activities of the new civilization. The motto urges unity and hard work.

29

30

31. *Gustave Courbet,* Portrait of Pierre Joseph Proudhon *(1809–1865), 1853 (Paris, Louvre). Founder of a system of mutual benefits for society, Proudhon was one of the great figures of socialism, an anarchist, and an opponent of Marx. His 1858 work,* On Justice in the Revolution and in the Church, *was dedicated with irony to Cardinal Mathieu of Besançon; he was forced to take exile in Brussels. Courbet depicts him wearing a worker's blouse, with the glasses of an intellectual, surrounded by books and children playing peacefully—all symbols of a more just society.*

32. *Karl Marx (1818–1883), first edition of the first volume* On Capital, *a critique of the political economy, Hamburg, 1867. The second and third volumes were completed by Friedrich Engels (1820–1895).*

33. *Little girls employed in factory work (engraving of the time). The prettiness of the drawing and of the children, surrounded by the boss and foreman, hides the terrible conditions of the work schedule, including night work, and the low salaries imposed on these children. Doctor Villermé speaks of "homicidal exploitation" in his 1839 report that resulted in the 1841 French law limiting child labor. In England, many voices rose up to object to children working in the mines.*

34. *The village of New Lanark, Scotland, 1825. Robert Owen (1771–1858) founded this textile factory meant to be a self-sufficient community and a site for putting his reformist ideas into practice, in particular, the reinvestment of profits to improve the condition of the workers. It was very successful. He also founded a school for children where there were no rewards or punishments. In 1824, Owen attempted to establish a communalist colony in the United States at New Harmony, Indiana, but it failed.*

31

32

33

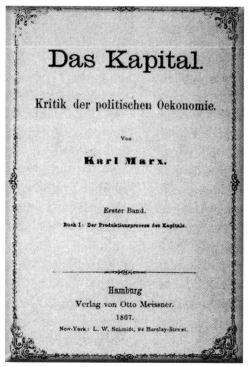

34

35–38. Portraits of some leaders of the Catholic social movement. Throughout both Catholic and Protestant Europe, the misery of the workers and their painful working conditions caused by the industrial Revolution inspired initiatives to address their most pressing needs, but also to develop principles for social analysis. (35) Saint John Bosco saw the urgent need for the education of youth, and as early as 1854, he implemented his ideas in a working quarter of Turin. His reputation for holiness, his activities, and the congregations that he founded made him a saint for the universal Church (seen here in a statue at the sanctuary of Fatima, Portugal). (36) As a young student, then later as a university professor, layman Frederic Ozanam in Lyons, beatified in 2003, chose to visit the poor in their homes, putting his ministry under the patronage of Saint Vincent de Paul. (37) Bishop von Ketteler of Mayence, political activist and influential preacher, began in 1848 to reflect on principles for a social Christianity. (38) Through his encyclical Rerum Novarum *in 1891, Pope Leo XIII synthesized the different issues touching social justice (salary, work, unions) and most of all gave these ideas the status of official Church teaching.*

38

35

36

37

Catholic responses to poverty, moreover, were as swift as they were limited, coming for the most part from the conservative and nostalgic milieux of the old political and economic order. Focusing on charity and alms, with a respect for established situations that were judged to be willed by Providence, the relief of misery was real and was assumed with great generosity. In France, we can point to the celebrated Sister Rosalie and Frederick Ozanam. There was also the dedication of the charitable and teaching congregations, especially of women, that multiplied the world over as well as the foundation of the Salesians in 1859 by Saint John Bosco (1815–1888). Between 1830 and 1850, bishops almost everywhere were concerned with the social situation and moral degeneracy.

The reflections of Wilhelm Emmanuel von Ketteler (1811–1877), bishop of Mainz, based on pastoral and even political experience, were more detailed. He inspired the first beginnings of the Church's social teaching, to be adopted by movements throughout Europe. Notable among these was the Union of Fribourg, gathered around the future Cardinal Mermillod. Leo XIII, in *Rerum novarum* (1891), gave it a solemn form. The question of trade unions held a prominent place in debates, and the shadow of "socialism" could also be discerned therein. The term was adopted by certain utopian Christians but still considered as dangerous. Social organizations inspired by Christianity sprang up in Germany and formed the beginnings of Christian trade unions.

39. *Interior scene of a boat transporting Negro slaves to the American continent, watercolor contemporary with the slave trade (Castle of Fronborg, Danemark, Maritime Museum).*

40. *A meeting between Indian and English representatives concerning the Punjab, the northwest part of the subcontinent, currently divided between India and Pakistan. In 1849, it was annexed to Great Britain and, after the revolt of 1857–1858 and its suppression, it became a colony directly administered by the British Crown.*

39

41

40

42

The Geographical Revolution

In the second half of the nineteenth century, explorations multiplied, making possible the colonization of Africa with zones of influence being distributed at the Congress of Berlin in 1885. This political and economic takeover was matched by Protestant and Catholic evangelization of unprecedented scope. Missionary congregations multiplied, all the more numerous, active, and lively as vexing political opposition instigated by anti-clerical governments attempted to hinder religious initiatives in Europe. As the century opened, the quite simple idea of Pauline Jaricot in Lyons of collecting even modest funds for "the Propagation of the Faith" gave Catholics the opportunity to take part in the great missionary ventures.

Education, hospital care, and training in social work accompanied evangelization. The Church perfected a system

41. *At Buganda in Uganda, King Mukesa I welcomes the British explorers John Hanning Speke (1827–1864) and James Grant (1827–1892). This drawing by Grant was published in 1863 in Speke's work,* Journal of the Discovery of the Source of the Nile.

42. *A caricature published in the magazine* Jugend *in 1896, ironically spoofing German efficiency in bringing order to the chaos of colonial African. Everyone stands at attention, even the giraffes, elephants, and monkeys.*

43. *The medieval section of the city of Lyons, a cradle of social and missionary action from the beginning of the 19th century. Pauline Marie Jaricot (1799–1862), as early as 1819, conceived of a way to financially help the distant foreign missions by the modest offering of a penny a week for the "Propagation of Faith." She also sponsored Christian workshops to alleviate the moral misery of the silk-factory workers.*

43

45

45. Cardinal Lavigerie (1825–1892) in Africa, illustration from an 1891 newspaper. The two officers who accompany him probably belong to the Order of Malta.

44

44. View of the Palace of the Propagation of the Faith Congregation in Rome. Bishop Jean Baptiste Vivès (1545–1632), while ambassador in Spain, bought Bernini's Ferratini Palace in 1613. After the creation of the Congregation for the Missions in 1622, with which Vivès had been associated, he gave this building to Pope Urban VIII. It became a missionary college that accepted young candidates from far away churches. In front of the palace, there is a column supporting a statue of the Immaculate Conception.

of institutional development for local centers of Christianity, first on the apostolic missions, then for vicariates, and ultimately created new and usually enormous dioceses, while taking into account national rivalries and susceptibilities between congregations. In a broader perspective, Cardinal Lavigerie, Archbishop of Algiers and founder of the White Fathers and White Sisters, spent himself in working for the abolition of the slavery of blacks under Moslem domination in Africa. Roman centralization, beginning with Gregory XVI, former Prefect of the Propagation of the Faith, had made possible the unification of missionary thought and practice. In spite of the limitations due to the mentality of the period, the missions were the most fruitful and promising of the Church's activities in the nineteenth century.

The missionary epic mobilized remarkable energies and heroic deeds to the point of martyrdom (as in Uganda in 1882) while at the same time arousing the interest of European Christians and moving them to participate through donations. But apart from this daring movement, the Church's attitude

46

47

46 and 47. Examples of medieval inspiration in religious architecture. (46) The tower of the neo-Gothic oratory from Tittoni Traversi Villa in Desio (Milan) by the architect Pelagio Pelagi (1775–1860). (47) St. Matthew's Church, known as Queen's Cross Church, Glasgow (Scotland) 1898 by Charles Rennie Mackintosh (1868–1928). This architect, who will introduce Art Nouveau in Great Britain, chose here an English Gothic style and adapted it, especially for the tower, to modern taste and needs.

toward the revolutions when viewed rather superficially seems disappointing or in any event timid save for a few solitary voices. It cannot be denied that for understandable reasons the Church was rather on the defensive in the nineteenth century and sought moreover to resurrect an idealized past as reflected in the neo-Gothic and then the neo-Romanesque movements in art. This was in keeping with the medieval taste that dominated all forms of culture at this time from literature to music, from Sir Walter Scott to Richard Wagner.

However, we should not overlook the very quiet but widespread generosity that was shown, not only in the missions but in religious life and the commitments of the laity. All through Europe a renewal of Catholic teaching could be observed as a result of the freedom that had been acquired slowly and with difficulty. At first this renewal involved secondary education only in France and Belgium. Later, following the example of Germany, "freedom" in teaching was extended to the university level.

48

48. *Karl Friedrich Schinkel (1781–1841), German Medieval Cathedral and City on a River Bank, oil on canvas, 1815. After Napoleon's defeat, German nationalist sentiment comes to be expressed in Gothic architecture. The artist puts a fluttering flag on one of the towers and encircles the cathedral with a rainbow, a sign of heavenly blessing. The return to the Gothic style represents opposition to the ancient Greco-Roman taste that characterizes the French Revolution and the Napoleonic Empire, but Schinkel himself will help to bring back the Greco-Roman architectural styles in the monuments he builds in Berlin in the coming years.*

49. *The Curé d'Ars parish (Department of Ain), in which Jean-Marie Vianney ministered from 1818 until his death in 1859. Ars became a parish in 1820. At that time, the Curé d'Ars had the church restored, added lateral chapels, and had the sanctuary transformed. In 1843, another chapel was built a few meters away from the church. Despite these additions, the church was still too small for the huge crowds that, from 1827, came in pilgrimage to confess their sins to the holy pastor who spent 11 to 12 hours a day in the confessional.*

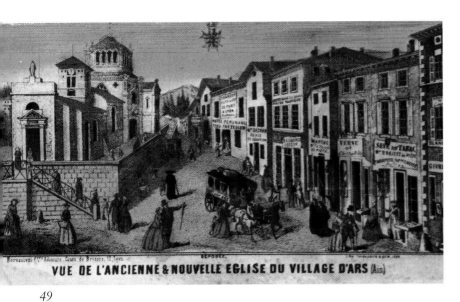

VUE DE L'ANCIENNE & NOUVELLE EGLISE DU VILLAGE D'ARS (Ain)

49

50. *Autographed letter from Sister Marie Bernard Soubirous (1844–1879) (Archives of the Sisters of Nevers). After the apparitions at Massabielle grotto in Lourdes in 1858, Bernadette entered the convent of the Sisters of Charity of Nevers in 1866.*

51. *Sister Therese of the Infant Jesus (1873–1897) in a group portrait taken at the Lisieux Carmel in 1896, one year before her death. This saint has often been presented as "sweet, flowery, almost insipid," but authentic photos reveal her serenity and inner strength.*

50

51

The response of the Church in the nineteenth century was not expressed primarily in its documents or leading names but rather in those sons and daughters who were recognized very early despite the poverty of their condition or manner of speech. The Curé of Ars, Jean-Marie Vianney (+1859), was a priest of overwhelming humility to whom crowds flocked to confess their sins. Bernadette Soubirous, shepherdess of Lourdes, heard the Blessed Virgin Mary, whose Immaculate Conception had just been proclaimed (1854), address her in the patois of the Pyrenees (in 1858). And at the end of the century, Thérèse Martin of the Child Jesus and the Holy Face (+1897), in a style now judged slightly sentimental, gave the Church so powerful a teaching that she was named patroness of the missions and became universally recognized in the twentieth century, being declared a Doctor of the Church by Pope John Paul II in 1999.

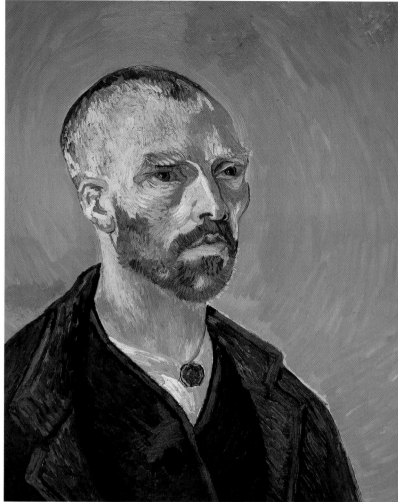

52. *Edward Munch (1863–1944),* The Scream, *1893, oil pastels on panel (Oslo, Edward Munch Museum). In the last decade of the 19th century, using a new style, Munch tries to communicate his tragic feeling about existence. Because of the depth of colors and the sinuous forms, the anguish of the cry seems to affect the spectator's hearing.*

53. *Vincent Van Gogh (1853–1890),* Self Portrait, *September 1888, work dedicated to "my friend Paul Gauguin" at the time of their happy association in Arles. Here, the artist gave himself a sort of Japanese look, an idea arising perhaps from his admiration for Japanese engravings. In the depth and stillness of the eyes, he reveals not only his psychological anguish, but also the mystical torment that was at work in him.*

54. *Paul Gauguin (1848–1903),* Where Are We Coming From? Who Are We? Where Are We Going? *1897–1898 (Boston, Museum of Fine Arts, The Tompkins Collection). In Tahiti, Gaugin learned of his daughter Aline's death and, considering suicide (which in fact, he attempted soon after), he created what he considered to be his artistic testament. The title affirms his metaphysical preoccupation.*

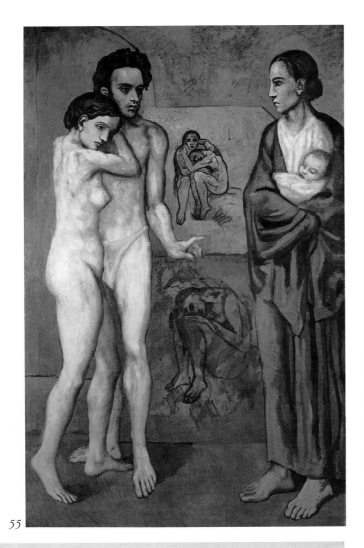

55

Twentieth-century art explicitly claimed a modernity capable of restoring a spiritual dimension. In 1910, after he had painted his first abstract work, Vassily Kandinsky wrote a short book whose title announces a whole program: On the Spiritual in Art and in Particular in Painting, *subtitled "At the Heart of Pictorial Creation." It prophesies a new "age of the Spirit."*

55. *Pablo Picasso (1881–1973),* Life *(Paris, 1903), oil on canvas (Cleveland, Museum of Art). Almost contemporary with Gauguin's work on a similar theme, this canvas from the blue period, despite the sadness it projects, insists on the affectivity that bonds human beings together—man and woman, mother and child.*

57

56

56. *Casimir Malevich (1878–1935),* Black Square, *1915 (Moscow, Tretiakov gallery). This work is the emblem for the movement called "absolute" painting, named "suprematism" by Malevich, meaning the "supremacy of pure sentiment." On the edge of self-contradiction, it assigns a quasi-mystical dimension to painting, which will be fulfilled later on when the painter comes back to figurative painting that recalls the art of icons.*

57. *Vassily Kandinsky (1866–1944),* The Last Judgment, *1910 (Switzerland, Merzbacher Collection). Contemporary to his work,* On the Spiritual in Art, *Kandinsky gives a biblical title to his search for "the pure and eternal forms of art."*

1

2

1. *Caricature of Bismark launching the* Kulturkampf *(Berlin, Staatsbibliotek). Stepping on freedom of speech, the chancellor pulls on a rope to pull down the Roman Church. Satan observes him, puzzled, and asks how long it will take to demolish it. "Three or four years," Bismark answers. "Well," replies the devil, "I have tried for eighteen centuries and have not succeeded yet."*

2. *Fribourg University, Switzerland. Following the Sonderbund war, which they lost in 1846, and the consequences which were similar to a Kulturkampf, Swiss Catholics reacted by creating this university in 1889. The laymen who established it were inspired by the ideal of a "Christian republic." The buildings above were constructed between 1938 and 1941 by the architect Denis Honegger (1907–1981).*

3

3. *Giuseppe Pellizza (1868–1907),* The Fourth Estate, *1898–1901, oil on canvas (Milan, Municipal Gallery of Modern Art). At the turn of the century, the worker and peasant movement claimed the status of a Fourth state, no longer the* people, *but the* proletariat. *The figures hold out their hands, their only power. The painting, depicted as a moving parade, has a cinematic character and thus could be used as a billboard for the Bertolucci film,* Novecento *(1976).*

Chapter 10

THE CHURCH AND THE CHALLENGE OF IDEOLOGIES

The end of the nineteenth century and the entire twentieth century were marked by ideologies which in many instances arose out of the preceding period, as was the case with Marxism. The Church found itself in a position of weakness in confronting them, not to mention a kind of isolation which was often experienced as a state of siege.

From a Church Besieged to a Church in Isolation

Trials

As the conciliar minority had foreseen, when the First Vatican Council proclaimed the infallibility of papal teachings pronounced *ex cathedra,* the reaction of European governments was very negative. Almost everywhere, people appeared to think that relations between Church and State had been substantially changed and that national bishops had become in some sense civil servants of a foreign government. This was all the more paradoxical given that this same pontifical government had just been robbed of its territory with the taking of Rome by Italian troops forcing their way through the Porta Pia on September 20, 1870.

The twenty years following Vatican I were difficult for Catholics in many countries. Historically, the anti-Catholic campaign has been given the name of its German version, the *Kulturkampf,* but it appeared in other forms elsewhere. In the new German Empire built upon the ashes of the French Second Empire and the defeat of Austria, Chancellor Bismarck, in the "May laws" of 1873, imposed administrative and academic control over the Catholic Church. He did this under the pretext of remedying the clergy's lack of "culture." In Switzerland, a deliberate policy of the federal and cantonal authorities favored the schism of the "old Catholics" who, under the influence of Döllinger (+1890), refused to accept the First Vatican Council. "Articles of exception" against the

Jesuits and against religious houses were introduced in the Constitution of 1874.

It was also religious congregations and then religious instruction itself that suffered in France thanks to the anti-clerical spirit that became enshrined beginning in 1877–1879 with the defeat of those upholding "the moral order." Although Pope Leo XIII intervened in 1890, rallying Catholics to defend the legitimacy of the Republic, the conflict grew sharper with the Dreyfus affair (1894–1898). In this veritable civil war of opinions, Catholics lining up behind the army and the Assumptionists of the newspaper "La Croix" were at first convinced of the Jewish captain's treason in favor of Germany. But as it happened, Dreyfus was found not guilty. From this time on a separation between Church and State was inevitable. In 1905, the abolition of the Concordat was imposed upon the Catholic Church. Pius X rejected the legal solution proposed by the Combes government whose policy hardened the aggressivity of French secularism still further. Particularly odious to believers were the inventories of nationalized ecclesiastical property. In Italy too, Pope Pius IX had rejected the law of guaranties offered by the Italian government after the annexation of the Papal States, an annexation ratified by plebiscite. From that time on he considered himself a "prisoner in his Vatican palace."

At the end of the nineteenth century, however, the Church experienced renewed energy through initiatives coming from Rome. Pope Leo XIII encouraged a true intellectual revival in Catholicism, a revival already perceptible since the middle of the century. After the re-foundation of Louvain in 1834, other universities followed in being explicitly Catholic. Such was the case in 1854 in Dublin where John Henry Newman wanted to incarnate his "idea of a University." At the end of the century institutions such as the Institut Catholique in Paris were created. They were destined to replace those controlled by the state. On the other hand, at Fribourg in Switzerland, the University founded in 1889 came about through the explicit

4. *Cover of* The Gospel and the Church, *Alfred Loisy (1903). This short book attempted to refute* The Essence of Christianity *written by the Protestant historian Adolf von Harnack (1851–1930). Loisy's subsequent explanations* (Autour d'un petit livre) *could not convince those who read in his book an attack against the dogmas of the Catholic Church and a negation of Christ's divinity.*

5. *The library of the* Civiltà Catholica *located on the Via Ripetta in Rome, during the era of the modernist controversy. This bi-monthly magazine was founded in 1850 by the Italian Jesuits, and came to be considered in the 19th century an official organ of the Holy See struggling against modernist ideas.*

4

5

will of Swiss Catholics, implemented by laymen engaged in politics. The return to the sources of medieval theology, and above all to Aquinas, which had been recommended by Leo XIII, promoted renewal in Catholic intellectual circles, whose members were equally aware of the problems posed by modern science. Catholic intellectuals met in international Congresses, soon to be interrupted by the modernist crisis.

The sense of being besieged by enemies from without was intensified during the pontificate of Pius X by the threat from within, a danger all the more serious and insidious in that it seemed to attack the faith itself. Modernism was, as often happens, a term forged by those who opposed it and was eventually used by the accused themselves. Difficult to define, it was more a question of a tendency, a climate, a choice arising from a clash between the traditions of the faith and modernity. According to a famous definition, a modernist was a person who, in the event of conflict, was ready to abandon, modify, or in any case adapt a particular tradition or its consecrated expression.

At the beginning of the twentieth century, modernism was prevalent in certain areas of study and in certain countries, such as France, England, and Italy. Its birth certificate was to be found in biblical criticism with the interpretations of Alfred Loisy (+1940), popularized in 1902 in *The Gospel and the Church* (*L'Evangile et l'Eglise*). But other areas too were affected by problems of interpretation. A case in point was the mysticism studied by the English Jesuit Tyrrell (+1909), with its corollary in the history of religions in which Baron Friedrich von Hügel (+1925) took special interest. Von Hügel played the role of coordinator and supporter of the modernists at the international level.

In Italy the movement took a more practical, committed form with Romolo Murri (+1944) for example, but it also resembled "Le Sillon" of Marc Sangnier (+1950) in France. This movement wanted to reconcile the Church and democracy and to build "a new city." As long as it was concerned with popular education it was tolerated, but its political connections from 1906 on earned it the suspicion of the French bishops, suspicions exacerbated by quarrels within the movement itself.

In 1907, two documents from the Holy See, the decree *Lamentabili* and the encyclical *Pascendi* of 8 September, denounced a series of positions. Loisy saw in the documents an artificial and unreal reconstruction of a system which Pius X named modernism. A series of excommunications followed which included Loisy and Tyrrell. Suspicion was in the air and

6

6. *Cover of Romolo Murri's work containing negative comments on Pius X's encyclical* Pascendi Dominici Gregis *(September 8, 1907), in which the Pope condemned the "modernists."*

7. The Ecole Biblique in Jerusalem, tower and basilica. Marie-Joseph Lagrange, a Dominican, was asked to set up a post-graduate school for Biblical studies in Jerusalem (1890). It was built on the venerated site of the martyrdom of the protomartyr Saint Etienne. Suspected of sympathizing with the new modernist exegetical methods, Lagrange successfully maintained both critical rigor and fidelity to Catholic Tradition.

8. Photo of Alfred Loisy (1857–1940). After resigning his teaching position at the Ecole pratique des hautes études *in Paris in 1904, he abandoned priestly ministry in 1906. Excommunicated in 1908, he became a professor at the* Collège de France *the following year.*

9. Cover from the novel by Antonio Fogazzaro (1842–1911), The Saint, *published in Milan in 1906; this work was put on the Index list that same year.*

poisoned the ecclesial climate up to the First World War. Before and after the formal condemnation, many Catholic intellectuals were subjected to the trial of mistrust and suspicion as to their orthodoxy. Among these were Marie-Joseph Lagrange, the Dominican founder of the Ecole biblique in Jérusalem and Msgr. Duchesne, a historian of the early Church. Thinkers of great worth such as Laberthonnière (+1932) of the Oratory were also condemned. The latter was accused of reducing revelation to religious experience. Condemned, as well, were laymen like Edouard Le Roy (+1954), reflecting in 1905 on *What is dogma?* or again, the philosopher Maurice Blondel (+1949) who was suspected of immanentism. (His book, *Action,* had been written in 1893.)

In 1901, the Sillon was condemned for having nurtured confusion between Christianity and democracy and developing a false conception of authority and freedom. Marc Sangnier submitted at once and pursued his political activities as a private person. Shortly before this, some French laymen had created the Semaines sociales, and the Jesuits had produced l'Action Populaire, to stimulate social Catholicism while distinguishing it from modernism.

It was also in 1910 that an "anti-modernist" oath was instituted for all the clergy. It is now known that a small group of intransigent Catholics surrounding Msgr. Benigni, who held for a time an important post in the Roman Curia, undertook the detection of modernist dangers. La Sapinière, through its network of people and publications, succeeded in creating a hateful climate of denunciations and fear, to such a point that it would be more accurate to speak of an "anti-modernist" crisis.

This is not to say that the danger of an erosion of the Catholic faith was pure illusion. In any case, a whole generation of laity and priests were marked by this confrontation with a modern world apparently ever more alien to Christianity, or at least to religious orthodoxy. Literature bears witness to this. An Italian novel contemporaneous with the crisis, *The Saint* by Fogazzaro (1905), sketches the portraits of reformers inspired by the new ideals. A generation later in France, Joseph Malègue with his *Augustine or the Master Is Here* portrays the passage of faith, entrapped by modernist doubt, to faith rediscovered in the Church.

From the end of the nineteenth century and up to the First World War, it is possible to detect particularly in France an extraordinary burgeoning of authors who had come to the Christian faith from the most diverse horizons. The leader, whose influence was personal rather than literary, was Léon

10. Léon Bloy (1846–1917), writer and polemicist whose journals from 1852 on were titled "The Thankless Beggar" and "Pilgrim of the Absolute." He was led back to Catholicism under the influence of Barbey d'Aurevilly (1808–1889) and the Salette apparitions. "Escalating invective to the point of genius," Bloy tries to defend the poor against bourgeois self-preoccupation.

11. Jacques Maritain (1882–1973), drawing from a photograph. With his wife Raissa, he converted from atheism under the influence of Léon Bloy and began to study and teach Saint Thomas Acquinas' philosophy. From 1945 to 1948 he served as France's ambassador to the Holy See. After Raissa's death, he joined the Little Brothers of Jesus, a religious congregation inspired by Charles de Foucauld's spirituality.

12. Portrait of Charles Péguy (1873–1914) from a painting by Jean-Paul Laurens. Product of the secularized ideas of post-revolutionary France, Péguy defended the innocence of Dreyfus in the Dreyfus affair debates. Detaching himself from socialist politics, he fought for justice in the Cahiers de la Quinzaine (1900–1914). *Returning to his childhood faith, he became the poet of Chartres and of Jeanne d'Arc.*

13

10

11

12

Bloy (+1917). He was able to rise above his despair through a mystique of the absolute. During this period, there is a kind of genealogy of conversions. By his example Bloy drew to the faith Jacques Maritain (+1973), his wife Raïssa and his sister-in-law Vera, all of whom were Jewish. They in turn attracted to Catholicism Ernest Psichari (+1914), the grandson of Renan. G. K. Huysmans (+1907) converted from naturalism to Catholicism and proposed a "spiritual naturalism," championing the impressionists in painting. It was in company with him and Bloy that the painter Georges Rouault (+1958), by his own account more of an "expressionist," sought to convey on canvas his mystical obsession and religious faith. He was certainly among those artists who best perceived the tragedy of contemporary man, transparent nonetheless with light.

In 1886, Paul Claudel (+1955) returned to the Catholic faith. Without interrupting his diplomatic career, he constructed a vast work of poetry and Christian drama, including the plays, *l'Annonce faite à Marie* of 1912 and the Trilogy of Coûfontaine (1906–1916). In England the Anglican G.K. Chesterton (+1936) defended orthodoxy with humor and eccentricity. In 1909, he published *The Ball and the Cross,* and came into the Catholic Church in 1922. But by far the most

13. Georges Rouault (1871–1958), "Are we convicts?" Miserere, plate II, engraving, 1926. Deeply religious, Rouault was friendly with Bloy and Maritain. Nearly expressionist in style, Rouault's images depict his tragic and spiritual vision of the world. His large series of engravings under the title Miserere, created between 1922 and 1927, expresses the human disruption caused by the First World War. The figure in this engraving seems to represent all of humanity attempting to protect its children. A halo of light suggests hope. (see fig. 34 p. 207)

14. Kifwebe mask, painted wood (Congo, Songye). The discovery of African art played an important role in legitimating modern art. The expressiveness of this mask, in a genre beyond either figurative or abstract, between the familiar and the exotic, calls the viewer to ponder the depths of humanity and of civilization.

15. A missionary building in Khartoum, where Daniele Comboni (1831–1881) died. The Missionaries of the Sacred Heart of Jesus were founded in 1867, and the feminine branch of the institute was founded in 1872, to evangelize Black Africa, in particular, the Sudan. In that country, Comboni tried to establish Christian villages reminiscent of the Jesuit Reductions.

14 15

unclassifiable and most original of these Christian poets was Charles Peguy (+1914). At first a socialist of the mystical type, he returned to the faith in 1908, producing within a few years a powerful meditation on the Incarnation and Redemption. We have to marvel at how during these years of interior difficulties, particularly within the Church of France but also in the anti-modernist torment in which priests seemed at loggerheads with their age, ecclesial grace paved the way for congenial spirits, free and very far from being conformists.

Responses

Actually, the great majority of believers was not affected by this internal crisis, which in the main concerned intellectuals. The Church found within itself a profound dynamism enabling it to come up with original answers to new needs without necessarily confronting directly the theological and philosophical questions raised by modernism. This would be a deep and even subterranean movement, focusing on the needs of the hour.

Mission appeals were met by generous responses of all kinds, in terms of personnel as well as financial assistance. At the end of the nineteenth century and even beyond, each year

saw new religious congregations of men or women founded for the foreign missions. Daniel Comboni (+1881) and Charles Lavigerie (+1892) were among the best known of these pioneers. It was as if the superabundant energies within the Church, unable to find an outlet in Europe, poured themselves out generously in evangelization abroad especially in Africa where systematic exploration and then colonization had occurred in the last quarter of the nineteenth century. This spirit of colonization was symbolized by the Congress of Berlin of 1885.

Climate and diseases decimated the first volunteers, who were remarkable for their heroism, abnegation, and incredible spirit of sacrifice. Despite these trials, missionaries built churches, hospitals, and schools; they baptized, cared for the sick, and taught. Of course, evangelization took place simultaneously with colonization. Yet it also is true that, at least up to 1918, it was carried out in a context of frigid relations between the Church and European states, even though arrangements were more flexible in foreign climates. The Catholic missions did not count very much on the help of colonizing states except in the Congo, which was for a time the personal property of the King of Belgium. Missionary zeal should not

16. *Diego Rivera (1886–1957), detail from one of the frescoes in the National Palace in Mexico City (circa 1934) describing Mexico's history. After the beginning of the revolution of 1913 in which he participated, Rivera created a national painting that illustrated Mexico's painful past, using a technique of mural frescoes that would expand across the country. The picture is clearly anticlerical: evangelization is plainly shown, but accompanied by Cortes on the right, the symbol of colonial power, and by armed violence as well.*

17. *Chicago and Lake Michigan (lithograph by Currier and Ives, 1892). In this quasi-aerial view, we can feel the intense activity in the harbor and the rapid development of this industrial city. In its reconstruction after the big fire of 1871, Chicago became a key commercial center. The great waves of immigration coming from Europe will create in the U.S. a Catholic Church forced to face challenges never seen before.*

16

be interpreted as a form of nationalism, although it necessarily took on the sociological and intellectual characteristics of the period. In the minds of those who consecrated their lives to the missions, their work stemmed from the need to proclaim the Gospel to the nations.

The missions to Asia and Africa were a European project. During these years, the Church of North and South America was preoccupied with adapting to particular situations. In Latin America, the Church had to face the challenge of anticlericalism or the influence of positivism and freemasonry, as in Mexico and Brazil. At the turn of the century, new waves of immigration helped to strengthen the ecclesial and social consciousness of Catholicism. A sign of this new consciousness is the first Plenary Council of Latin American bishops which met in 1899. Yet it was in the United States that the greatest effort could be noted to adapt to a society whose values and criteria did not stem from Roman Catholicism.

Possessing a hierarchical organization early on, the Church in the United States had to face massive immigrations from Ireland, Germany, Poland, and the Ukraine, which created a melting pot of diverse cultures within the country—although this concept is now a point of contention. In an attempt to surmount all these differences as well as the scorn of certain Protestant groups, Catholics thought they could succeed in integrating themselves into the larger society by way of adaptation. It was probably this tendency toward adaptation which

became suspect in Rome under the name of "Americanism." Emphasis was placed on Christian activity and the modern values of democracy and freedom of opinion while the values of humility and obedience were minimized. In 1899, Leo XIII issued a warning of the dangers that underlay this tendency, but in the United States "Americanism" was thought to be a 'phantom' heresy. It was feared that the condemnation might include the entire American way of life. Through the founding of religious congregations originating in the United States and through the creation of typically American universities, Catholics attempted to gradually integrate themselves into political and social life. The defeat of Alfred Smith in the presidential election of 1928, largely due to his Catholicism, showed that their goal of integration had not yet been attained.

The papacy, dispossessed of its states, tried instead to take advantage of opportunities to affirm its international role. Leo XIII, for example, agreed in 1885 to mediate between Germany and Spain regarding the Caroline Islands in Oceania. Similarly, he encouraged the efforts of Lavigerie in his struggle against slavery in Islamic Africa and his attempts, though unsuccessful, to participate in international conferences regarding the African continent.

During the First World War, Benedict XV worked to restore international peace. This was in no way facilitated by the warring powers, particularly after 1915 when Italy, rejoining the French-English entente, laid down the condition

18 and 19. Photographs of Italian immigrants on the ship that brought them to the United States (L. Nole, 1905). The medical check-up at Ellis Island in the East River became an administrative and public health control to screen the incoming immigrants.

17

18

19

that the Holy See should be excluded from future negotiations. The Pope, however, distressed at seeing Catholics killing one another and disturbed by the idea of the disappearance of the Catholic Austrio-Hungarian Empire, proposed an ambitious plan for general peace, dated August 1, 1917, and prepared by the nuncio in Munich, Msgr. Eugenio Pacelli, the future Pius XII. The main idea was to resolve the conflict in a face-saving way for all parties. Several of his measures, such as obligatory arbitration in the future, simultaneous disarmament, and the principle of freedom of the high seas, would in fact be examined by the victors after World War I. But his plan was deliberately ignored or bitterly rejected as in France where the government and even Catholic opinion severely rebuked the Pope for not having explicitly mentioned the return of Alsace-Lorraine to the Republic. It seems, however, that the acceptance of this plan would have avoided the carnage of the last months of the war, the dismantling of Austria-Hungary, and above all the humiliation of Germany, which was to give rise to horrendous political and social consequences.

Thus when a new era opened in 1919 the papacy was certainly not officially heard or recognized internationally. However, it knew how to make itself heard in social matters for example. With the appearance of the encyclical *Rerum Novarum* of May 15, 1891, on the conditions of the working classes, the social teaching of the Church had its charter. The document was a great success by very reason of Leo XIII's

21 and 22. (21) Henri Gaudier-Brzeska (1891–1915), Machine Gun in Use, *pencil drawing, 1914. In his time, he was one of the most surprising sculptors in Europe. French, but trained in England and Germany, he died in the war at the age of twenty-three. This drawing, made in a trench, suggests the impersonal and mechanical aspect of the fratricidal combats that began with the First World War. (22) From the other side, the German Hermann Keil,* The Origin of the War, *1919: This expressionist painter expresses his anti-war feelings through the image of a figure, ironically wearing a halo marked "in heroism" (Tapferkeit), with multiple arms like a Hindu divinity, who successfully cuts humanity into pieces. A citation from Victor Hugo denounces the hero as often being a murderer.*

20. Benedict XV Portrait (1854–1922), taken from a photograph. Elected in 1914, the successor of Pius X confronted the horrors of the First World War and its consequences. He remains the most underrated pope of the 20th century.

20

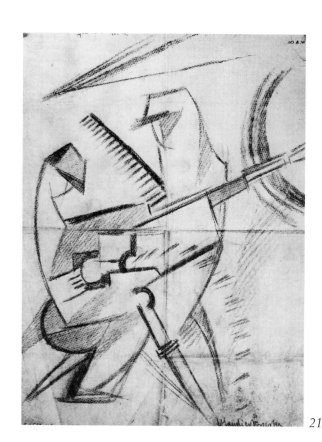

21

22

engagement of the modern world on this issue. The Pope recalled the importance of manual labor, which needed to be given its proper value in the eyes of the other social classes.

After the war, Catholics were able to overcome a certain intellectual inferiority complex. However, in a paradoxical and painful way, in the various countries engaged in war, they had to pay for their social and national reintegration through active participation in battle and in the trials of civil populations. The anticlerical cry in France, "rucksacks for the priests," which resulted in compulsory military service for the clergy, would prove in the end to be the most direct way of effecting a human and even spiritual understanding between laymen and clerics.

From an Isolated Church to a Consolidated Church

In the years following World War I, which saw the immense Tsarist Empire of Russia swinging toward a Marxist regime, the Catholic Church and the European states were reconciled, or at least came to terms with one another. It was a period that saw the negotiation of new concordats and looser interpretations of the terms of separation, as in France. It is also in the context of this same evolution that we must situate the success of Pope Pius XI's efforts to settle the Roman Question with the Italian government of Benito Mussolini. The Lateran Treaty of 1929 created a sovereign state in Vatican City, giving the Holy See the temporal base it deemed indispensable for conducting its activities.

24

23

25

The Conflict of Ideologies

For all that has been said, the struggle between the Catholic Church and political powers was not over, but it was carried on at a more general level, moving beyond the simple anti-clericalism of the nineteenth century. Antagonistic ideologies drew the world into a second global war, then split it into two or three solid, uncompromising blocks.

From 1919 to 1945, the Church affirmed the primacy of the spiritual order, to borrow an expression of Jacques Maritain, and this in the face of all ideologies, most of which sought to do battle with the Church or, worse still, annex it. In this regard, the condemnation in 1926 of the newspaper and the ideas of *l'Action française* directed by Charles Maurras, is both illustrative and a forewarning of things to come. It was in no sense the royalist tendencies of the movement that were challenged, but rather the neo-pagan philosophy undergirding it. While Pius X had already been preparing before the first World War to denounce this spirit, which was leading certain Catholics astray, Pius XI followed through in strongly opposing a vision that was making the Church the simple

depository of hierarchical values and of civilization, while rejecting its transcendent message. Even though the phenomenon was limited chiefly to the French context, we can still date the polarization between two different currents of Catholicism from the time of this condemnation, although they were already present a bit earlier. The opposing trends were a political and doctrinal intransigence called fundamentalism and a liberalism called progressivism.

Throughout this period, the Church denounced the idolatry of even just and good values, such as the Fatherland and the Nation, as well as those that were unacceptable, such as race or class struggle. The denunciations were made with greater or lesser vehemence according to the dangers that were involved—and these were not only spiritual. In 1931, Italian fascism was condemned in the encyclical *Non abbiamo bisogno.* In 1937, came the double condemnation of German National-Socialism *(Mit brennender Sorge)* and atheistic Marxism *(Divini Redemptoris),* just a few days apart.

These tragic years began with the terrible Spanish Civil War from 1936 to 1939. Seemingly at stake was the takeover of Catholic Spain by Marxist ideology. The Spanish Republic,

26. *Pablo Picasso (1881–1973), study for* Guernica, *India ink, Paris, May 9, 1937. This sketch, made in preparation for the huge canvas at the Museum of Modern Art in New York, was drawn by Picasso immediately after the German air raids called for by the nationalists in Guernica y Luno, a small town in the Basque country. It killed about two thousand people on April 27, 1937, and became the symbol of the horrors of the Spanish Civil War.*

27. *Madrid, November 1936, after the bombings by General Franco's (1892–1975) nationalist forces, photo, private collection.*

28. *Antonio Gaudi y Cornet (1852–1926). This architect, also a painter and sculptor, participated into the "Catalonian Renaissance" and employed all the different styles of religious art to build the* Church of the Holy Family *in Barcelona. It is still unfinished and remains unclassifiable as sacred art, but nonetheless inspiring. Starting with Gothic art, Gaudi let his imagination dictate astonishing forms, admired by the surrealists.*

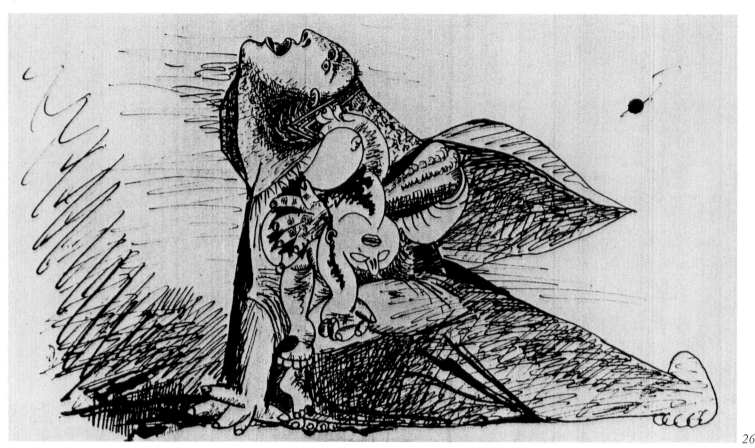

26

27

legitimate according to law, fell into the trap of a savage religious persecution that caused official Catholicism, particularly the hierarchy, to lean toward the nationalists who seemed to be defending the values of country and religion. No other conflict so divided Catholic opinion in democratic European countries. The novelists Mauriac (+1970) and Bernanos (+1948) did not hesitate to denounce the atrocities committed by Franco's troops and they underscored the resulting amalgam of nationalism and Catholicism.

The years between 1925 and 1930 saw a renewed interest in the Church among writers and artists. The philosophical and literary circle grouped around the Maritains at Meudon exerted a remarkable influence. In 1925, the Norwegian novelist Sigrid Undset (+1949) became a member of the tiny Catholic community upon which the glory of her Nobel Prize for Literature in 1928 shone. Sacred art did not experience the

28

29

29. *James Ensor (1860–1949),* Christ Calming the Sea, *1891, oil on canvas (Oostende, Museum of the Fine Arts). Three years after his* Christ's Entry into Brussels, *a parody of the society of his time painted completely in red, this half-English, half-Flemish artist from Oostende, created a painting that can't be called religious, but which nevertheless shows Christ in an amazing play of sea and light, the expression of his almost metaphysical vision of painting.*

same flourishing, even though there were attempts at architectural renewal. Antonio Gaudi, who died in 1926, leaving unfinished the celebrated and unusual Church of the Holy Family in Barcelona, begun in 1883, is not truly representative. Yet the review *l'Art Sacré* was founded by the Dominicans in Paris in 1935 and bore fruit after World War II. We should also note that the Benedictines of Solesmes, returned from exile in 1922, pursued their work of the restoration of Gregorian chant in spite of the death of Dom Joseph Pothier (+1923).

By inviting the world to recognize the royalty of Christ, the Church desired to point the way to a true hierarchy of values and the building of the kingdom of God. Pope Pius XI instituted the feast of Christ the King of the Universe in 1925 with the encyclical *Quas primas*. From this spiritual kingship, however, follow certain duties for national and international society in its march toward progress.

It is from this theological perspective that we need to understand the support that Pius XI gave to Catholic Action, a movement that encompassed the laity in the Church. It assumed different forms according to times and places. Differences also could be seen in the content of its "mandate," the manner of its collaboration in the apostolate of the Church, and its relationships with the hierarchy. Under the umbrella of Catholic Action were branches for men, women, young men, and young girls. This is how Italian Catholic Action was reorganized in 1923 and this model was followed elsewhere.

But Catholic Action would also become specialized, with groups for workers, people living in the country, and after World War II, for the liberal professions. Joseph Cardijn (+1967), vicar in a popular suburb of Brussels, perceived the need for a "Young Christian Workers" group (JOC), and organized it in 1924. The initial impact was powerful. In France the movement came into being in 1927 and it is from this period that we can date Pope Pius XI's encouragement of young lay Catholics to dedicate themselves to "making their fellow workers Christian once again," in the words of a popular refrain of the time. In spite of its defects, its succinct vocabulary, its militant attitude, and the crises experienced after 1950, Catholic Action would bear remarkable fruits of generosity, enthusiasm, and even heroism.

The pontifical magisterium pursued its work of social reflection as well, even though the encyclical *Quadragesimo anno,* written in 1931 to celebrate the fortieth anniversary of *Rerum Novarum,* seemed to favor a corporate model that would inspire the conservative regimes of Spain and Portugal. This model entrusted the re-evangelization of the workplace to the Christians who worked, the idea being that they were to be like leaven in dough.

30. William Congdon (1912–1998) came with the army as a volunteer ambulance driver to the concentration camp at Belsen. He chose as his title for this upsetting drawing of a Hungarian Jewish face: Morning Death (Morgen Tod).

30

The Second World War, waged by the German Nazi regime against the European democracies, which were already basically fragile and given over to party conflicts, and then against Soviet Russia, which would ultimately ally itself with the prosperous United States of America, placed the Church in considerable dilemmas. As a mother, she had to continue to instruct her children in the truth as she had always done, but also to protect them in the hour of danger from privations and trials never before endured to such a degree in an era of pitiless military technology.

After the war, Pius XII was reproached for his silence as "the Vicar of Christ" in regard to the mass exterminations of Jews, which had remained hidden from the public. From 1943 on, the Pope made it clear that he had renounced the idea of public denunciation in order to avoid the reprisals that would have been the lot of German Catholics or Catholics of other countries occupied by the Hitler regime. But individual voices only resounded all the more forcefully. There were prelates such as Msgr. von Galen, Bishop of Münster, who spoke out in his sermons of 1941, or Msgr. Saliège, Archbishop of Toulouse, who spoke out in 1942 in occupied France. There were also the reproaches of almost anonymous martyrs such as the

31

34. Georges Rouault, Ecce Homo, *1950 (Vatican, Contemporary Religious Art Collection). The mystical painting of his last years, and in particular his faces of Christ, took on special meaning as an interpretation and a symbol of the martyrs of the 20th century, innocent people persecuted either for their race, their class, or their faith.*

31 and 32. Sister Teresa Benedicta of the Cross, Edith Stein's Arrival at Auschwitz (1892–1942) (Rome, General Curia of the Discalced Carmelites). This hagiographic portrait tries to portray the profound vision of this Jewish philosopher, who was Husserl's disciple. She became a Christian in 1922 and entered the Carmelite Monastery in Cologne in 1934. In the preceding year, she had warned Pius XI of the gravity of the situation for Jews and Christians in Germany. Arrested with other converted Jews, she was taken to the gas chamber as soon as she arrived in Auschwitz. (32) Photograph of Father Maximilian Kolbe (1894–1941), Polish Conventual Franciscan. Known for his theology about the Immaculate Virgin, urging the consecration of one's total existence to God, Father Kolbe was deported to Auschwitz. There he volunteered to take the place of a prisoner condemned to die from hunger who was the father of a family.

32

34

33. In the tradition of seeing Mary as Queen of Poland, the Black Virgin of Czestochowa, *venerated at the Shrine of Jasna Gora (the Hill of Light), is identified with the Polish nation's spiritual and political resistance to Communism (along with the Union called* Solidarity*). You can see marks of defacement (from 1430) on the face of this icon brought from the Ukraine.*

33

German Karl Leisner, the Austrian Jägerstatter, the very young French "Jociste" (Young Christian Workers) Marcel Callo, the Carmelite nun Edith Stein in solidarity with her Jewish people, and the Polish Franciscan Maximilian Kolbe, who crowned a life of total devotion imbued with Marian theology with a sacrifice of substitution at Auschwitz.

In the face of so many persecuted innocents, the sacred painting of a Georges Rouault (+1958), who, beginning in the 1930s, multiplied religious or biblical themes, seemed to prefigure a body of Christ whose members would be tragically disjointed—a Christ whose Resurrection could only be surmised in the splendor of colors. The world and the Church emerged shaken by the terrible trial, which came to an end with the bombing of Hiroshima. This was followed by the revelation of extermination camps as well as the betrayals and collaborations that so often resulted in purges for the sake of squaring accounts in the absence of a civil war.

Europe was reshaped, but soon two groups were to confront one another. One sought to be free, attempted to rebuild ruins, and dress its wounds. This group was led by the United States, which had not experienced enemy occupation and had poured all of its resources into obtaining victory. The other group was formed under the leadership of the Soviet Union,

35

36

37

which benefited from the glory of resistance to the Nazis to annex for itself an empire in eastern Europe. The two camps would engage in a global struggle from then on by means of a "cold war" that, paradoxically, was resolved by a nuclear "balance of terror." From non-aligned countries a Third World emerged, concerned above all with development and claims to national independence.

Following the war, the Church, and particularly the papacy under the reign of Pius XII, neither would nor could rely on those circles that had been compromised by collaboration with the enemy, choosing instead to promote in traditionally Christian or Catholic countries a "Christian democracy." The earliest members of the resistance, among whom were Alcide de Gasperi in Italy, Konrad Adenauer in Germany, and Robert Schuman in France, united to found an ideological movement that soon saw the only hope of success in the organization of a Europe destined to become progressively united. Like the new Christian trade unions, these parties with confessional labels were encouraged by the Holy See, which was on guard against the new "opium of intellectuals" denounced by Raymond Aron and also by Christian intellectuals such as the French Jesuit Gaston Fessard. These men warned against a theoretical Marxism which was seducing those Christians who

35 and 36. (35) The Pan Am Building, built by Walter Gropius (1883–1969) and his agency, the TAC (The Architect Collaborative), between 1958 and 1963, a symbol of America in the Kennedy years (President from 1960 to 1963). The Soviet Union, the U.S.'s Cold War rival, built seven gigantic buildings in Moscow in "Stalinist Gothic" between 1949 and 1953, including (36) Moscow State University, designed by a group of architects under Rev. Roudnev's direction. This was one way for the two rival states to symbolize their power.

37. Between 1952 and 1965 the film versions of the humorous accounts by Giovanni Guareschi (1908–1968) of Italian social life, depicting conflicts between a village pastor, Don Camillo *(played by Fernandel) and the communist mayor, Peppone (Gino Cervi), were very successful. They evoked the Italian political reality, where the Communist Party won over a majority of electors but still had to compromise with the Church, or rather with the Christian Democrats.*

38. The dogma of the Assumption of the Virgin Mary, proclaimed by Pius XII in 1950, was based on long tradition, an iconographic tradition in particular—as for example this Monteluce altarpiece, by Raphael (1483–1520) (Rome, Vatican Pinacotheca). In the upper part, Christ crowns his mother; below, the apostles marvel at finding the tomb empty, her body now taken up to heaven.

38

had been invited by certain Communist groups to become "fellow travelers" in the struggle against capitalism and imperialism. This was the policy of "the outstretched hand."

It is obviously in this context that we should judge the condemnation of certain aspects of the experiment of the worker-priest movement, which began with the "Mission of France" during the difficult years of the war. In 1954, in order to avoid Marxist infiltration, very strict conditions were placed on the work of priests in factories. They were forbidden to adhere to any political party or labor union. Solidarity with working companions sometimes overrode communion with the Church. But soon in 1956 came the dramatic turn of events, when Krushchev denounced the abominations of the Stalin regime. This, along with the invasion of Hungary by Soviet troops, began to reveal a less attractive image of the Soviet Union and Marxist-Leninism. People soon realized that the iron curtain had not been lifted and that a hardening against the Churches was underway in the Soviet Union and its satellites.

The Church rediscovered a certain rootedness in social issues, which grew stronger as it demonstrated an apostolic dynamism. Yet public opinion seemed to take no notice, despite the appearance of new congregations and the prestige of pontifical pronouncements. Pius XII, intellectual aristocrat and mystic, governed and centralized the Church. In the course of his innumerable audiences, there is hardly a subject on which he did not comment. His manner was very careful and nuanced in those areas in which he anticipated the thought of Vatican II, for example in directives on social morality or religious liberty. He also taught the Church through such encyclicals as *Humani generis* (1950). This Jubilee Year in which the dogma of the Assumption of the Virgin Mary was proclaimed marked the end of preparations for an eventual Council. The magisterial teachings, both extraordinary and ordinary, of Pius XII seemed to have addressed the most urgent problems in the field of theology and Catholic devotion.

There was, however, a whole series of currents of thought from both clergy and laity—some overt, others more underground—pondering a return to the sources, the Fathers of the Church in particular but also the Bible. Perceptible even before the war with the publication of such works as *Divided Christendom* (1937) by Yves Congar and *Catholicism* (1938) by Henri de Lubac, or even in Romano Guardini's synthesis of spiritual theology, *The Lord,* as well as the works of Erik Przywara (+1972), a theological movement was branching out into various disciplines. It was particularly apparent in biblical research which, after the Qumran discoveries of 1947, attained

41. Fragments of a manuscript of the Psalms from Qumran. Discovered in caves near the Dead Sea (beginning in 1947), these Old Testament manuscripts written in Hebrew and Aramaic, belonged to a Jewish community at the time of Christian beginnings (maybe the Essenes), and gave new textual sources for a number of books of the Bible.

39 and 40. The Jesuit Henri de Lubac is one of the noteworthy representatives of the theological renewal that prepared the way for Vatican II. Steeped in the Fathers of the Church and preoccupied with the non-Christian religions, he took on one of the central questions of Catholic theology through his re-reading of the classic texts in his The Supernatural *(1948) and* The Mystery of the Supernatural *(1965).*

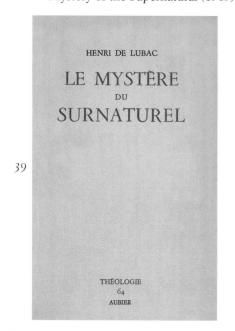

39

41

40

a renewal of perspectives. The Jerusalem Bible appeared in French in 1948 and would later be translated into other languages. In patristics, Danielou and Mondésert; for the history of theology and of institutions, Chenu and Congar in France, Hugo Rahner and Joseph Lortz in Germany, and Roger Aubert in Belgium; in more speculative theology, Karl Rahner and Henri de Lubac: all of these explored or re-explored Catholic or Eastern traditions and compared them with more modern or contemporary trends.

Two rather exceptional voices were heard in Switzerland. Charles Journet (+1975), who founded the review Nova et vetera in 1925, distinguished himself in the spiritual resistance to totalitarianism. He published *The Church of the Incarnate Word,* placing it under the patronage of Saint Catherine of Siena, in 1941. His approach to Aquinas, beyond the influence of Garrigou-Lagrange (1964), was closer to that of Maritain. The other great name is that of Hans Urs von Balthasar (+1988) who, with de Lubac (+1991), proposed a new way of doing theology in the West, but one profoundly anchored in tradition. Marked by the mystical intuitions of Adrienne von Speyer (+1967), Balthasar, who left the Society of Jesus in 1950 in order to found the Community of Saint John, constructed a monumental work begun in 1937. It would be recapitulated, so to speak, beginning with the first volume of *The Glory and*

42 and 43. In The Glory and the Cross, *Hans Urs von Balthasar introduced the idea of beauty into theology with "Theological Esthetics" as the subtitle of the work. His series continued with "Theo-Dramatics," developing the mystical approaches of Adrienne von Speyr. Both authors were published by Basel publisher Johannes Verlag: here, a book of Marian theology by Speyr.*

44. The Jesuit Pierre Teilhard de Chardin (1881–1955) (drawing by Giovanna Belcastro). He was a well known paleontologist who worked in China and elsewhere in Asia for a long time. His posthumous theological work, which ties the scientific theory of evolution to a spiritualization of matter, was much acclaimed during the years preceding Vatican II, despite warnings from Holy See in 1962.

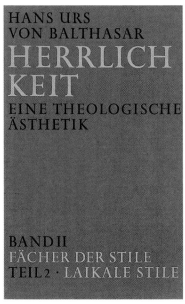

42   43   44

the Cross, *(Herrlichkeit)* in 1961, in which all the great currents of thought of European culture are compared with Catholic dogma.

With Joseph-André Jungmann of the University of Innsbruck, the history of liturgy revised its methods and prepared, through the study of sources, a renewal destined to be the most visible and most contested aspect of the work of Vatican II. A first step had been taken with the restoration of the Easter Vigil by Pius XII in 1951.

It was these same intellectuals who were preoccupied with dialogue with other Christians and maintained that the Catholic Church should not slacken its efforts for unity, efforts which were also being manifested within Protestantism.[1] The Roman Curia was disturbed by their boldness and a number of theologians were, if not condemned, at least exiled and forbidden to teach on the occasion or in the wake of the termination of the worker-priest experiment.

The most interesting case, however, is that of the posthumous publications of Pierre Teilhard de Chardin (+1955). A Jesuit whose scientific competence as a geologist and paleontologist enjoyed worldwide recognition, Teilhard, very much preoccupied with the divorce between science and the faith, attempted to reunite them in original writings such as *The Divine Milieu* (1926–1940) and *The Human Phenomenon*

(1938–1940), which did not receive an imprimatur. Disseminated in mimeographed copies, they were published after his death and met with remarkable success, demonstrating the expectations of a public attracted by the idea of a progressive spiritualization of the material element. His writings escaped being placed on the Index but the Holy Office pointed out their "ambiguities and serious errors." However, all the work of the generation of theologians between 1945 and 1960 which had matured under difficult circumstances was at long last to produce its delayed harvest.

Upon the death of Pius XII in 1958, John XXIII, who was thought to be "a transitional Pope," could rely on the support of an entire current of thought pursued by those who had worked, reflected, experimented, and above all hoped for the victory of a vision of the Church that they believed to be broader and more profound.

The Second Vatican Council

Very shortly after his election, John XXIII announced the meeting of an "ecumenical" Council, the first since Vatican I which had been interrupted in 1870. He began to envisage it in January of 1959 together with a synod for his diocese of

45

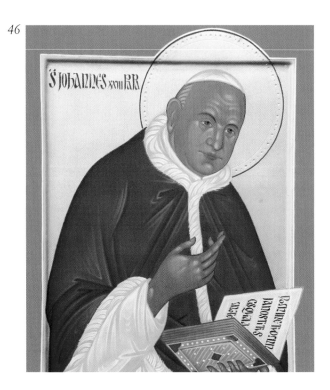

46

Rome. Pope Roncalli was a diplomat, a pastor, but also and more profoundly, a historian. He knew the relativity of certain theological perspectives and ecclesial practices which had taken on a kind of permanence and understood how to return to the great constants which the life of the Church discovers in meditating on the Gospel. These included ongoing reform, the meeting of Councils, the role of the Pope, which does not contradict that of the bishops, and the importance of the Bible and of patristic theology, including that of the East.

To the astonishment of many, it was announced that invitations to the Council would be sent to non-Catholic Christian communities. Preparations for Vatican II began in June 1959. The bull of convocation of the Council issued on Christmas 1961 indicated its three aims: the Church's attempt to address the problems of the world, the renewal of ecclesial structures, and preparing the way for Christian unity. In his talks, John XXIII often emphasized that the Council should be more pastoral than dogmatic. Vatican II took place over the course of four periods often incorrectly called sessions, a term that more properly designates public meetings for solemn

45. *The nave of St. Peter's Basilica in Rome was turned into a huge auditorium for more than two thousand Conciliar Fathers at Vatican II. A new dimension: the balconies provided a place for non-Catholic observers and lay auditors.*

46. *Blessed John XXIII, icon from the Monastery of Bose (Italy). The popularity of "Papa Giovanni" during his pontificate and after his death coincided with the rediscovery in the Latin West of Eastern spirituality and icons. After John XXIII's beatification in 2000, this community, founded by Enzo Bianchi in Bose, has venerated him in this icon.*

47. *The flight of refugees during the Vietnam War (photo by Henri Bureau for* Gamma*). After the country was divided in two in 1954, many Catholics from the North took refuge in the South. Here, the Saigon population fled the combat zone in 1975, before the fall of the city and the reunification of the country under a Communist regime.*

48. *The new Church of the Virgin of Vena (Cevenatico, Italy, project of C. Cabassi and M. Piccioni, Studio A.I.R.). The organization of space follows the directives of Vatican II and the practice that became universal all over the Catholic world: the altar facing the community, the tabernacle placed to the side, the pulpit moved to the front, the removal of the communion rail and benches for concelebration.*

47

48

49

ceremonies or the promulgation of texts that have received a majority vote.

The first period lasted from 11 October to 8 December 1962. From the first working day, certain bishops refused to ratify the planned assignment of Council Fathers to the commissions. The Pope accepted the consultation of the national Episcopal Conferences on the matter. In this way the Council wished to make it clear that it intended to retain the initiative and not see it confiscated by the rule of the Roman Curia. The first significant vote was that which adopted the broad outline of the Constitution on the Liturgy by 2,162 votes out of 2,215 on 14 November 1962. The documents on Revelation and on the Church met with more objections. There was apparent opposition between the Doctrinal Commission, which held ultimate responsibility for projects prepared under the leadership of Cardinal Ottaviano and the new Secretariat for Christian Unity, presided over by Cardinal Bea.

The next stage of the Council took place after the death of John XXIII and the election of Paul VI. These events only delayed by a few weeks this second period. It was held from

49. *Brother Roger Schutz addressing a youth gathering in Taizé. Founded in 1940 near Cluny, the great historical center of the Western monastic tradition, this Protestant community almost immediately discovered its ecumenical vocation, as its recruitment of members from both Protestants and Catholics and its construction of the Church of the Reconciliation (between 1960–1962) attest. The huge gatherings at Taizé, particularly at Pentecost, are one of the signs that today's youth are still preoccupied with religious questions.*

50

51

50. *Kiev (Ukraine), Cathedral of Santa Sophia, a general view of the altar in the circular apse. Christ the Priest gives the Eucharistic cup to his apostles. This heavenly liturgy is a model for the earthly one, and may serve as a symbol of the communion among the bishops gathered in synod.*

51. *The historic meetings between Paul VI, bishop of Rome, and Athenagoras, patriarch of Constantinople, spurred immense hopes for reconciliation. However, the lifting of the reciprocal excommunications of 1054 did not bring the expected results. The mutual embrace of the two pontiffs has often suggested the icon of Peter and Paul, the two great apostolic leaders.*

29 September to 4 December 1963. The methods and organization of the Council were improved, thanks particularly to the institution of four Moderators. The Council Fathers also succeeded better in working together. The greater part of the discussions focused on the document on the Church, *Lumen Gentium,* particularly the problem of the collegiality of bishops. The result would be a new equilibrium to the ecclesiology of Vatican I, as seen also in the practically unanimous affirmation that the episcopate is indeed a sacrament (30 October 1963). The permanent diaconate was restored at this time. The Council also decided to treat of the Blessed Virgin Mary in the final chapter of *Lumen Gentium* rather than in a separate text. The problem of religious freedom began to cause division and disturb the minority.

During the year 1964, Paul VI met with Athenagoras, Patriarch of Constantinople, and created the Secretariat for Non-Christian Religions. These two decisions had repercussions on the activity of the Council, which took up its work in a third period, lasting from 14 September to 21 November 1964. It was now time to fine tune certain texts discussed in the preceding periods: the Constitution on the Church, *Lumen Gentium,* to which Paul VI annexed a note clarifying the interpretation to be given to collegiality, the Decree on Ecumenism and that on the Eastern Churches in union with Rome. The Council Fathers also began to discuss Schema XIII, so named from the number of the document that would eventually become the Constitution *Gaudium et Spes.*

52. In an unprecedented initiative, twice, in 1988 and 2002, Pope John Paul II invited representatives from the great world religions to gather and pray for peace (according to their own rites and beliefs) in Assisi, a site filled with the spirit of Saint Francis (who went to the Sultan of Egypt to talk to him about Christ).

52

In 1965, Paul VI set up a Secretariat for Non-Believers. The fourth and last period of the Council was held from 14 September to 8 December 1965. After having announced a synod of bishops, which would assemble regularly as an instrument of collegiality, Paul VI reaffirmed the value and obligation of ecclesiastical celibacy in the Latin Church. It was then that the Council voted on the definitive documents that would form its teaching. Among the most important are *Dei Verbum,* on Revelation, which had been in the making since 1962; *Dignitatis Humanae,* a consiliar Declaration on Religious Liberty; and finally, *Gaudium et Spes.* These last two texts were promulgated on the eve of the closing of the Council, at a session that also witnessed the reciprocal lifting of the anathemas of 1054 between the Latin and Greek Churches.

The unique experience of the conciliar gathering of Vatican II with its 2,500 bishops from all parts of the world, its non-Catholic observers, and its men and women lay auditors, was a determining event in the history of the Church and also of the world in the twentieth century. All opposition did not abate after the closing of the Council. In addition to rejecting the liturgical reform set in motion by the Council, Msgr. Marcel Lefebvre and some of his partisans basically rejected collegiality and above all the Declaration on Religious Liberty which they denounced as "the marriage of the Church and liberal ideas." Their opposition ended in schism in 1988 after the meeting of world religions took place at Assisi at the invitation of John Paul II. This meeting was an irrefutable

proof for the "traditionalists" of the new relativism. It was clear that the Church had fairly well modified the image it had presented of itself since the Council of Trent. In place of a vision of "a society" that was called "perfect," there was now an ecclesiology, also traditional, of communion. The ministry of unity and the magisterium of the Pope were not eliminated for all this. But the attention given to religions, the recognition of evangelical and Christian values in Protestantism, and the emphasis placed on the building up of the "world" and human development, gave quite a different tonality to the post-conciliar Church.

The period after the Council was marked by a dramatic crisis for the Church. However, it is difficult to lay responsibility for this at the door of that tremendous gathering of Catholic bishops achieved by John XXIII. There has been talk of a shattered Church (Emile Poulat). But surely it is premature to attempt the untangling of the causes and contributions leading to this situation, which differ moreover from one country to another. Some have accused the Catholic Church of deviation, while others rejoice on having found "a free space." These divergent interpretations are themselves a part of the history of the contemporary Church.

CONTEMPORARY SACRED ART

Breaking with the previous century's medieval imitations that were sometimes successful but often servile, 20th-century artists dedicated their own creative genius to the service of the Church with the support of religious authorities who believed that liturgy and prayer could be served by contemporary innovations. Sometimes the faithful were less than convinced.

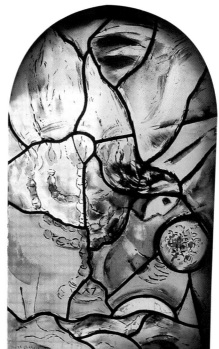

53

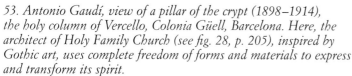

55

53. Antonio Gaudí, view of a pillar of the crypt (1898–1914), the holy column of Vercello, Colonia Güell, Barcelona. Here, the architect of Holy Family Church (see fig. 28, p. 205), inspired by Gothic art, uses complete freedom of forms and materials to express and transform its spirit.

54. Marc Chagall. Chapel of Our Lady of All Graces, Assy (France), 1956–1957. Two drawings for the stained-glass windows of the baptistry: on the left, an angel holding a candelabrum; on the right, an angel with holy oil. This is one of many works of art that can be found in this church, built in 1950 by Maurice Novarina (1907–2002). In two stained-glass windows placed on either side of the baptistry, Chagall evoked the angels' movements in heaven, using themes relevant to both the Old and New Testaments.

55 and 56. Henri Matisse (1869–1954), Rosary Chapel, Vence (France), Convent of the Dominican Sisters, 1951. Sensitive to the luminosity of this Mediterranean region, Matisse gave vivid coloration to the Tree of Life (1949 sketch) for the stained-glass windows at the side of the altar, while the faces of Saint Dominic and the Mother and Child are totally absorbed by the light — a symbol of the divine — to the point of eclipsing their features.

56

57

57 and 58. Le Corbusier (1887–1965), Our Lady of the Heights Church, Ronchamp (France), 1955. An artist in concrete in his large urban constructions, Le Corbusier, in this pilgrimage chapel, integrates rustic materials with the purity of abstract art, searching, as he wrote, "through mathematics, the Creator of the ineffable mystery of space." The interior is bathed in soft light.

60

58   59

61

59 and 60. Eero Saarinen (1910–1961), Chapel for the Massachusetts Institute of Technology, Cambridge, 1955, exterior and interior. Decoration in the apse is replaced by a "waterfall" of small strips of metal hanging from wires which, as they catch light from above, form a non-figurative mosaic. This effect places the light behind the altar and refracts it as if it were the actual source of light.

61. Alfred Manessier (1911–1993), Chapel of St. Therese of the Infant Jesus, Hem, northern France. The stained-glass window covers the entire wall surface, playing on the contrast between the dark patches and the flow of colored light, in order to symbolize the darkness and light Lof the mystical life.

62

63

EUROPA '51

INGRID BERGMAN · ALEXANDER KNOX · ETTORE GIANNINI · GIULIETTA MASINA
TERESA PELLATI · SANDRO FRANCHINA · REGIA DI ROBERTO ROSSELLINI
È UN FILM PONTI · DE LAURENTIIS   DISTRIBUZIONE LUX FILM

64

65

63. *Robert Bresson (1907–1999) consecrated his life to the art of "cinematography," which he distinguished from cinema-representation. As much by his subjects, often adapted from Bernanos and Dostoyevski, as by the rigor and austerity of his pictures, Bresson created a true spiritual language for film. This sensibility, already present in* The Diary of a Country Priest *(1950), his adaptation of Bernanos' novel, never stopped growing.*

64. *Roberto Rossellini (1906–1977) is one of the most notable witnesses of this search for meaning. He creates neo-realism as a means to apprehend the questions of the human condition by means of an intentional humility in the images. His films with Ingrid Bergman produced in Italy (here,* Europa '51, *from 1952, which describes a woman's commitment to the outcast) are proof of his commitment to this idea. In* The Messiah *(1975), Rossellini applied his esthetic ideal of discretion to the life of Christ.*

62. *Influenced by surrealism, Luis Bunuel (1900–1983) always handled paradox with a devastating humor that attacks the established powers of the army, the Church, and the bourgeoisie, in Spanish and Mexican contexts. A declared atheist, he belonged to a generation that attacked Catholicism so much that it had to have been intrigued by it. In 1968, he produced* The Milky Way, *a sort of historical and ritual voyage through the Christian heresies.*

65. *John Ford (1895–1973). This American cinematic master, who exploited the popular genres of westerns and police dramas, touched a large public with the healthy, virile, and moving insight of his* The Grapes of Wrath *(1940), adapted from John Steinbeck's novel. He brings to the story of these farmers, expelled from their lands by poverty, a universal sense of suffering and, despite everything, hope.*

CINEMA

Film making is the 20th century art par excellence. Invented in 1895, from the beginning, it focused on religious themes with certain inexhaustible topics like Christ, Satan, Francis of Assisi, and Joan of Arc. Until the invention of television, films that were edifying or at least entertaining and decent were the glory of parish "movie theaters." Recognized as an art form, cinema had to make room for the spiritual dimension of humanity.

66

67

68

66. Andrei Tarkovski (1932–1986) expressed in a series of seven lyrical and demanding films the heart of Russian mysticism and his own religious search. Andrei Roublev (1969), a portrait of the 15th-century artist who became a monk and icon painter, is a major work in an era when all religious thought was banished in the Soviet Union. Tarkovski had to emigrate to the West to pursue his powerful poetic work.

67. Krzysztof Kieslowski (1941–1996) is first of all a moralist. This is the key to his ten movies produced for Polish television, The Ten Commandments *(1988). He shows an amazing intellectual and cinematic virtuosity, never giving a moralistic or an apologetic meaning to his work. Through fiction inspired by reality, he revealed the depth of human questions about the biblical commandments.*

68. Wim Wenders (born in 1945), a German film producer strongly influenced by the American film industry in which he worked, dared to bring angels into films. The Sky over Berlin (1987) shows them (thanks to their invisibility) bridging the wall of separation that divides the city into two antagonistic regimes. Guardian angels protect people as much as they can and comfort them with their fraternal touch, as seen in this picture. These are not the angels of theology, but of poetry and compassion for the world.

69

A Shattered Church?

From a statistical viewpoint it is certain that, at least in Western countries, there has been a sharp decline in religious practice, both in rural districts and in cities. The crisis is clearly manifested in the scarcity of priestly and religious vocations and above all by the massive departure of men and women who had entered the priesthood or the consecrated life. Only crises such as those occasioned by the events of the Protestant Reformation or the French Revolution have given rise to a comparable exodus. The theological questionings born of a confrontation with the human sciences and the influence of Protestant thinkers like Bultmann (+1976), have played a definite part in this.

Yet at the same time and in the same countries, numerous new religious communities are flourishing. The biblical and theological formation of the laity is developing. A blending of traditional forms of devotion with new approaches to the sacred and to piety, such as the Charismatic movement, are at work. It does indeed seem that the Catholicism, which is a bit scornfully referred to as "sociological" and which underlies

the debate of historians over the "Christianization" of medieval Europe or the classical age, has lived on. It is as if a more elitist religion has been set up.

It is paradoxical that the vitality of Catholicism should appear simultaneously in the young African churches, where countries gained their independence in 1960 or thereabouts. There, Catholicism has received the teachings and intuitions of Vatican II with joy and success. Paradoxical too is the prestige of the papacy which, after John XXIII, has not lessened, even though some positions of Paul VI and John Paul II may have been contested by a public opinion more—if not better—informed by the media on the subject of religious problems.

The first of the modern Popes to leave Italy, Paul VI made use of his always very brief visits to symbolize the profound attention he directed to contemporary problems. There was the pilgrimage to the Holy Land where he met with Patriarch Athenagoras of Constantinople in 1964. For the first time since the Council of Florence, he entered into a true dialogue with this representative of Greek Orthodoxy, the two co-authoring what has been called "The Book of Charity." At the end of the

70

71

69. The Catholic mission in New Dongola (Sudan). Evangelization and Christian community life are difficult in countries with Moslem majorities. In this photo, notice on the right a large map of Africa on which a cross can be seen, and in the center, the dove, symbol of the Holy Spirit and of peace.

70. Allahabad, at the junction of the Ganges and the Yamuna rivers (India) (Matteo Rodella photo). In this sacred place that becomes a gigantic pilgrimage site every twelve years, we see two faces in a bus, one of an old woman and (on top) one of a young girl.

71. Abouna Elias Chacour speaks during the Peace Walk at Jerusalem (August 1972). This Palestinian priest, an Israeli citizen, has devoted his whole life to building a large school complex that welcomes Jewish, Moslem and Christian teachers and students.

same year he went to Bombay for the Eucharistic Congress. There he encountered the melting pot of religions that is India as well as the misery of the Third World to which he would devote his encyclical *Populorum progressio,* 26 March 1967, in the tradition of Lebret. In 1965, he visited the United Nations in New York, where the tensions of war and peace are in permanent confrontation. In 1967, he went to Fatima in Portugal on a Marian pilgrimage to attest the power of prayer, then to Istanbul to meet with both the Eastern Church and Islam.

In 1968, the Pope visited Bogota in Columbia and then Uganda in Africa in 1969, stressing both the problems of underdevelopment and the hopes of the young Churches. Between these two visits he went to Geneva, to the International Office of Labor and to the Ecumenical Council of Churches. These two institutions, one social and the other religious, typify the efforts of our times. Finally, in 1970 he visited the Philippines, escaping assassination in Manila, and then went on to Australia. From then on, he contented himself with brief trips in Italy.

The Pope had thus encountered—or more precisely confronted—the great problems of his time: the future of Israel and Palestine, those places where men were endeavoring to solve political, social, and economic tensions at an international level. He showed his concern as well to know the new continents, so filled with poverty and hope. Pope Paul VI also spoke out on the subject of birth control. After much work and consultation, he published the controversial encyclical *Humanae Vitae* on 25 July 1968. It appeared just a few months after the social or rather cultural explosion that had taken place the previous May in Western countries, a symbol of the liberation of mores. The traditional teaching of sexual self-control recalled by the Pope sounded at the time like a challenge and gave rise to a long-lasting misunderstanding on the part of public opinion.

As for the personality of Paul VI, his exceptional intelligence and his literary and artistic sensibilities are generally acknowledged. He appreciated the philosophers and theologians of the French tongue so dear to him: Jacques Maritain, and Charles Journet whom he made a Cardinal. He has been criticized for a kind of indecisiveness and an anxiety which is very understandable for one who had to face after the Council "storms, tempests, and darkness" and to be Christ's witness to "this sorrowful, dramatic and magnificent world" of which he spoke in his Testament.

After the very brief pontificate of John Paul I, elected on 26 August 1978 and found dead on the morning of 29 September, Cardinal Karol Wojtyla, Archbishop of Krakow, was elected on 16 October as the first non-Italian Pope since

72. John Paul II, Pope from 1978 to 2005, had one the longest pontificates in the history of the Church. He was also the first Polish pope and the first non-Italian since 1523.

73. Makati neighborhood (Manilla, Philippines), February 1986. Five years after John Paul II's first visit to the Philippines, religious women and priests are in the front rows of a peaceful demonstration against violence and for free elections, following the advice of Cardinal Sin and the bishops. Following this, on February 25, 1986, the regime of the dictator Marcos was dismantled without the shedding of blood.

72

73

Adrian VI, elected in 1522. Beginning in January 1979, the Polish Pope embarked on a series of pastoral journeys that would be interrupted for only a few months by the wound he received on 13 May 1981, during an attempted assassination, whose origin has never been officially declared.

The journeys of this Pope have taken on an extreme ecclesial and political significance, not only in Haiti or the Philippines but also in his own country. Doubtless only later will due justice be given to his spiritual role in the thaw of Communism in Eastern Europe which marked the years 1989 and following. His encyclical *Centesimus annus* of 1991, written for the centenary of *Rerum Novarum,* gives an amazing review of this recent period. It is a faithful portrait of the role of spiritual service to the world and humanity that the Catholic Church has rendered in the course of the age of ideologies—all of which end up, it seems, by disintegrating. With or without resistance, Marxist-Leninism is disappearing, but its Far Eastern version still persists.

Struggles go on, particularly against the unequal distribution of the goods of the earth and the appetite for pleasure, which seems to have obsessed the world like a modern form of the paganism we have seen continually reviving throughout the course of this panorama. The political and also religious face of the world has in fact profoundly changed. We can now speak of post-Christianity. In many countries, especially Latin America, the hunger for religious belief feeds upon all sorts of sects that are quasi substitutes for Christianity. The prevailing mentality of our time gives a determining place to practical behavior, technical to the extent that Western technology does not belie its power and in that way fascinate, shape, and at the same time impoverish minds. Since the decline of "the Gutenberg galaxy," the means of communication are paramount on the global scene, even though we are aware of their limitations and above all their dangers. Islam uses them, but reacting against the secularized character of the century's end with a simple and absolute response, it affirms its dominant role in its traditional regions and also in Africa and Asia, as well as in Europe through emigration.

Writing his celebrated *1984* in 1948, George Orwell prophesied a catastrophic "Utopia." After the discovery of the gulag, it would be unfair not to admit how lucid his vision was. Yet at the same time, after the failure of Messianisms, do we not get the impression that the contemporary world at last seems to understand that respect for the rights of the person,

74. *An apartment building in a neighborhood of Paris. Despite the colors and the variety of materials used, the anonymity of the urban metropolis can be felt.*

75. *This photo is part of a report on Koldo Chamurro, a community founded at the Mato Grosso of Brazil by a Claretian priest, Pedro Casaldaliga, who became bishop of St. Felix of Araguaia. He denounced the evils of unrestrained* laissez-faire *economics and he provided shelter for the most impoverished children of the world.*

74

75

76. *Mother Teresa (1910–1997), probably the most unanimously respected person of the 20th century Church. Of Albanian Catholic origin, she entered an Irish missionary congregation in 1928 and worked in Calcutta. Soon after the massacres between Moslems and Hindus that she witnessed in 1946, she was given permission to found an Indian congregation, the Missionaries of Charity, who take care of the poorest of the poor—who are so totally deprived in the Indian Subcontinent. She was beatified by John Paul II on October 19, 2003.*

76

including his religious rights, is one of the legitimate aspirations of humanity? In this sense, the commitment of Christians and religious institutions in the domain of human rights, justice, and peace, or a veritable "theology of liberation," may still bear fruit provided it does not once again become a source of internal conflict and alienation.

In the last years of the twentieth century, despite the fact that the Catholic Church's current disturbances come more from within than from external challenges, it is true to say and to believe that the Christian message, spread so powerfully by John Paul II, can find support in ecclesial communities, numerous movements, and most certainly in anonymous, hidden holy people whom hope has not deserted.

1. *Saints Cyril and Methodius, modern icon (private collection). These two brothers are considered the "Apostles of the Slavs." Constantine (826–869), on the left, who took the name of Cyril when he became a monk, holds in his hand the "Cyrillic" alphabet that made possible the translation of the Bible and of the liturgy for the Slavic populations. Methodius (circa 815–885) was named Archbishop of Pannonia and ministered in fact to all the newly evangelized territories.*

Chapter 11

THE CHURCH AND THE CHALLENGE OF CULTURES

In Chapter 1 we saw how the Church, at the beginning of its history, had been confronted by the problem of inserting itself into the ancient world. This world had witnessed the emergence of Christianity from the womb of Judaism, a particular religion of salvation which had instituted multiple signs of membership from circumcision to forbidden foods. In the name of the universality of Christ's message, the early Church had clothed itself in a Greco-Latin civilization, with its languages, law, and general way of life. Yet within this framework there was the need to discern what was compatible with the demands of the Gospel and what was not.

Twenty centuries later, the universality of the Church is no longer a simple, theoretical concept, albeit theological, but rather a very concrete reality. Because of the means of communication (from jet planes to fax and e-mail), and the knowledge, superficial or profound, that can be had of what is going on in the world, sometimes even an immediate knowledge (from television to travel), contemporary human beings have never felt more closely connected to the rest of the world. This universality at times might be nothing more than cosmopolitanism or the state of being crushed beneath a mass of information. However, with it comes a keener sense of the diversity and specificity of cultures, often more claimed than actual. For example, in the laborious construction of Europe there has been a twofold movement toward unification and the emergence of intermediary entities characterized by differences in language, tradition, history, and way of life.

Catholic ecclesiology has taken note of this twofold requirement. While Vatican II rejected nothing of the role of the Roman pontiff, guarantor and guardian of unity, it nevertheless showed its openness to the life of particular and local Churches, to a balanced exercise of collegiality between the episcopal body and its head, and to the diversity of traditions. Undoubtedly the Council's choice of the vernacular in the liturgy, which has developed through practice, has broadened or at least echoed the phenomenon of greater recognition of cultures.

The Pastoral Constitution on the Church in the Modern World, *Gaudium et Spes,* develops the theme of culture in its second part, which is devoted to "some more urgent problems." After having defined culture and immediately stated (art. 53) that it can be used in the plural—"we speak of a plurality of cultures," the Council considers the relationship between the Gospel and culture (art. 58). "God, revealing himself to his people to the extent of a full manifestation of himself in his incarnate Son, has spoken according to the culture proper to different ages. Living in various circumstances during the course of time, the Church, too, has used in her preaching the discoveries of different cultures to spread and explain the message of Christ to all nations. But at the same time, the Church sent to all peoples of every time and place is not bound exclusively and indissolubly to any race or nation nor to any particular way of life or any customary pattern of living, ancient or recent. Faithful to her own tradition and at the same time conscious of her universal mission, she can enter into communion with various cultural modes, to her own enrichment and theirs too."

One cannot better mark the tension, even the dialectic, which exists between the universal affirmation of the faith and "inculturation"—a term in use for some time but not found in the Vatican II text. This term was used in 1985 by Pope John Paul II in the encyclical *Slavorum apostoli* when he evoked the missionary figures of Saints Cyril and Methodius, patrons of Europe. There, the word designated an incarnation of the Gospel in native cultures and the introduction of these cultures into the life of the Church. In 1990, the Pope took up this reflection once more in *Redemptoris missio,* stressing the reception of the Good News through and in the culture being evangelized.[1]

On what conditions and in what way can the Church insert itself into other cultures seriously and without condescension? Should it and can it be inserted into any type of culture whatsoever? Finally, what does history tell us on the subject? We now need to explore in depth what we could only touch on

2   3

2. Eduardo Cano de la Pena (1823–1897), Christopher Columbus at the Friary of La Rabida, *1856 (Madrid , Prado Museum). There was a mystical and religious dimension to the project of discovering Asia by way of a western passage. In this romantic reconstruction, Columbus, back from Portugal, explains to the Rabida Franciscans— Juan Perez, presumed to have been Isabella of Castille's confessor, and Antonio de Marchena—his navigational plan. On the left, Columbus' son Diego, whom he brought along after his wife Felipa's death.*

*3. Drawing from a portrait of Alvar Nunez Cabeza de Vaca (around 1500–1560). The conquistador who discovered Florida and explored Latin America, through his narratives (*The Shipwrecks *and then* The Commentaries), *gave in his time, some of the best information on the cultural shock caused by the Europeans' discovery of the continent.*

briefly in the preceding chapters when addressing other questions. As has already been noted at the start, this present historical chapter of our work brings us full circle to the first challenge met by the Church in the earliest centuries, which was that of becoming a universal Church.

Since Christianity, coming from Europe, has progressively penetrated the various continents, it is appropriate to follow both its chronological and geographical course. In the sixteenth century, both the Church and Europe discovered what was for them a new world—the Americas. In the seventeenth century came the penetration into Asia, more permanent than it had been in previous centuries. Finally, in the nineteenth century, following explorations came installation—the word is not inaccurate—in sub-Saharan Africa. Afterward, we shall return to Europe, for the Church, which both accompanies and has helped to shape the modern world, has become in the nineteenth and particularly in the twentieth century in some sense opaque to that world.

The Americas

We can hardly imagine the shock of the discovery of an unknown world for men of the late fifteenth and early sixteenth centuries. Particularly astounding were its inhabitants,

4–8. (4) A General History of Affairs in the New Spain, 1565–1577, in the Codex Florentinus, a work by Bernardine de Sahagun (1499–1590). These vignettes from Volume III show successively the Aztec messengers of the Emperor Montezuma II (1503–1520) who are offering gifts to Hernando Cortés (1485–1547): See in the center the sun that they worshipped. (5) Spanish conquistadors riding horses, an astonishing sight for the "Indians." (6) A meeting between Montezuma and Pedro de Alvarado, Cortés' lieutenant. (7) Alvarado's army on the road from Tacuba to Tenochtitlan, the Aztec capital located in the middle of a lake on a plateau in central Mexico (see fig. 17, p. 231). The colonial city of Mexico was built on the ruins of Tenochtitlan after it had been completely destroyed. (8) The massacre of the Aztecs by Guerrerieri-Aquila. The native rebellion against the Spaniards in 1520 ended with a slaughter and the ruin of the Aztec Empire in the summer of 1521.

called Indians because of the error of Christopher Columbus who thought he had reached Asia.[2] The astonishment was reciprocal. People of both groups wondered if the others belonged to the same human race! Recall the relief of the Indians on seeing the Spaniards dismount from their horses and become simple bipeds or the reverential fear of the last Aztec emperor, Montezuma II, at the arrival of the Spaniards taken to be gods. Foretold in so many prophecies,[3] these gods had long been awaited and dreaded. The most impressive account of this twofold fascination and the cruel but inevitable defense reflexes that sometimes ensued is given to us by Alvar Nuñez Cabeza de Vaca, who crossed the entire expanse of North America[4] and wrote of his adventures between 1527 and 1537.

In view of these reactions, we have less cause for surprise at the lengthy debate held between Spanish philosophers and theologians over the thorny problem: Were the Indians, who went about naked, worked only for food, and had little or no interest in gold, an inferior class of human beings? What kind of creatures were they?

Faced with this unheard of manifestation of God's providence in opening up new lands to receive the Gospel, temporal and spiritual powers were quick to react. Referring to colonization in her will, Isabella the Catholic (+1504) declared:

"Our chief intention was to attract the peoples of these regions and to obtain their conversion to our holy religion." Already the "Alexandrine gift" of 1493, through several bulls of Alexander VI Borgia, affirmed the duty of evangelization. It was for this purpose that the Pope divided up those parts of the new world already discovered and those to be discovered in the future between Spain and Portugal. But in the view of the *conquistadores,* an appetite for wealth and for evangelization were by no means incompatible. Bernal Diaz, second in command to Hernan Cortes in Mexico and his chronicler, put it crudely: "We came here both to serve God and to grow rich!"

The "conquest," an expression later forbidden by Charles V, decimated populations. Even if the figures advanced by Las Casas were contested, the reality remains. The first cause was malnutrition combined with exhausting work in the mines to which the American Indians were unaccustomed. Slavery, or at the least serfdom, engendered social inequality. Despite the official texts abolishing it, it continued with the system of repartition known as the *encomienda* which had its equivalent in the feudal system.

Furthermore, evangelization itself was quite brutal. The *Requirimiento,* a crude summary of the history of salvation, was trotted out before the frightened Indians as a summons to them to be converted to the God of the white men. It soon

9. *Plan of Santo Domingo (Hispanolia), founded in 1497 by Bartholomew Columbus, Christopher's brother. This first urban establishment of the Spaniards in America has been preserved intact until now. This engraving (1585), made at the time the English pirate Francis Drake attacked, depicts an ideal colonial city plan.*

10. *City of Sancti Spiritus in Cuba, a regional county seat from where Las Casas started his mission in Cuba. One can still see the cathedral (16–17th centuries) and the access road to the "Old Bridge" built in the 16th century. Near to Sancti Spiritus, Las Casas received an "encomienda" (government of a territory) as a reward for his contribution to the colonization of the island.*

had to be abolished. Las Casas for his part rose up against the precipitous destruction of idols and putting crosses in their place. To erect crosses without any preparation, explanation, or catechesis, he declared, was "useless and superfluous, for the Indians might well think that a new idol depicting the god of the Christians was being proposed to them."

Reflection on the methods of evangelization and its theological presuppositions and also on the relationship of religions and cultures was needed. Only with difficulty would a balance be found.

An initial temptation surfaced, based on a rereading of Aristotle by those who endorsed the neo-pagan humanism issuing from the school of Padua. Philosophers made use of an obscure text of Aristotle on "natural servitude," applying it to the American natives. In the course of a famous debate in Valladolid in the summer of 1550, Las Casas took his stand against Sepulveda, a canon of Cordova, and was declared the victor. How could the Church evangelize an inferior race? Had not God created man in his image and likeness? Las Casas found support for his claim in the bull *Sublimis Deus* published by Paul III in 1537, affirming the eminent dignity of the person of the Indians.

The same obviousness underlies the very well thought out position, both theological and juridical, of Francisco de Vitoria, the eminent Dominican who taught at Salamanca. In his "Lectures on the Rights of the Indians" of 1539, he held that the Indians had "a kind of religion" and stated that theirs was an invincible ignorance of the Gospel. Vitoria established the right to peaceful evangelization while insisting on respect for natural rights, and thus the possibility of normal relationships between men. This is a fundamental principle of international law and Vitoria was one of its precursors.

In contrast to this intellectual advance made in favor of a balance between the rights of reason and the demands of grace, another temptation arose: the desire to base evangelization on a false theology of history, close at times to religious fabrication. The Franciscan Geronimo de Mendieta, the Jesuit Jose de Acosta, and others, delighted in a pseudo-scriptural providentialism. An apocalyptic vision of the end from the Middle Ages also played its part in this. Christopher Columbus prepared for his first voyage by jotting down in his favorite book, Pierre d'Ailly's *Imago Mundi,* phrases drawn from the apocrypha composed by the disciples of Joachim of Fiore.[5] This was to give evangelization a very fragile and above all deceptive foundation.

All of this helps to explain an eventual turn to pastoral solutions more conformed to the balance between faith, grace,

9

10

11. *Chiapas, Las Casas' episcopal see, had been a former territory of the Mayas at the time of their power, but nothing but ruins remained, since the Mayan kingdoms of the 16th century were only to be found in the Yucatan peninsula. What the Conquistadors found at Chiapas was later covered over by the forests and only rediscovered in the 19th century. The principal roadway for Chiapas is the river Usumacinta Axchilan, seen here in a timeless landscape, near the ancient Mayan city of Yaxchilan.*

12. *Illustrated detail from frontispiece of* The Very Brief Narrative of the Destruction of the Indies, *written by Bartolomé de Las Casas (Seville, 1552). This accusatory document, denouncing the massacres and destruction that took place during the Spanish colonization of Latin America, was this Dominican bishop's way of carrying out his role as the "Protector of the Indians."*

12

11

and nature. The personal journey and actions of Bartholomew de Las Casas represent a first endeavor in this direction.

This Spaniard of Seville, whose father and uncles were among the first to embrace the adventure of colonization in the newly discovered American continent, followed in their footsteps and also crossed the Atlantic. Ordained in 1512, he has the distinction of being the first newly ordained priest to celebrate Mass in the New World. Working in Hispaniola (the present Haiti and Dominican Republic) and later in Cuba, he practiced the system of colonization that despoiled the Indians. For this reason, a Dominican priest who had challenged this state of affairs with Montesinos in 1511 refused to give Las Casas absolution. Thereupon, Las Casas changed his views, was converted, freed his slaves, and embarked for Spain to plead their cause.

Called "the Protector of the Indians" by the Regent of Castile, Las Casas tried to bring to a successful issue an experiment of cohabitation of Indians and Spanish peasants, an endeavor that failed from the outset. It was at this time that he also proposed to replace Indian slaves with others from Africa, a plan he repented of very quickly. He then felt that he was not ready for the task to which he wanted to devote himself, the struggle for justice and peaceful evangelization.

After having joined the Dominicans in 1522, Las Casas entered upon a period of silence and study. He later came out of seclusion and engaged the world once more. In a fundamental treatise, *On the Unique Means of Evangelization,* the "means" being charity, he commented on the bull *Sublimis Deus* of Pope Paul III. Next, he obtained from the Emperor Charles V the "New laws" protecting the Indians. In 1543, he was named bishop of Chiapas (south of present Mexico and Guatemala) and became a member of the Council of the Indies.

It was at this point that Las Casas experimented with peaceful evangelization in his diocese with tribes reputed to be very aggressive. His efforts led indeed to pacification, and to the preaching of the Gospel in this territory, which took on the name of "Vera Paz." Las Casas multiplied discussions, memos, and reports, and in 1547 returned definitively to Spain. In 1550 he renounced his bishopric. Henceforth he devoted himself to the defense of the Indians. On the one hand, he revealed the acts of destruction and the violence perpetrated against them in his writings, *A Very Brief Account of the Destruction of*

13. The Chain of the Andes seen from the top of Huarochiri. In the middle, Mount Pariarca with its two peaks, a sacred mountain that is still venerated today.

14. Part of the steps that lead to the Incas "Royal Road."

13

14

15. Folio manuscript by the Franciscan Bernardine de Sahagun (1500–1590) containing catechetical and liturgical texts in Nahuatl (John Carter Brown Library, Brown University, Providence, R.I.).

15

16. Illustration from the work of the Dominican chronicler Diego Duran (1537–1588), A History of the Indies of New Spain and of the Islands of Terra Firma (1585). Here we see the meeting between Hernando Cortes and Malinche, called Dona Marina, the name given to the Conquistador (the Captain of Marina). According to Bernal Diaz, a witness of the Conquest, Marina, a young Indian woman given to Cortes, was very talented and served as his interpreter. She became a mythic figure of the Conquest, by initiating the Spanish-Indian mestizo (mixed blood) adventure, critical for understanding Latin America.

the Indies, published in 1552, and *A History of the Indies,* printed after his death. On the other hand he occupied himself with demonstrating the absence of legitimacy in the *Conquista* and the obligation to restore all that had been taken from the natives, as seen in his *Treatise of Twelve Doubts* of 1564.

Did this concern to prevent the exploitation and decimation of the Indians go hand in hand with respect for their culture? Las Casas was interested in the customs of the Indians but viewed them somewhat apologetically. For him, an idol was really a clumsy representation of God, and in every way possible he stressed the progress shown by carefully worked out religions such as that of the Aztecs in comparison with the more primitive cults.

There are from this period veritable ethnographic treatises composed by the missionaries which are mines of information for the modern historian. The Franciscan, Toribio of Benabente (+1568), called by the Indians Motolinia or "the poor man," wrote a *History of the Indians,* while his confrere Bernardino of Sahagun (+1590) produced the *History of Events in New Spain* in both Spanish and Nahuatl. The case of Garcilaso de la Vega, the Inca (+1616) and his *True Stories of the Incas,* is still more notable. Being the product of two cultures since his maternal tongue was Quechua, he attempts to demonstrate—not without the risk of syncretism—the providential preparation for the future of Christianity through the Incan civilization. He also brings to light the importance of natural religion.

The history of inculturation in the Americas calls for a careful examination of the diversities, developments, and debates involved. A study of the concept of idolatry enables

17. An old map of Tenochtitlan (see fig. 7, p. 227). This engraving is part of the first edition of the Letters of Cortés, *published in Nuremberg in 1524, and then thought to have been based on the conquistador's own descriptions.*

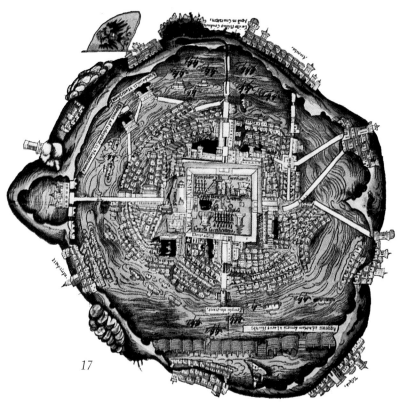

17

16

us to follow its progress.[6] Though the American Indians were dispossessed of their way of thinking—and this is a byproduct of colonization—the Christianity of the American Indians nevertheless was not the Christianity of Europeans. It existed in its indigenous form and cultural shifts took place.[7]

There are many lessons to be drawn from intermarriage, a widespread phenomenon in South America as compared with North American countries. In *The Labyrinth of Solitude (El Laberinto de la Soledad)* Octavio Paz speaks of Mexicans as "the sons of Malincha," the mistress of Cortes who revealed to him the secrets of the Aztecs. In their descendants, conqueror and vanquished, traitor and betrayed lived on. Another Mexican thinker, Vasconcelos, considers the Metis, on the contrary, as "a race of bronze," the supreme realization of humanity.

What interests the Church historian more, however, is the beginning of a certain inculturation by means of communion, a symbol of which might be the image of the Virgin of Guadalupe, so venerated in the Americas.[8] The image left by the Virgin on the mantle of the poor and devout Indian, Juan Diego, is specifically Catholic. However, an Aztec hieroglyphic, subtle but central, can be discerned, representing the Sun nourished by the blood of human sacrifices. It is as if, beyond the too narrow perspective of concepts of idolatry, superstition, and assimilation, another language and another approach were possible, if we think in terms of the mysterious preparations for Christianity.

When the faith was sung to native melodies in "The Land of True Peace" founded by Las Casas, or when the Guarani Indians listened to the baroque sacred music of the Jesuit

18. First page of the Nican Mopohua, *a narrative published in 1646. The Indian writer, Antonio Valeriano, wrote it when witnesses of "the miracle of the roses" were still alive. He described how the Virgin of Guadelupe's image appeared on Juan Diego's tilma. This apparition of the Virgin of the Apocalypse (venerated at the Monastery of Guadalupe in Spain) to the young Indian in 1531 on Tepeyac Mountain, near Mexico City, gave birth to the most popular of all Catholic devotions in the Americas.*

18

NICAN
MOPOHVA,
MOTECPANA INQVENIN
YANCVICAN HVEITLAMAHVIÇOLTICA
MONEXITI INÇENQVIZCA ICHPOCHTLI
SANCTA MARIA DIOS YNANTZIN TOÇI-
HVAPILLATOCATZIN, IN ONCAN
TEPEYACAC MOTENEHVA
GVADALVPE.

Acattopa quimottititzino çe
maçehdaltzineli itoca Iuan Diego; Auh çatepan monexiti initlaçò Ixipilarain ynixpan yancuican Obifpo
D. Fray Iuan de Sumarraga. Ihuan inixquich tlama-
huiçolli ye quimochihuilia.

Y E iuh màtlac xihuitl in opehualoc in
atl itepetl Mèxico, ynyeomoman
in mitl, in chimallà, in ye nohuian
onelamatcamani in ahuàcan, intepe-
huàcan; in maçaçan yeopeuh, y ɔko-
tla, ye cuepeui intlanelteouiliztlè,
inixinmachocatzin inipalnemohuani
nelli Teotl DIOS. in huel iquac inipan Xihuitl mill
y quinientos, y treinta y vno, quiniuh iquezquilhuioc
In metztli Diziembre mochiuh oncatca çe maçehual-
A   tzintli,

19. Manuscript of Psalm 116 (Vulgate) from Domenico Zipoli (1688–1726). This Italian musician, who entered the Society of Jesus in 1716, arrived in America the following year. His musical work has been rediscovered in the Archives of the Chiquitos Indian Reductions, presently in Bolivia, villages that were founded in 1690. He set his music for the liturgical ceremonies of the Reductions according to simple popular Baroque melodies.

19

20. *The resurrected Christ (17–18th centuries). Wooden sculpture from the Jesuit missions in Paraguay.*

21. *Cloister from the College of the Society of Jesus in Arequipa, in southern Peru, founded by the Conquistador Francisco Pizarro (c. 1475–1541) in 1540, at an altitude of more than 6,000 feet.*

20

21

Domenico Zipoli (+1725) performed on their instruments, was this not an exchange between peoples at the level of the soul?

The Reductions in Paraguay

Among the most astounding events in the history of the Church is the extraordinary venture of a Republic composed of thousands of Indians under the direction of the Jesuit missionaries. It lasted for a century and a half, from 1610 to 1768. Let me first make a clarification: Paraguay here should be understood in a broad sense, since the territory covered a vast stretch of the basin of the great rivers of South America where the present countries of Paraguay, Uruguay, Argentina, and northern Brazil meet. Furthermore, the word "reduction" does not correspond to this reality but designates, in the sixteenth century and beyond, colonies of Indian tribes which had been nomadic up to that point but were in the process of becoming settled.

The chief purpose of the reductions was to create a concrete and durable setting for peaceful evangelization. It was the Franciscans who first came up with the idea for the tribes of the Guaranis, employing an ingenious system that incorporated native customs along with true Christianization. Behind the scenes here, we can observe the interest in utopias, literary or actual, which from the time of Thomas More had fascinated Christian thought.[9]

Succeeding the Franciscans, the Jesuits wanted to perfect this original system of evangelization whose characteristic feature was the protection of the Indians from all armed or mercantile intrusion. The first village, named Loretto, was organized with the agreement of Philip III in 1610 by the Italian Fathers Simon Maceta and Joseph Cataldino. The monarch drew up a special statute for the reductions, placing them under the direct sovereignty of the king of Spain and entrusting them to the care of the Society of Jesus. These arrangements were renewed in 1631, 1633, and 1647.

This venture has been made known to us through a work entitled *The Spiritual Conquest* (1639) by Ruiz de Montoya, superior general of the mission to the Guarani from 1620 to 1637. The Indians were grouped in cities numbering at times several thousand inhabitants. The layout of common buildings was uniform and included church, school, cemetery, town hall, hospital, home for widows, Jesuit residence, and so forth. All activities were carried on in the Guarani language. In accordance with the renowned Jesuit pedagogy great importance was attached to sports, the theater, and feasts.

Doubtless in continuity with the former economic system, the land belonged to the community and everything was held in common. Each family had the use of a house, given at the time of marriage. Life there was simple, devout, and austere. Work properly so-called, which was obligatory for all, even the traditional chiefs (caciques), took up six hours of the day. Daily Mass was obligatory for children, with much singing

23. *Drawing, from a portrait of Ludovico Antonio Muratori (1672–1750). This famous scholar in the history of Law and Liturgy had studied with the Jesuits in Modena. He became the advocate of the Paraguay Reductions, this real "utopia" that resembled the egalitarian and fraternal ideal of the early Church.*

23

22

and music. The catechism was also sung in the local language. Clothing was uniform and alcohol was forbidden in the reductions. The Jesuits tried to adapt local customs and Christianize them, but polygamy remained one of the chief obstacles to Baptism. Capital punishment did not exist in the territory.

We can imagine that this reserve of territory and above all the potential in manual labor stirred up much envy. The first threat took concrete shape in 1628. Some Portuguese of mixed race in Brazil as well as some Paulists (from the region of Sao Paulo), also called Mamelukes (from the word *maloca:* slave), while considering themselves good Christians, decided to put an end to this entity so foreign to colonization. Overcome by this armed band, the Jesuits organized the withdrawal of populations into Spanish territory. Eighty thousand people traversed forests and rivers between 1629 and 1631. In 1635, the Jesuits obtained royal authorization to supply the Indians with firearms, enabling them to win the decisive battle of Mborore in 1641. Apart from another attempt ten years later and a few skirmishes, the Indians in the reductions were able to live peaceful lives under the leadership of the missionaries for a century.

The enemies of the reductions had to wait almost this long to defeat them. The Jesuits, much criticized in the Catholic world and attached directly to the papacy, and in this case also to the king of Spain, were investigated regarding their activities in Paraguay. They were faulted for their authoritarianism and a certain paternalism, which hindered them from receiving priestly and religious vocations among the Guarani. But the

Cedula Grande of King Philip V in 1743 gave them justice. In 1744, several Indian Republics were established: that of the Chiquitos, the Mojos, the Baures, and also groups in the Andes, each of them having several tens of thousands of inhabitants.

It was at this point that the Marquis of Pombal (+1782), the all-powerful master of Portugal from 1755 to 1777, who is also a perfect example of the anticlericalism of the Enlightenment, succeeded in breaching the walls of this edifice through diplomatic tactics. On 13 January 1750, he reached an accord with Spain known as the Treaty of Madrid, which modified borders and cut away from the Guarani Republic almost half of its territory. The Jesuits received an order to submit from the General of the Society, Visconti, but the inhabitants decided to resist. From 1754 to 1756 the troops of the kings of Spain and of Portugal faced an armed resistance which was at first victorious in 1753 and 1754. But the Guarani were soon overcome in the eastern reductions in the battle of Caybate and were forced to flee.

When in 1761 the new king of Spain, Charles III, denounced the Treaty of Madrid, and while the other reductions were flourishing, they nevertheless fell victim to the hatred that was pursuing the Society of Jesus in Europe. In 1767, the Jesuits were banished from all Spanish territories, a measure that was applied to the reductions in the following year. Finally, the Society itself was suppressed by Clement XIV in 1773.

Montesquieu, Voltaire, d'Alembert, and writers of articles in the *Encyclopedia,* had nothing but praise for the political

26

24

25. Husayn Naqqash (+1665), Tobias's Angel, *around 1590 (Paris, Guimet Museum). This painter was part of Akhbar's court (1542–1605), the Moghul Emperor of India, who practiced a surprising religious tolerance—even syncretism with Hinduism, Chrtistianity, and Islam—and thus he welcomed the Portuguese Jesuits. In this multicolored painting, the Archangel Raphael ordered Tobias to take hold of the fish that leaped out of the Tigris and whose heart, liver, and gall will heal his blind father (Tobit 6:4). A mix of influences are put to the service of the biblical text: the style is that of Persian miniatures, but the draping of the mantle is Western.*

25

organization of the reductions. The "myth" about them, if we may use the term, found expression in the work of the great ecclesiastical scholar, Ludovico Muratori (+1750), who wrote "The Happy Christianity of Paraguay," *Il cristianesimo felice nel Paraguay,* in 1747. It was an exceptional experiment in which the religious pastoral mission of the Jesuits never seemed to have been challenged. This was not the case with their apostolate in the Far East.

Asia

After the travels far and wide of Marco Polo and his companions in the Middle Ages and the epic journeys of the Franciscans in the Far East, the first attempt at evangelization was due to Francis Xavier.

Having joined Ignatius of Loyola during their years of study at the University of Paris, Francis was the first missionary of the new Society of Jesus. He was ardent, passionate, and full of initiative. At the invitation of John III of Portugal, he left Lisbon on 7 April 1541 to evangelize the Indies. In May 1542, he reached Goa, whence he fanned out in the direction of Malaya, Indonesia, and Ceylon. In 1549, he was in Japan studying the language. He once again left Goa in 1552 to attempt an entrance into China but had to be satisfied with

Crux miraculosa S. Thomæ Apostoli Meliaporæ in India.

27 28

26. *The Church of the Assumption at Kyoto (Namban Dera or foreign temple in the south), depicted on a fan (Kobe, Municipal Art Museum). Here, we find real architectural inculturation, since externally this church resembles other Japanese religious buildings. The figures in the courtyard are Jesuits in the attire they adopted.*

27. *The miraculous cross of the Apostle Thomas in Meliapora, India (Athanasius Kircher, China monumentis . . . illustrata, Amsterdam, 1667). The Jesuit Kircher (1602–1680) (see fig. 26, p. 169) is one of the most distinguished scholars of his time, in the exact sciences as well as in the arts, a fact demonstrated by his curiosity cabinet depicted in Museum Kircherianum (1678). The Apostle Thomas was thought to have come to southern India to evangelize those called "Thomas Christians" and who honor his tomb in Meliapora, on the east coast of India.*

28. *Reprint of an engraving showing Nobili in Hindu dress. In 1623, Pope Gregory XV granted the Italian Jesuit's request for a prudent adaptation of Indian clothing, in particular for the habits of the missionaries. As seen here, Nobili wears a turban, a shawl, a Brahmanic cord, made however with Christian symbols, and finally the Saddhu's copper vase. In his right hand, he holds a long stick mounted with an inscription. Nobili wanted to be allowed to celebrate the liturgy in Sanskrit, and he himself wrote catechetical booklets in Tamul.*

seeing it from afar as he lay dying on the Island of Sancian (San-Tchao), off Canton. His attempt to reach the continent was fruitless. In the fascinating correspondence he exchanged with Ignatius of Loyola, we can feel Francis burning with the desire "to extend the limits of Holy Mother Church" and to work for "the spread of our holy faith." He has been criticized for acting too quickly and multiplying baptisms. He was of the race of pioneers rather than of consolidators, but the many Jesuit missionaries who succeeded him would attempt to plant the faith in civilizations more ancient than Christianity.

Nobili and India

Born in Rome in 1577, the young Roberto de Nobili, having been entrusted to the tutelage of his cousin Cardinal Sforza, obtained his reluctant permission to enter the Society of Jesus in Naples in 1596. In 1603, at his own request, he was sent to India. He arrived in 1605 and would remain there as well as in Ceylon until his death in Madras in 1656.

Installing himself first in the kingdom of Madurai in southeastern India, Nobili wanted to experiment with a new method of evangelization that today would be called inculturation. He sought to become integrated in the population by adopting the clothing and gestures of Hindu penitents (*sannyasis*, those who practiced renunciation). He studied Sanscrit, the sacred

books of Hinduism, and the languages of the country such as Tamil. Nobili's concern to adapt to the civilization which he wished to evangelize by avoiding a religious appearance and following purely local customs aroused much criticism, similar to that which the controversy surrounding the Chinese rites had brought down upon the Jesuits. However, Pope Gregory XV (+1623), following the advice of the Jesuit cardinal, Robert Bellarmine, and being very solicitous for the missions, encouraged the Jesuit practices of "accommodation" in India in a nuanced manner in a bull of 31 January 1623.

It was thus possible to develop a missionary apostolate that varied according to whether they were dealing with the higher caste of the Brahmins or with other castes. The Jesuits' way of life differed according to which caste they were addressing, since they were confronted with the redoubtable problems of the religious and social divisions in India and of the pariahs (untouchables). At the time of Nobili's death, the number of Christians at Madurai was estimated at one hundred thousand. John de Britto (+1693), following in his footsteps, evangelized the lower castes.

In the eighteenth century a quarrel developed in India over the so-called "Rites of Malabar." Under Clement XII in 1734 and 1739, and Benedict XIV in 1744, the papacy resolved the debates with clarity and the Jesuits throughout the world submitted to its decision. This episode shows both the daring

30. The sphere of the Zodiac at the astronomical observatory built by the Jesuits in Beijing. The Jesuits inserted themselves into the Chinese traditional astronomical interests: The first observatory in Beijing was built at the end of the 13th century of our era. In the 19th century, the Jesuits created a meteorological and astronomical observatory in Zikkawei, near Shanghai.

29. In 1579, in Macao, a Portuguese commercial city, Father Michel Ruggeri began to study Mandarin Chinese, the language of the literate. He invented his own method, without any books or interpreters. From top to bottom, the Roman letters of the sound of the ideogram, then the ideogram itself, and finally its graphic representation.

29

30

and the occasional recklessness of the missionary impulse in the seventeenth century, and also the prudence required of the Holy See, lest the customs or rites that the missionaries judged they might safely adopt should give a false idea of the Christian religion. This was precisely the problem with the Chinese rites.

The Controversy over the Chinese Rites

The controversy within the Roman Church regarding missionary methods in the Far East lasted an entire century between 1639 and 1742 with far reaching repercussions in the public opinion of the period. From Pascal to Voltaire, all the Western "intellectuals" took part in the controversy at a time when people had such a keen interest in the middle Empire that it is possible to speak of a "Chinese Europe."[10] Actually, it was a matter of knowing how far adherence to Christianity would permit the integration of the rites and customs of native culture. If, during this same period, Roberto de Nobili seemed to be able to resolve the question more easily in India, this was doubtless due to the fact that in China the approach to the sacred and to philosophical wisdom differed in nature from that of Hinduism.

From the time of the arrival of the first Jesuit missionaries in China, questions arose as to how they should act and even how they should dress. Michele Ruggieri (+1607), and especially Matteo Ricci (1552–1610), perceiving that the Buddhist monks whose appearance they had adopted were despised by the people, decided it would be better to adopt the dress of the "scholarly Confucians." As a matter of fact, the activity of these first Italian Jesuits was crowned with success, especially after Ricci had composed a sort of summary of Christian doctrine in Chinese, *The True Meaning of the Teaching of the Lord of Heaven (Tianzhu Shiyi).*[11] The mathematical and astronomical competence of Jesuits such as Adam Schall (+1666) was greatly

31. Giuseppe Castiglione (Lang-Shi ning, 1688–1766), The Games at Mulan. The Emperor Qianlong (+1795) presides at a wrestling game. Silk painting, around 1752 (Paris, Guimet Museum). This Jesuit artist for the Chinese emperor of the Manchu dynasty, who was also his architect for the Summer Palace near Beijing, blends together two cultures here. This setting for traditional sports is treated with Western techniques, but also with the delicacy of Chinese drawing (see fig. 34, p. 238, and fig. 25, p. 169). Does this purely secular painting explain the reproach made to the Jesuits of the time of forgetting their first mission—to proclaim the Gospel?

32. Confucius and Lao Tsu protecting the child Shakyamuni. Painted scroll, ink and colors on silk, Ming dynasty (London, British Museum). This painting depicts the very popular theme of the interdependence of the three wisdom traditions—Confucianism, Taoism, and Buddhism. The size of the figures reflects a certain hierarchy. Kung Fu Tsu, latinized by the Jesuits into Confucius (555– 479 BC), holds the future Buddha in his arms (556–480 BC), since Buddhism cannot be found in China before the first century of our era, and he shows him to Lao Tsu (circa 4th century BC).

31

32

appreciated by the authorities. Numerous conversions took place at that time within the context of inculturation. The exceptional permission to celebrate the Catholic liturgy in the Chinese of the well-lettered, granted in 1615 and called the privilege of Paul V, was in keeping with this spirit, even though it could not be put into practice and gave rise to much debate.[12]

It was only when missionaries of other religious Orders arrived upon the scene that questions began to be raised. Dominicans and Franciscans who penetrated the Chinese continent after 1630 discovered to their stupefaction and horror that the Jesuits had allowed new converts to continue making their offerings to Confucius and to their ancestors. The newcomers judged these offerings to be superstitious, at least as they saw them being practiced among the simple folk whom they were evangelizing. It is true that the cult of Kung-Fu-Tzu (latinized as Confucius), the great thinker of the fifth century BC, and respect for ancestors had so shaped Chinese thought that the Jesuits believed these rites purely cultural or

"civil" and in no way incompatible with the sincere profession of the transcendent God of the Christians. The other missionaries posed, implicitly, a valid question: Why had the Jesuits favored Confucianism to the neglect of Buddhism and even of Taoism, so present in Chinese religious thought? Another quarrel related to these points of contention arose over the translation of the Word of God into Chinese.[13]

There followed an entire century of conflicting influences being brought to bear on the papacy, interventions on the part of the Emperor of China himself, and misunderstandings. Behind the scenes was a threat, sometimes actualized, of persecution of the Christians. The fall of the Ming dynasty in 1644 and its replacement by that of the Manchurian led to the persecutions of 1665 and 1724, which produced many martyrs for the faith.

Consider how the successive decisions regarding the Chinese rites must have appeared contradictory and damaging to Christianity's credibility. After the intervention of the

33. St. Ignatius Church in Beijing presents the typical characteristics of Jesuit architecture, with its facade both elegant and severe.

34. Castiglione (see fig. 31, p. 237), Scroll of The Hundred Horsemen (Paris, Guimet Museum). Tartar envoys offer their horses to the Emperor Qianlong.

33

34

Dominicans in 1639, Innocent X condemned the Chinese rites in 1645. This decision, however, was nuanced by Alexander VII in 1656 after the Jesuits had presented their version of the facts. Moreover, it was at this time that Pascal, in the fifth letter of his *Provinciales* against the theology of the Jesuits, accused them of "suppressing the scandal of the Cross," "as they had done in the Indies and in China, where they had allowed Christians to commit idolatry." In 1669, after the reconciliation of the missionaries of all Orders following the persecution, Clement XI wisely tried to harmonize the two decisions, asking that the diversity of concrete cases be considered.

The quarrel was revived when the Priests of the Foreign Missions of Paris received responsibility for Chinese Catholics. Monsignor Maigrot, Vicar Apostolic, drew up in 1693 a Mandate that curbed the use of the Chinese rites. It was ratified by a decree of Clement XI in 1704. Furthermore, a pontifical legate in China, Monsignor de Tournon, both clarified the decision and exacerbated the situation in 1707. Now the Jesuits were in very good standing with the Emperor Kang Xi (+1722), whom the philosophers of the Enlightenment admired from afar as "the charming King of China." They loved him because he had granted an edict of tolerance whose significance in Chinese society they did not understand and because he defended Confucius, a model of Reason as opposed to Revelation. After an attempt at conciliation in

1721 (the eight permissions of Monsignor Mezzabarba), and the revival of the problem in 1735, Pope Benedict XIV, of whom we spoke in Chapter 10, condemned the Chinese rites. His bull, *Ex quo singulari,* of 9 August 9 1742, was intended to purify the Christian faith of superstitions. It was definitely too late, however, for by now Christianity was illegal and subject to persecution.

In the twentieth century, the Church recognized the civil and neutral character of the Chinese rites as well as those of Japan,[14] but the quarrel shows how the Church was trapped by the battle against superstitions being waged by the philosophers. Despite the differences in appreciation of the rites as they were truly practiced at the time by the converts of varying social classes in China, the Church of the eighteenth century let slip the opportunity of a true and intelligent "inculturation" in a desire to escape any suspicion of connivance with superstition in its proclamation of faith in Jesus Christ. This closed the "new world" of the Far East to the Church for a long time to come.

Why should such a failure have taken place? In the mid-eighteenth century, the Congregation for the Propagation of the Faith, organized in 1622 and still operating under the guiding hand of its first secretary, Francis Ingoli (+1649), had warned vicars apostolic leaving for Cochin China in 1669 in a celebrated instruction: "Do not be eager to convince these

35

people that they should change their rites, customs, and habits unless they are obviously contrary to religion and morality. What could be more absurd than to transplant France, Spain, Italy, or any other European country into China? There is no more powerful reason for alienation and hatred than to introduce changes in customs that are proper to a nation, especially those that have been practiced for generations."[15]

In all probability the philosophers' criticism of religion and of superstition unsettled Catholic authors of the period, and even the Holy See, far more than the philosophers themselves suspected. The combination of divergent motives resulted in a true paradox. In the name of purity of religion, which was a response to the philosophers, inculturation, upheld by the philosophers for motives other than those of evangelization, became a thing of the past.

Africa

It was the Portuguese who began to penetrate the African continent from the Atlantic in the fifteenth century. Yet for centuries the continent appeared to explorers as inaccesible and remained unknown. This, indeed, is the meaning of the allegory of the Nile with veiled head, placed by Bernini in the fountain of the Piazza Navona in Rome around 1650. At the time, the source of this great river was unknown. And yet, from the fourteenth century on, the image of the Black made its appearance in Western art in depictions of Balthazar, one of the three magi of Matthew's infancy narrative, and of Saint Maurice, who belonged to the Theban legion recruited in the valley of the Nile.

The first missionaries arrived in the kingdom of the Congo in 1482. Less than ten years later the king's son was baptized. Having become king himself under the name of Alfonso I (1506–1543), he was described in 1535 by Paul III as "a good king but also a shepherd of souls" because he encouraged and preached the Christian religion. His own son, Don Henrique, the first bishop of the black race, died in 1531 shortly after his arrival in Rome. In 1624, a bilingual Portuguese/Kikongo catechism was printed.

From the time of the first, coastal colonization until the eighteenth century, relations between Africa and the West were marked by the slave trade, or triangular traffic in "ebony" as it was called. European ship owners exchanged merchandise in Africa for slaves whom they resold in America for prime commodities such as tobacco, sugar, and rum.

Despite the bull *Veritas ipsa* of Paul III in 1537, slavery, and thus this regulated, lucrative commerce in slaves, were justified by theologians such as Molina at the beginning of the seventeenth century. While the theologians did not justify

36. Andrea Mantegna (1431–1506), The Adoration of the Magi *(about1550) (Brentwood, California, Paul Getty Museum). Mantegna is one of the first painters to represent a black king, traditionally called Balthasar, whereas Casper is an Asian type, or at least oriental as shown by his turban. In its iconography as in its liturgy, the feast of Epiphany brings out the universality of salvation offered in Christ.*

36

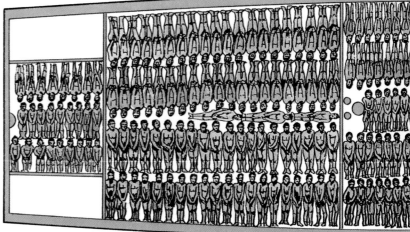

37

37. Theodore (1528–1598) and Jean (1561–1623) de Bry, The Portuguese Show Homage to the King of the Congo *(from the Latin edition of* The Narrative of the Kingdom of the Congo, *1598, F. Pifagetta and D. Lopez). The Congolese King is represented as a European monarch, with scepter and crown. While the foreigners stand up, the indigenous people prostrate themselves. In the background, a friendly intermingling is sketched out. This edition, illustrated by the Flemish engravers, is a Latin translation of an Italian account of the Portuguese merchant Duarte Lopez' odyssey. Lopez was sent by the Mani Kongo (the King of the Congo) to be his representative to the pope.*

slavery *per se,* they admitted of so many exceptions that consciences were put at ease. At the end of the seventeenth century, as this human commerce grew more extensive, the Church's condemnations became more solemn. We can see this in the instruction of the Holy Office of 20 May 1686. As often happens, some saw the point more clearly, sooner, and more effectively. This was true of Alphonsus of Sandoval, who published his book on the proclamation of salvation to the Blacks in 1627,[16] Peter Claver (+1654), and of his successor at Carthagena, the warehouse port for slaves in what is now Columbia. Born in Catalonia, Claver made profession as a Jesuit in 1622, signing himself "forever the slave of the Blacks." A catechist who taught in the Angolan which he had studied, a physician, and a priest, he gave himself to the service of these transplanted and exploited peoples.

In the nineteenth century the interior of the continent of Africa was definitively penetrated. A first stage was that of the mystical thrust that had ripened in the sufferings, exiles, and traumas born of the French Revolution and its consequences. Missions in Africa and elsewhere became places of reparation, substitutes for apostolates that could not be undertaken in one's native land. The Catholic countries of Europe, particularly France, which had been affected by anti-religious measures,

38. The placement of the Negro slaves in a slave ship, drawing from an 18th-century engraving (Paris, Museum of the Arts of Africa and Oceania). The ship is designed to carry the greatest possible number of slaves. This arrangement was intended to make any kind of revolt of the slaves physically impossible.

39. First published portrait of Saint Peter Claver (17th-century woodcut). Out of his mouth comes forth this prayer in Spanish: "Lord, I love you very much."

40. François Libermann, drawing from a portrait. A convert from Judaism who became a missionary, he concentrated on the formation of catechists in Africa. In 1843, he made an agreement with the French Navy and the Senegal Colonial authorities for transportation and material support of the missionaries who were sent to open schools.

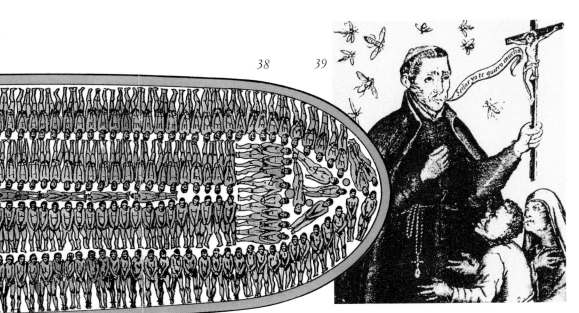

were the most generous in sending out missionaries at the time of the monarchical restorations. Their spirit of abnegation was remarkable and absolute.

It was in this spirit that men's and women's missionary congregations were founded. These would come to play a very important role. In 1847, Monsignor Truffet, vicar of the Two Guineas, wrote to Rome: "The apostle's first duty . . . is the abnegation of his entire being, which leads him to descend to the level of his neophytes and to identify himself humanly with them, so as to identify them spiritually with himself. This reciprocal assimilation is the means for coming to know, to unite, and to make fertile the religious and social elements which God has deposited wherever He has created those who are his children and images, regardless of differences in skin color."[17] This "reciprocal assimilation" which Monsignor Truffet goes so far as to compare to the Eucharistic mystery, was the final goal of missionaries to Africa who so generously made the choice of sacrifice.

Long before the fusion of the Congregation of the Holy Ghost Fathers with that of the Holy Heart of Mary, Jacob Libermann (+1852) had recommended both the formation of an indigenous clergy and the dependency that missions ought to have in relation to the initiatives of the Holy See. For missionaries, this was the guarantee of being "more fervent, more zealous, and more detached from this world and from ourselves." The ultramontanism of the nineteenth century was one of the most important elements of this period. Foreseeing and fearing the problem of colonial nationalities that would arise a little later, it was essential that the missionaries be independent.

Presenting his project to Rome for "the conversion of the Blacks" (the word he used was "Negro race," *nigrizia*), in 1864, Daniel Comboni (+1881) proposed this formula promising a beautiful future: "Could not the conversion of Africa be promoted by Africa . . . there where the African lives and has his home, there where the European works and survives?" In 1878, ten years after having founded the White Fathers and then the White Sisters, Monsignor Charles Lavigerie (+1892), archbishop of Algiers, wrote a confidential memorandum to the Sacred Congregation for the Propagation of the Faith. His terms were explicit: "To transform Africa," that is, to render it Christian, "overall education of our young Negroes (future leaders or catechists) should be African, essentially African. On the contrary, their religious education should be essentially apostolic."[18] In contrast with the "philanthropic civilizers" of his time, Lavigerie clarified the measures that

41 and 42. African religious objects. (41) A wooden dish for the kola nut (Igbo, Nigeria). The Igbos give great symbolic importance to the kola nut. In their myths, it has always been one of the primordial offerings that their people brought to the goddess Chukwu through the ages. The kola nut makes communion with the gods possible and enhances social communication among humans. It is consumed during hospitality rites as a purification act. (42) An anthropomorphic wooden cup (Horo, Nigeria). The Koros sculpt cups for palm wine, used during sacrifices and the second funeral rites that celebrate the arrival of the deceased in the hereafter. The container represents the womb of the feminine figure.

ought to be taken to avoid the "acculturation" (to be understood here as the opposite of inculturation), in regard to dress, language, and mentality, that is so detrimental to human and Christian identity.

The second phase of penetration into the African continent extended up to World War II. It began almost simultaneously with the martyrdom of the neophytes of Uganda, which took place during the persecutions between 1885 and 1887. These martyrs, both men and women differing in ages and functions under the leadership of Charles Lwanga, underwent very cruel executions. There were more than a hundred victims: Catholics, Protestants, and Anglicans. The executions took place at the very time of the Berlin Conference (1884–1885), which was dividing the continent among the different European countries according to zones of influence, and actually accelerating the process of the division of Africa already at work. This missionary period coincided with the height of colonial imperialism

The problem of the link between missionary expansion and colonization has often been broached. Without denying their reciprocal dependency, we have to admit that faced with the governmental anti-clericalism of the late nineteenth century, even in its watered down version overseas, missionaries sought to preserve their independence. This led them to develop a kind of Christian private law that sought to distance itself from the common law upheld by the colonials. Yet the missionary congregations' works of instruction and education were supported by the national administrations. It was no accident that in 1919 Pope Benedict XV, in his encyclical *Maximum illud,* and again in the following year in his instruction *Quo efficacius,* recommended to the missionaries that all nationalism and intervention of a political nature should be avoided. He wrote: "The apostolic missionary should not admit of any other intention nor propose to himself any other goal than the conversion of men to God and the salvation of souls."

Actually, after the First World War the picture had changed with the discovery in Africa of a Christian pluralism that led to a certain tolerance. The Protestant missions were often older than those of the Catholics. Many of them had been financed and developed by the Missionary Society of London, founded in 1795 and functioning on an interconfessional basis. The key figure representing these Protestant missions was David Livingstone (+1873), explorer, physician, and missionary all in one.

The universalist and mystical aspect of the missionary enterprise also deepened and was rendered tangible when Pius XI proclaimed Saint Thérèse of the Child Jesus patroness of the missions in 1929. But tensions continued as can be seen

43. *The Arabs visit Kwihara, Unyanyembe where Stanley discovers Livingstone; a vignette in Stanley's memoirs:* How I found Livingstone *(London, 1872). The famous reunion of the two British explorers at Ujiji, near Lake Tanganyka in the heart of Africa, on November 10, 1871, when Stanley was sent to rescue Livingstone who was trying to discover the source of the Nile, has become legendary. Stanley makes clear the rivalries and difficulties of the explorers and of the African mission in the 19th century.*

44. *English officers attending a catechism lesson in a Protestant mission parish in Africa, lithograph, 1880.*

42

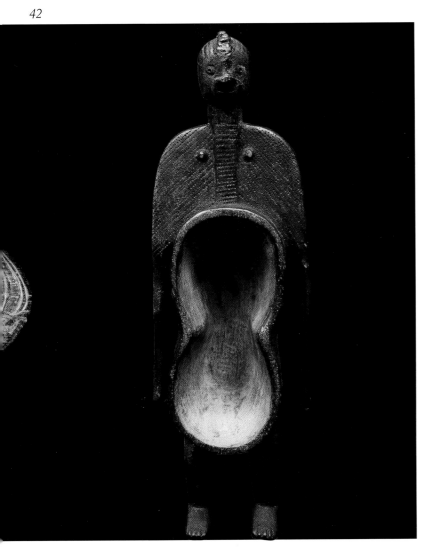

44

in the Belgian Congo. In opposition to Monsignor Jean de Hemptinne, a personal friend of King Albert of Belgium, Vicar Apostolic to Katanga from 1932 to 1958, and defender of "Christian civilization," there rose up the Flemish Franciscan, Placide Tempels, author of the controversial work, "The Bantu philosophy," and also the "prophet" Simon Kimbangu, founder of a new religion in which the Christian elements were strongly Africanized.

Although prior to 1945 the missionaries had been fully aware that they had come first to evangelize before civilizing, the question of an in-depth Africanization of the Churches on the continent now surfaced. This would be the point of debate of the third stage of penetration into the continent following the Second World War and contemporaneous with decolonization. Missionary models were modified and the "young Churches" began to take shape. At times, however, the changes were made in the context of veritable tragedies, such as the civil war that devastated the Congo, and for which the white missionaries were blamed. It was not yet the moment for a nuanced judgment of the colonial period. Admittedly, it was not a disinterested enterprise, but in its paternalistic aspects it nevertheless revealed the Africans to themselves.

Another note was struck at Vatican II where ten percent of the Council Fathers represented Africa. At Vatican I there had been none to speak of, nor had there been time to discuss the schema on the missions. By contrast, the decree *Ad Gentes* on the Church's missionary activity was carefully elaborated at Vatican II. It did not make specific reference to the various regions of the world where missions were in place but stated very clearly the foundations of "inculturation" (n. 22) "The young Churches, rooted in Christ and built up on the foundation of the apostles, take to themselves in a wonderful exchange all the riches of the nations which were given to Christ as an inheritance (cf. Ps. 2:8). From the customs and traditions of their people, from their wisdom and their learning, from their arts and sciences, these Churches borrow all those things which can contribute to the glory of their Creator, the revelation of the Savior's grace, or the proper arrangement of Christian life. If this goal is to be achieved, theological investigation must necessarily be stirred up in each major socio-cultural area, as it is called. In this way, under the light of the tradition of the universal Church, a fresh scrutiny will be brought to bear on the deeds and words which God has made known, which have been consigned to sacred Scripture, and which have been unfolded by the Church Fathers and the teaching authority of the Church . . . Thanks to such a procedure, every appearance of syncretism and of false particularism can be excluded, and Christian life can be

45. Upper end of a ceremonial baton, wood (Senufo, Ivory Coast). It represents Katieleo, the "village mother." Even though the creator god Kulotiolo remains inaccessible, Katieleo maintains relations with humans by regenerating their world.

46

46. On a pastoral trip in Africa at the beginning of September 1990, John Paul II, in Burundi (at Bujumbura in the photo here) and in Rwanda, exhorted these countries, in great majority Catholic, to reconcile after the bloody ethnic massacres that took place among them. The Rwanda genocide between April and July, 1994, cruelly proved him wrong.

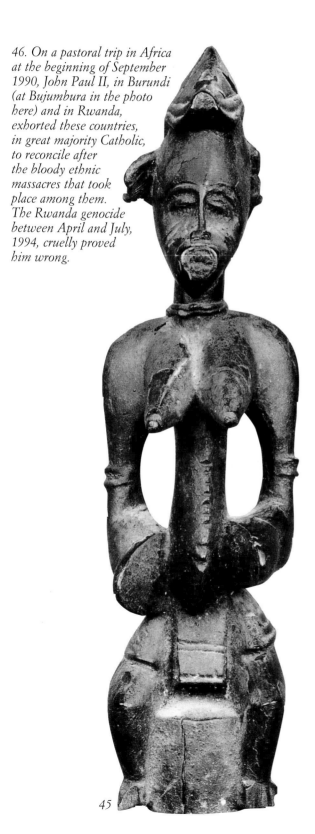

45

accommodated to the genius and dispositions of each culture." This last sentence is a reference to the allocution given by Pope Paul VI in 1964 for the canonization of the martyrs of Uganda who had been beatified by Benedict XV in 1920. It seemed as if their protection was accompanying the great moments of ecclesial life in Africa.

The Pope would in fact deepen this intuition, first by his message to Africa of 31 October 1967. In it he gave a nuanced appraisal of the missions during past centuries and enumerated the difficulties of the present moment. He then visited Uganda from 31 July to 2 August 1969, and there affirmed that communion with the Holy See not only did not suppress the African character but actually promoted it. He also proclaimed that "Africans are now their own missionaries." This was also the language of John Paul II in the course of his pastoral visits to Africa.

On 13 August 1985, addressing the intellectuals of Yaounde in Cameroon, the Pope made explicit the bond between Christian faith and culture: "Any rupture between the Gospel and culture would be a tragedy. The positive elements, the spiritual values of the African people should be integrated, ever more integrated. Christ came to fulfill. An untiring work of inculturation therefore remains to be done." John Paul II called this the second evangelization of Africa and charged the Africans themselves with carrying it out. This is the very same program he had been proposing to Europe since 1979.

Europe

The situation of Europe in the twentieth century is still more complex, for Europe was the cradle of Christianity. Space

47

48

49

does not permit me to assess, even historically, factors that have contributed to the divorce between contemporary attitudes and the Church or even Christianity in general. We have seen certain elements of it appear in Chapters 10 to 12. It is certain that in the nineteenth century the Church saw itself in an awkward position vis-à-vis the errors of the modern age, as is seen with the *Syllabus,* source of so much misunderstanding. Perhaps because he had had the experience of unbelief, Lacordaire was one of the few Catholics to sense the generosity and the grandeur of certain values of his time.

By way of example, we could recall in Western Europe an attempt that was unsuccessful in France at the time, but which now pursues its patient course of inculturation—the experiment of the priests who shared the workers' conditions.

Stemming from the profound changes engendered by the French Revolution and the industrial revolution, the effects of de-Christianization were felt in different Western countries and particularly in France. From the end of the nineteenth century, the phenomenon became incontestable among the working classes. This was a deep concern of Pius XI and of the Belgian priest Cardijn who founded Catholic Action there. Its goal of evangelization, shared by many other pastors, was "to make our brothers Christian once more."

This was true of Cardinal Emmanuel Suhard (+1949), who was named archbishop of Paris in 1940, the year of the French defeat. In the following year he obtained the foundation of "the Mission of France," located at Lisieux under the patronage of Saint Thérèse of the Child Jesus to form priests for the most de-Christianized dioceses and areas. In 1943, Henri Godin and Yvan Daniel, chaplains of the "JOC" (Young Christian Workers), published a small book that sounded a cry of alarm: *France, a Mission Country?* Basing themselves

47. Pascal Dagnan-Bouveret (1852–1929), Nuptial Blessing, 1880–1881 (Moscow, Pushkin Museum). This realist painter shows how the major events of human life were marked by the Church's rites and religious beliefs.

48. Attilio Pusterla (1862–1941), The Soup Kitchen of Porta Nuova, 1887 (Milan, Modern Art Gallery). In the 19th century, all the European countries had to face the problem of poverty and, with private initiatives, to try to ease the day to day difficulties of the poor.

49. Reprint of a photograph of Cardinal Suhard (1874–1949), Archbishop of Reims from 1928 to 1940 and then of Paris at the time of the French defeat. Emmanuel Suhard addressed the phenomenon of de-Chritianization first in rural and then later in urban contexts. Deeply concerned, he encouraged apostolic action among the working classes.

on the findings of sociology, the authors asserted that the only way to mitigate the terrible "uprooting" which was "the principal cause of the de-Christianization of the proletariat" was to establish base communities in the workers' milieu. Then in January 1944, Cardinal Suhard set up "the Mission of Paris," from which the first worker-priests came. A similar experiment was occuring simultaneously in Germany where the Nazi government had refused to allow chaplains to minister to young people leaving for compulsory labor. So some priests joined their number. The Jesuit Henri Perrin recounted this experience in 1945.[19]

At this time, French priests decided to work in factories and to embark on a long term evangelization by their presence and their sharing of the workers' life. One of the first of these was Henri Barreau, who took part in the very difficult strikes carried on in the climate of social confrontation in the years following the Liberation of France. Many worker-priests joined trade unions, even the one which was the organ of the Communist party in France, still basking in prestige for its participation in the Resistance and the powerful influence wielded by the Soviet Union in Eastern Europe.

It is indeed in this climate of the "cold war" between the North Atlantic Treaty Alliance (NATO) and the Warsaw Pact set up immediately after World War II that we should situate the problem that was to arise between the French worker-priests and Roman authorities. The lifestyle of the worker-priests and their involvement in trade unions and politics were absolutely unheard of and posed new questions as to priestly identity, the model for which had been provided by the Catholic renewal stemming from the Council of Trent, in a far different world.

Pius XII was concerned about the attraction Marxism might have for these priests. Their speeches, without doubt full of generosity, appeared to be something of a diminishment of the Church's message. Beginning in 1953, initial measures were taken to slow down the experiment and on 23 September the Nuncio in Paris, Monsignor Paolo Marella, announced that priests were forbidden to work in factories.

Catholic intellectuals rebelled. The French cardinals went to Rome to explain the situation to the Pope. On 1 March 1954, Rome stood fast to its decision. Some of the French worker-priests, perhaps sixty percent, disobeyed and continued to work. Public opinion, it seemed, could not understand the reaction of ecclesiastical authorities.

Beginning in August 1954, the seminary of "the Mission of France" was reopened, but salaried work, limited to a few hours a day, was subject to certain conditions, one of which was the assignment of these priests to a parish. Progressively,

50. *An assembly line in Detroit (photo from Robert Frank, born in 1924,* The Americans, *1958). A photograph symbolic of the "capitalistic" practice of "Fordism," a system for maximizing profit through mass production, which was later adopted by European countries.*

51. *Workers, men and women, protesting in front of a factory in the 1950s and '60s (drawing by Giorgio Baldanzi). The European unions, unlike the American ones, succeeded in creating solidarity among the workers. This ideal inspired some priests to share the workers' experience.*

51

52 and 53. Ignored or unknown during Charles de Foucauld's lifetime (1858–1916), his spirituality blossomed into several foundations that unite humble work and contemplative prayer. (52) The Fraternity of The Little Sisters of Jesus, workers in Korea. (53) Pope Paul VI's visit in Tre Fontane, a suburb of Rome in September 1973. From left to right, Little Sister Magdeleine Elisabeth Hutin (1898–1989), foundress of the Little Sisters in 1939, Dom Domenico, abbot of the Trappist monastery in Rome and motherhouse of the Trappist Order, Paul VI, and Father Voillaume (1905–2003), founder of the Little Brothers of Jesus in 1953.

52

53

despite reminders in 1959 that the discipline was still in force, things quieted down. After John XXIII's encyclical *Mater et magistra* (1961) and Vatican Council II, together with political changes occurring throughout the world, the existence of worker-priests no longer caused a problem, but the requirements of prudence were maintained.

I have only wished to give a single example, among others which affected different countries, of one of the demands of the Church's confrontation with the contemporary world in Europe and elsewhere. The fact remains, however, that European society, becoming less and less agricultural, has also become less and less industrial. To what milieu should the Church address itself as a priority? To technicians, to scientists, to those working in the field of communications?

As we bring this panorama to a close, a question arises inevitably in the mind of the historian, even though he makes no pretense of predicting the future: What will the challenge of the next century be? I have said in the course of this book, which does not claim to be exhaustive—I need hardly repeat it—that save for a few exceptions, the challenges encountered by the Church throughout its history do not seem to disappear, but rather to surface in other forms. This is why they are open to a certain typology. But we can guess what these future challenges will be. The challenge of inculturation, of which "liberation theology" is perhaps a form, is far from having been

57. Historical reconciliation with Orthodox Churches was one of John Paul II's priorities. Despite difficulties and rivalries, he tried to establish or maintain contacts with the Patriarchs. Here, On June 27, 1995, at the Vatican, he meets the Patriarch of Constantinople, Bartolomew I, to pursue the dialogue inaugurated by their two predecessors, Paul VI and Athenagoras (see fig. 51 p. 214).

54. Marc Chagall (1889–1985), The Creation of Man, *one of the pastels preparatory to the large canvas of the same name (1954–1967) (Nice, Marc Chagall Museum, The Biblical Message). This Jewish artist, a Russian emigrant, recreated in his work a spiritual world inspired by the Bible, by Hasidism, and by Russian fairy tales. In a synthetic religious vision, the artist shows in this representation of Genesis a pre-figuring both of the Ten Commandments and of Christ's death on the Cross.*

54

55

56

55. Mural in a Mexican-American neighborhood in San Diego, California. The popular Mexican mural tradition (see fig. 16, p. 200) affirms the Latino identity of the immigrants. This mural by an anonymous artist shows Aztec symbols as well as the Virgin of Guadalupe (see fig. 18, p. 231).

56. Berlin, Demolition of the wall (Giovanni Chiaramonte photo). Built in order to prevent escape to the West and in itself a symptom of the weakness of the Communist regime, the Berlin Wall was a tangible sign of European ideological divisions. Its demolition, begun on November 9, 1989, was perceived by everyone as an historical moment and the beginning of a new era of freedom in Europe.

57

successfully met. It is in part connected with the problem of development and of the gap between, if not North and South, at least between the richest and the poorest. The challenge of Europe once again comes to the fore with the almost complete thaw of the Marxist iceberg, symbolized by the events of 1989 and echoed again in John Paul II's *Centesimus annus.* Finally, like a gaping hole for so many centuries, the challenge of Christian unity or ecumenism has yet to be met and demands from all sides at least a reciprocal knowledge.

NOTES

ABBREVIATIONS

CCSL   Corpus Christianorum Series Latina
CSEL   Corpus Scriptorum Ecclesiasticorum Latinorum
PL   Patrologia Latina

CHAPTER 1

1   Salomon Wittmayer Baron, *A Social and Religious History of the Jews,* New York: Columbia University Press, 1952.

2   On this important subject that exceeds the scope of this book, see Jean Miguel Garrigues (and others), *L'Unique Israël de Dieu,* Paris: Criterion, 1987.

3   Erik Peterson, *Die Kirche aus Juden und Heiden,* Salzburg: A. Pustet, 1933.

4   Irenaeus, *Adversus Haereses* IV, 21, P. 7, col. 1043–1046; Cyprian, *Testimonia ad Quirinum,* Bk 19, CCSL 3, 19; Tertullian, *Adversus Judaeos* I, CCSL 1, 1339–1341.

5   For an analysis of the Acts of the Apostles and of the Lucan attitude toward preaching to the pagans, see Bruno Wildhaber, *Paganisme populaire et prédication apostolique, d'après l'exégèse de quelques séquences des Acts.* Geneva: Labor et Fides, 1987.

6   Franz Cumont, *The Oriental Religions in Roman Paganism,* Chicago: The Open Court Publishing Company, 1911.

7   "Du christianisme," a Memorial of André-Jean Festugière, *Cahiers d'orientalisme* X, Geneva, 1984, 275–281.

8   Robin Lane Fox, *Pagans and Christians in the Mediterranean World from the Second Century* AD *to the Conversion of Constantine,* London: Penguin, 1988, 23.

9   The German novelist Alfred Döblin, in a book written in 1949 after his conversion, has described this conflict magnificently in fictional form, drawing freely on the authentic personage Etheria, who at the end of the 4th century left an account of her pilgrimage to Jerusalem: *Die Pilgerin Aetheria,* Olten: Walter, 1978.

10   *Histoire des religions,* vol. 2 (Encyclopédie de la Pléiade, 34), Paris: Gallimard, 1972, 77–78. Michel Meslin, "Réalités psychiques et valeurs religieuses dans les cultes orientaux," *Revue historique,* 512, octobre-décembre 1974, especially 308–314, rather stresses the coexistence and rivalry of these cults with Christianity.

11   Jerome Murphy-O'Connor, *St. Paul's Corinth: Texts and Archeology,* Wilmington, Delaware: Michael Glazier, 1983. On these subjects, the classic book remains André-J. Festugière, *Personal Religion among the Greeks,* Berkeley: University of California Press, 1960. See also the last chapters of his little collection, *L'enfant d'Agrigente,* Paris: Iles d'Or, 1950.

12   Daniel Bourgeois, *La sagesse des Anciens dans le mystère du Verbe. Evangile et philosophie chez Saint Justin, philosophe et martyr,* Paris: Pierre Tégui, 1981.

13   Endre von Ivanka, *Plato christianus.* Uebernahme und Umgestaltung des Péatonismusdurch die Väter, Einsiedeln: Johannes Verlag, 1964.

14   Jean-Michel Poffet, *La méthode exégétique d'Héracléon et d'Origène, commentateurs de Jean 4; Jésus, la Samaritaine et les Samaritains,* Fribourg: Éditions Universitaires, 1985.

15   Robin Lane Fox, *Pagans and Christians, op. cit.,* 202 ff; 647–651; 681. It was the apologist Lactantius (+ c. 325) who made use of the Sybiline oracles. See also A. de Waal, *Ara Coeli oder die Sibylle des Augustinus,* 1902.

16   *Orpheus. The Metamorphoses of a Myth,* ed. by John Warden, Toronto: University of Toronto Press, 1982. Christ was pictured beside Orpheus in the domestic oratory of the emperor Alexander Severus (+235).

17   During the reign of Tiberias, the sailor Thamos, off Paxos in the Ionian Sea, heard a cry: "Great Pan is dead!" This incarnation of the universe had been conquered. This is how Plutarch reports it (+125), (*On the Cessation of Oracles,* 17).

18   For a detailed description of this life, cf. Roland Minnerath, *Les chrétiens et le monde (1er et IIe siècles),* Paris: J. Gabalda, 1973.

19   *Apologeticum,* 50, 13, CCSL, 1, 171.

20   Jacques Moreau, *La persécution du christianisme dans l'Empire romain,* Paris: Presses Universitaires de France, 1956 and William Hugh Clifford Frend, *Martyrdom and Persecution in the Early Church. A Study of a Conflict from the Maccabees to Donatus,* Oxford: Blackwell, 1965.

21   *Letter of Ignatius to the Ephesians,* 11.

22   Philippians 1:1.

23   *First Epistle of St. Clement* 60, 4–61,1.

24   Henri-Irénée Marrou, "Autour du monogramme constantinien," *Mélanges Gilson,* Paris, 1959, 403–414.

25   "Ahi! Constantin! di quante mal fu matre/Non la tua conversion ma quella dote/Che da te prese il prima ricco Patre!" See also *Purgatory* 32, 136–139 and *Paradise* 20, 55–60; *De Monarchia,* III, 10.

26   It may be useful to recall briefly the chronological listing of the "seven ecumenical councils":

     1. Nicea I in 325, condemnation of Arianism

     2. Constantinople I in 381, continuation of Arianism

     3. Ephesus in 431, against the Nestorian heresy

     4. Chalcedon in 541 against the monophysite heresy (only one nature—divine—in Christ)

5. Constantinople II in 553, continuation of monophysism

6. Constantinople III in 680 against the monothelite heresy (only one will in Christ)

7. Nicea II in 787, on images

Among many excellent texts, see Volume II of *History of the Church* of Hubert Jedin and John Dolan: *The Imperial Church from Constantine to the Early Middle Ages,* New York: Seabury Press, 1980; and the remarkable synthesis of the historian/theologian Jaroslav Pelikan, *The Christian Tradition* 1, *The Emergence of the Catholic Tradition (100–600),* Chicago: University of Chicago Press, 1971. See also Aloïs Grillmeier, *Christ in Christian Tradition,* London: Mowbray, 1975 (translated from the German: Jesus der Christus im Glauben der Kirche).

[27] Henry Chadwick, "The Origin of the Title 'Oecumenical Council'," *Journal of Theological Studies,* n.s., 23 (1972), 132–135.

[28] A convenient edition of texts in Greek, Latin, and English can be found in Volume I of *Decrees of the Ecumenical Councils,* Norman P. Tanner (ed.), London: Sheed & Ward; Washington D.C.: Georgetown University Press, 1990.

[29] Pierre-Th. Camelot, *Les conciles oecuméniques,* Paris: Desclée 1988, 27.

[30] Capreolus of Carthage, Epistle 1, PL 53, col. 845.

[31] Klaus Schatz, "Oecuménicité du concile et structure de l'Eglise à Nicée II et dans les *Livres Carolins*" in *Nicée II, 787–1987,* ed. by F. Boesphlug and N. Lossky, Paris: Éditions du Cerf, 1987, 263–270. The case of the Council of Constantinople IV (869-870) is not included here. It took place during the dispute between Rome and the Patriarch Photius and was included as "ecumenical" in Western medieval listings but was obviously not considered as such by the Orthodox Churches. We should note that Pope Paul VI substituted the more exact term "general" councils (of the Roman Church) for "ecumenical," in referring to the Councils following the seven (or eight) which were held in the East.

[32] *Commonitorium* 2, 3; CCSL 64, 149.

[33] *Lex orandi* (or *supplicandi*), *lex credendi*: "that which is uniformly celebrated throughout the world and in every Church," according to the formula of Prosper of Aquitaine, *Auctoritates* 8, PL 51, 209.

[34] Hans Urs von Balthasar, *In the Fullness of Faith, On the Centrality of the Distinctively Catholic,* San Francisco: Ignatius Press, 1988, 102–105.

[35] *Letter V, 44 to John of Constantinople,* CCSL 140, 332.

CHAPTER 2

[1] Letter 127 to Principia, 12, CSEL 56, 154.

[2] Foreword to the Commentary on Ezechiel, CCSL 75, 3.

[3] Letter 128 to Pacatula, 5, CSEL 56, 161.

[4] *Adversus Paganos,* VII, 41, CSEL, 5, 552–55.

[5] Sermon 105, 9, PL 38, 623–24.

[6] Sermon 81, PL 38, 505.

[7] The Christian poet Prudentius (+415) is a good example of the disgust aroused by the figure of the barbarian. "There is as great a distance between a Roman and a barbarian as between a quadruped and a biped, or between a man who can speak and one who is dumb" (*Contra Symmachum,* II, 816–817).

[8] Jaroslav Pelikan, *The Excellent Empire. The Fall of Rome and the Triumph of the Church,* San Francisco: Harper and Row, 1987.

[9] *Historia Francorum,* PL 71, 276c.

[10] Claude Dagens, *Saint Grégoire le Grand. Culture et expérience chrétiennes,* Paris: Etudes augustiniennes, 1977.

[11] Letter 1, 30, CCSL 140, 37.

[12] *Historia ecclesiastica Gentis Anglorum,* 1, 22 (and 1,4), PL 95, 52 (and 30).

[13] *Ibid.* 1, 30, PL 95, 70–71.

CHAPTER 3

[1] Text in E. Caspar, "Gregor II und der Bilderstreit," *Zeitschrift für Kirchengeschichte,* 52 (1933), 84–89.

[2] Jean Batany, "Des 'trois fonctions' aux 'trois états'?," *Annales,* 18 (1963), 933–938.

[3] *Carmen ad Robertum Regem,* Adalbéron de Laon, "Les Poèmes satiriques d'Adalbéron," G. A. Hückel (ed., trans.), in *Mélanges d'Histoire du Moyen Âge,* Achille Luchaire (dir.), Paris: Alcan (Université de Paris. Bibliothèque de la Faculté des Lettres, n° 13), 1901, p. 155–156. Cf. Claude Carozzi, "Les fondements de la tripartition sociale chez Adalbéron de Laon," *Annales,* 33 (1978), 683–702.

[4] *Mythe et Epopée,* 3 vol., Paris: Gallimard, 1968–73. For Georges Duby this schema is less a real division of society than an ideal and a means of analysis: Georges Duby, *The Three Orders: Feudal Society Imagined,* Chicago: University of Chicago Press, 1980.

[5] See note 11 in this same chapter, on Political Augustinianism.

[6] *Coronations: Medieval and Early Modern Monarchic Ritual,* János M. Bak (ed.), Berkeley: University of California Press, 1990.

[7] PL 104, 126.

[8] Alain Boureau, *The Myth of Pope Joan,* Chicago: University of Chicago Press, 2001.

[9] *Recueil des Chartes de Cluny,* A. Bruel (ed.), Paris: Imprimerie Nationale, 1876, l, 124.

[10] *Monumenta Germaniae Historica. Constitutiones Imperatorum,* I, Hanover, 1892, 159–161.

[11] Etienne Gilson, *Les métamorphoses de la Cité de Dieu,* Louvain/Paris: Publications Universitaires de Louvain, 1952, and Henri Xavier Arquilliere, *L'augustinisme politique,* Paris: J. Vrin, 1934.

[12] Yves Christe, *Les grands portails romans,* Geneva: Droz, 1969. [13] Hughes Delautre, "*Per visibilia ad invisibilia.* Solstices à Vézelay," *Zodiaque,* No. 122, October 1979. See also J. Cobreros Aguirre, "San Juan de Ortega ou le miracle de la lumière d'équinoxe," *Zodiaque,* No. 142, October 1984. [14] Marie-Madeleine Davy, *Initiation à la symbolique romane (XIIe siècle),* Paris: Flammarion, 1977, 51–52.

CHAPTER 4

[1] Léopold Genicot, *Les lignes de faîte du Moyen Age,* Paris: Casterman, 1968.

[2] Marcel Reinhard, André Armengaud, Jacques Depaquier, *Histoire générale de la population mondiale,* Paris: Montchrestien, 1968, p. 88. Cf. also Génicot, op. cit., p. 52.

[3] *De consideratione* IV, 3, PL 182, 776.

[4] Maurice Denis, *Histoire de l'art religieux,* Paris: Flammarion, 1939, p. 64.

[5] Jacques Heers, *La ville au Moyen Age en Occident. Paysages, pouvoirs et conflits,* Paris: Fayard, 1990.

[6] *Histoire de l'art. L'art médiéval,* Paris 1964, p. 278.

[7] Georges de Lagarde, *La naissance de l'esprit laique au déclin du Moyen Age,* vol. 5, Louvain/Paris: E. Nauwelaerts, 1956–1970.

[8] *The King's Two Bodies. A Study in Medieval Political Theology,* Princeton: Princeton University Press, 1957 (especially ch. 5) See also Ralph Giesey, *The Royal Funeral Ceremony in Renaissance France,* Geneve: E. Droz, 1969

[9] William of Ockham, *Dialogus,* I, VI, ch. 100.

[10] Philip Ziegler, *The Black Death,* London: Collins, 1969.

[11] On *The Imitation of Christ* and its possible Franciscan antecedents, see Jaroslav Pelikan, *Jesus through the Centuries. His Place in the History of Culture,* New Haven, Connecticut: Yale University Press, 1985 (ch. 11: The Divine and Human Model).

[12] Charles Journet, *Saint Nicolas de Flue,* Neuchâtel: Éditions de la Baconnière, 1947.

CHAPTER 5

[1] Carlo Ginzburg, T*he Enigma of Piero: Piero della Francesca: the Baptism, the Arezzo Cycle, the Flagellation,* translated by M.Ryle and K. Soper, London: Verso, 1985 (original Italian, Torino, 1981).

[2] Michael Baxendall, *Painting and Experience in Fourteenth-Century Italy,* Oxford: Oxford University Press, 1972. Cf. also *Patronage, Art and Society in Renaissance Italy,* F. W. Kent and P. Simons (ed.), Oxford: Oxford University Press, 1987.

[3] Lucien Febvre and Henri-Jean Martin, *L'apparition du livre,* Paris: Michel, 1958/1971.[2]

[4] See the works of Pierre Chaunu, particularly *Le temps des Réformes,* Paris: Fayard, 1975.

[5] *Sacrorum conciliorum, nova et amplissima collectio,* I.D. Mansi, (ed.) XXXII, 912–913.

[6] *Uomo del Rinascimento,* E. Garin (ed.), Rome: Laterza, 1988.

[7] The celebrated model of the "Velata" in the Palatine Gallery in Florence can indeed be found again in the same museum as "The Madonna of the Chair," and as the Sistine Madonna (Dresden, Gemäldegalerie). These paintings are almost contemporary.

[8] See the works of Bruno Nardi, *Saggi sull'aristotelismo padovano del secolo XIV al XVI,* Florence: G. C. Sansoni, 1958, and *Studi su Pietro Pomponazzi,* Florence: F. Le Monnier, 1965.

[9] See Ludwig von Pastor, *Geschichte der Päpste seit dem Ausgang des Mittelalters, 1886–1933,* St. Louis, Missouri: Herder, 1886–1933, translated into various languages: *The History of the Popes from the Close of the Middle Ages, Drawn from the Secret Archives of the Vatican and Other Original Sources.* London: K. Paul, Trench, Trübner & Co., 1891–1953.

[10] Donald Weinstein, *Savonarola and Florence. Prophecy and Patriotism in the Renaissance,* Princeton, New Jersey: Princeton University Press, 1970.

[11] Charles Journet, preface to *En Prison–dernière méditation de Savonarole,* Fribourg 1943, reedited.

[12] Ronald Lightbown, *Sandro Botticelli,* Berkeley and Los Angeles: University of California Press, 1978.

[13] Marcel Bataillon, "De Savonarole à Louis de Grenade," *Revue de littérature comparée,* 16 (1936), 23–39.

[14] Henri de Lubac, *Pic de la Mirandole,* Paris: Aubier Montaigne, 1974.

[15] This is the title of the first volume of Henri Bremond, *Histoire littéraire du sentiment religieux,* Paris: Bloud et Gay 1924. On the humanist paradox see my chapter on it in Pierre Chaunu, *L'Aventure de la Réforme,* Paris: Hermé: Desclée de Brouwer, c. 1986.

CHAPTER 6

[1] Lucien Febvre already sensed this when he said: "Pre-Reform, Reform, Counter-Reform; I, for my part, should say: Renewal, Revolutions, Revisions."

[2] *Sacrorum conciliorum, nova et amplissima collectio,* I. D. Mansi, (ed.), XXXII, 672.

[3] Nelson H. Minnich, "Concepts of Reform proposed at the Fifth Lateran Council," *Archivium Historiae pontificiae,* 7 (1969), 163–251 (p. 238).

[4] *Weimarer Ausgabe,* 54, 179–187.

[5] Georges Chantraine, *Erasme et Luther. Libre et serf arbitre,* Paris: Éditions Lethielleux; Namur: Presses Universitaires de Namur, 1981.

[6] Jaques Courvoisier, *De la Réforme au protestantisme,* Paris: Beauchesne, 1977.

[7] In his celebrated article of 1929, "Une question mal posée: les origines de la Réforme française et le problème de la Réforme," reprinted in *Au coeur religieux du XVIe siècle,* Paris: Sevpen, 1957, 3–70.

[8] H. O. Evennett, *The Spirit of the Counter Reformation,* Notre Dame: University of Notre Dame Press, 1970, c1968. On the problem of the vocabulary of historiography, see the reflections of Hubert Jedin, published in 1946 and repeatedly reedited in Italian: *Riforma cattolica o Controriforma,* Brescia: Morcelliana, 1987.[5]

[9] Louis Châtellier, *The Europe of the Devout. The Catholic Reformation and the Formation of a New Society,* Cambridge: Cambridge University Press, 1989.

[10] Giovanni Bricci, *Relatione sommaria del solenne apparato e cerimonia . . . ,* Rome, 1622.

CHAPTER 7

[1] Inspired by a saying of Cicero, *sua cuique civitati religio,* the principle had been formulated by the Lutheran canonist Joachim Stephani (1623) in 1559. See Joseph Lecler, "Les origines et le sens de la formule *Cuius regio, eius religio,*" *Recherches de science religieuse,* 38 (1951), p. 119–131.

[2] Allen S. Weiss, *Mirrors of Infinity: The French Formal Garden and 17th-century Metaphysics.* New York: Princeton Architectural Press, 1995.

[3] Yves Congar, *L'Eglise de saint Augustin à l'époque moderne,* Paris, 1970, p. 372 ff.

[4] Jean-Robert Armogathe, *L'Eglise catholique et la révocation de l'Edit de Nantes,* Paris, 1985.

[5] Letter to Cristina of Lorraine, Grand Duchess of Tuscany (May, 1615). Galileo Galilei, *Opere, Edizione nazionale,* Florence, V, p. 309–359. It should be compared with the letters of Galileo to Benedetto Castelli, (December 21, 1613), *Edizione nazionale,* V, p. 280–288, and to Monsignor Piero Dini (February 16, 1615), *Ibidem,* p. 291–295. For a recent interpretation, especially valuable because of the knowledge the book reveals of the problems of the time, Pietro Redondi, *Galileo heretic,* Princeton, 1987

[6] *The Satin Slipper,* Second day, Scene V.

[7] Alain Merot, *Nicolas Poussin,* Paris, 1990.

[8] Paul Benichou, *Man and Ethics in French Classicism,* Garden City, New York, 1971 (translation of *Morales du Grand siècle,* Paris, 1948).

[9] Louis Chatellier, *The Europe of the Devout. The Catholic Reformation and the Formation of a New Society,* Cambridge: Cambridge University Press, 1989, and François de Dainville, *L'éducation des Jésuites (XVIIe-XVIIIe siècle),* Paris: Les Editions de Minuit, 1978.

[11] See Chapter 11 of this book.

CHAPTER 8

[1] Paul Hazard, *The European Mind, 1680–1715,* Cleveland, 1963.

[2] Piero Camporesi speaks of baroque anthropology and baroque theology: *The Anatomy of the Senses. Natural Symbols in Medieval and Early Modern Italy,* Cambridge, Massachusetts, 1994; *The Fear of Hell. Images of Damnation and Salvation in Early Nodern Europe,* Cambridge/Oxford, 1990.

[3] Jean Deprun, "Classicisme et Baroquisme religieux: la controverse Bossuet-Leibnitz," in *La prédication au XVIIe siècle: journées Bossuet.* Actes du Colloque de Dijon 1977, T. Goyet/J.P. Collinet (ed.), Paris, 1980, pp. 361–373. See also by the same author, *La philosophie de l'inquiétude en France au XVIIIe siècle,* Paris, 1979.

[4] *Histoire du vieux Testament,* Rotterdam, ed. 1685, Preface, p. 3.

[5] Jean-Pierre Jossua, *Pierre Bayle ou l'obsession du mal,* Paris, 1977.

[6] Etiemble, *L'Europe chinoise,* vol. 1, Paris, 1988 and G. Minamiki, *The Chinese Rites Controversy,* Chicago, 1985. See Chapter 11.

[7] F. Boespflug, *Dieu dans l'art. "Sollicitudini nostrae"* of *Benoît XIV (1745) et l'affaire Crescence de Kaufbeuren,* Paris, 1984.

[8] Robert A. Kann, *A Study in Austrian Intellectual History,* New York, 1972.

[9] *Benoît Labre. Errance et sainteté,* Y.M. Hilaire (ed.), Paris, 1984.

CHAPTER 9

[1] *Lettres du curé Barbotin,* A. Aulard (ed.), Paris, 1911, p. 26.

[2] The *Te Deum* was sung at Notre-Dame de Paris on 4 August 1789 and 14 July 1790 for the feast of the Federation.

[3] The sorrows are noted in the Brief of Pius VI, *Quod aliquantum,* of 10 March 1791.

[4] Cf. the collected pieces in *La condamnation de Lamennais,* M. J. and L. Le Guillou (ed.), Paris, 1982.

[5] Hans Maier, *Revolution and Church. The Early History of Christian Democracy, 1789–1901,* Notre Dame, 1969.

CHAPTER 11

[1] The theological term, inculturation should be distinguished from the concept of acculturation, forged by social anthropology since the end of the nineteenth century, which designates all kinds of encounters between cultures, whatever the form: for example, acceptance, identification, or assimilation of one by the other, which in the terminology of the history of religions could be called syncretism. Note that the term culture itself, in the

social sense, only became important in the mid-nineteenth century, even though it was known previously. On these problems, cf. Hervé Carrier, *Lexique de la culture pour l'analyse culturelle et l'inculturation,* Tournai, 1992.

[2] 1492. *Le choc de deux mondes,* Acts of the Geneva Colloquium, September 17–18, 1992, Paris, 1993.

[3] Nathan Wachtel, *The Vision of the Vanquished. The Spanish Conquest of Peru through Indian Eyes* (1530–1570). New York, 1977.

[4] *Naufragios de Alver Nunez Cabeza de Vaca,* v. 1 of *de Historiadores primitivos de Indias,* ed., Enrique de Veda, Biblioteca de Autores espanoles, Madrid, 1946. An amazing literary transcription of certain episodes can be found in *El Entenado,* of the Argentine writer Juan José Saer (1983).

[5] J.I. Saranyana and A. de Zaballa, *Joaquin de Fiore y America,* Pamplona, 1992.

[6] Pierre Duviols, *La lutte contre les religions autochtones dans la Pérou colonial.* "L'extirpation de l'idolâtrie entre 1522 et 1660," Lima- Paris, 1972.

[7] Serge Gruzinski, *The Conquest of Mexico: the Incorporation of Indian Societies into the Western World (16th–18th Centuries).* Cambridge, Massachusetts, 1993.

[8] See "Nican Mopohua," first account of the apparitions, written in Nahuatl around 1560, presented by Clodomiro L. Siller Acuna, *Para comprender el mensaje de María de Guadalupe,* Buenos Aires, 1990.

[9] Silvio Zavala, *La Utopia de Tomàs Moro en la Nueva Espana,* in *Recuerdo de Vasco de Quiroga,* Mexico, 1965.

[10] Etiemble, *L'Europe chinoise.* Vol. 1: *De l'Empire romain à Leibniz,* Paris, 1988.

[11] A Spanish Dominican drew up an abridged version of Christian doctrine in Chinese, which was, in 1593, the first book printed (actually xylographed) in the Philippines. Fidel Villaroel, "Shih Lu. Apologie de la vraie religion du dominicain Juan Cobo," *Mémoire dominicaine,* 7 (1995), p. 39–58.

[12] François Bontinck, *La lutte autour de la liturgie chinoise au XVIIe et XVIIIe siècles,* Louvain-Paris, 1962.

[13] On these problems, cf. Jacques Gernet, *China and the Christian Impact. A Conflict of Cultures.* Cambridge UK–New York, 1985.

[14] George Minamiki, *The Chinese Rites Controversy from its Beginning to Modern Times,* Chicago, 1985.

[15] Of 10 November 1659. Cf. A. Rétif, "La charte des missions modernes," *Etudes,* 300 (1959), pp. 49–56 (Collectanea Sacrae Congregationis de Propaganda fide, Rome, 1907, I, n. 135).

[16] This treatise has been reedited (Bogota, 1956): "*De instauranda Aethiopum salute.* El mundo de la esclabitud negra en America." Cf. Marie-Cécile Bénassy-Berling, "Alonso de Sandoval, les jésuites et la descendance de Cham" in *Etudes sur l'impact culturel du Nouveau Monde,* I, Paris, 1981, pp. 49–60.

[17] Quoted by Jacques Gadille, "L'idéologie et la pratique missionnaire" in *Eglise et histoire de l'Eglise en Afrique,* (ed. Giuseppe Ruggieri) Paris, 1988, p. 50. See also the articles by Alphonse Ngindu Mushete and Francis Kabasele Lumbala.

[18] Xavier de Montclos, *Le cardinal Lavigerie. La mission universelle de l'Eglise,* Paris, 1968, pp. 100–101.

[19] Henri Perrin, *Journal d'un prêtre-ouvrier en Allemagne,* Paris, 1945. Also Jacques Loew, *Journal d'une mission ouvrière,* Paris, 1959. See also the works of Emile Poulat, especially *Naissance des prêtres-ouvriers,* Paris, 1965.

BIBLIOGRAPHY

GENERAL WORKS

Handbook of Church History, edited by Hubert Jedin and John Dolan, London: Burns & Oates; New York: Herder and Herder, 1981, 10 vol.

Histoire du christianisme, sous la direction de J.-M. Mayeur, Ch. Pietri, A. Vauchez, M. Venard, Paris, 1990–2001, 14 vol.

Balthasar, Hans Urs (von). *Man in History: a theological Study,* translated by W. Glen-Doepel, London, Sydney: Sheed & Ward, 1968.

Gilson, Etienne. *Les métamorphoses de la Cité de Dieu,* Louvain-Paris, 1952.

Lubac, Henri (de). *Medieval Exegesis,* translated by M. Sebanc, Grand Rapids, Michigan: W.B. Eerdmans; Edinburgh: T & T Clark, 1998.

Marrou, Henri-Irénée. *The Meaning of History,* Baltimore: Helicon, 1966.

Pelikan, Jaroslav. *The Christian Tradition; a History of the Development of Doctrine,* Chicago: University of Chicago Press, 1971–1989, 5 vol.

CHAPTER 1

Campenhausen, Hans (von). *The Fathers of the Church,* Peabody, Massachusetts: Hendrickson Publishers, 1998.

Ivanka, Endre (von). *Plato Christianus. Ubernahme und Umgestaltung des Platonismus durch die Väter,* Einsiedeln: Johannes Verlag, 1964.

Lane Fox, Robin. *Pagans and Christians,* San Francisco: Harper, 1995.

Rahner, Hugo. *Church and State in Early Christianity,* translated by L. D. Davis, San Francisco: Ignatius Press, 1992.

_____, *Greek Myths and Christian Mystery,* translated by B. Battershaw, London: Burns & Oates, 1963.

Texts

Athanasius (Saint). *The Coptic Life of Antony,* translated by T. Vivian, San Francisco: International Scholars Publications, 1995.

Augustine (Saint). *Confessions,* (English and Latin) translated by W. Watts, Cambridge, Massachusetts: Harvard University Press, 1999–2000, 2 vol.

The Epistles of St. Clement of Rome and S. Ignatius of Antioch, translated and annotated by James A. Kleist, Westminster, Maryland: Newman Bookshop, 1995.

CHAPTER 2

Deanesly, Margaret. *The Pre-Conquest Church in England,* New York: Oxford University Press, 1961.

Herri, Judith. *The Formation of Christendom,* Princeton, New Jersey: Princeton University Press, 1989.

Markus, R.A. *Gregory the Great and His World,* Cambridge: Cambridge University Press, 1997.

Texts

Augustine (Saint). *The City of God,* translated by M. Dods, with an introduction by Thomas Merton, Modern Library ed. New York: Modern Library, 1993.

Bede the Venerable (Saint). *Bede's Ecclesiastical History of the English People,* (English and Latin), New York: Oxford University Press, 1998.

Gregory the Great (Saint). *Dialogues,* translated by O. J. Zimmerman, Washington D.C.: The Catholic University of America Press in association with Consortium Books, 1977.

Gregory of Tours (Saint). *The History of the Franks,* translated by L. Thorpe, Baltimore: Penguin, 1974.

CHAPTER 3

Arquilliere, Henri-Xavier. *L'augustinisme politique,* Paris: Vrin, 1934.

Bloch, Marc. *Feudal Society,* translated by L.A. Manyon, London, New York: Routledge, 1989.

Duby, Georges. *The Three Orders: Feudal Society Imagined,* translated by A. Goldhammer, Phoenix ed. Chicago: University of Chicago Press, 1982.

Falco, Giorgio. *The Holy Roman Republic: A historic Profile of the Middle Ages,* translated by K. V. Kent, New York: A. S. Barnes, 1965.

Ganshof, François-Louis. *Feudalism,* translated by P. Grierson, University of Toronto Press in association with the Medieval Academy of America, 1996.

Texts

Abelard, Peter.

The Letters of Abelard and Heloise, translated by B. Radice, Harmondsworth: Penguin, 1987.

The Story of Abelard's Adversities, translated by J. T. Muckle, with a preface by E. Gilson, Toronto: Pontifical Institute of Medieval Studies, 1982.

Bernard of Clairvaux (Saint). *Five Books on Consideration: Advice to a Pope,* translated by J. D. Anderson and E. T. Kennan, Kalamazoo, Michigan: Cistercian Publications, 1976.

Hugh of Saint-Victor. *Didascalicon: A Medieval Guide to the Arts,* translated by J. Taylor, New York: Columbia University Press, 1961.

William of Saint-Thierry, *The Golden Epistle: A Letter to the Brethern at Mont-Dieu,* translated by T. Berkeley, Spencer, Massachusetts: Cistercian Publications, 1971.

CHAPTER 4

Duby, Georges. *The Age of the Cathedrals: Art and Society, 980–1420,* translated by E. Levieux and B. Thompson, Chicago: University of Chicago Press, 1981.

Huizinga, Johan, *The Autumn of the Middle Ages,* translated by R. J. Payton and U. Mammitzsch, Chicago: University of Chicago Press, 1996.

Kantorowicz, Hans K. *The King's Two Bodies. A study in Medieval Political Theology,* Princeton, New Jersey: Princeton University Press, 1997.

Lagarde, Georges (de). *La naissance de l'esprit laïque au déclin du Moyen-Age,* Louvain, Paris: 1956-1970, 5 vol.

Mollat, Guillaume. *The Popes at Avignon, 1305–1378,* translated by J. Love, New York: Harper & Row, 1965.

Oberman, Heiko. *The Harvest of Medieval Theology: Gabriel Biel and late Medieval Nominalism,* Durham, North Carolina: Labyrinth Press, 1983.

Texts

Dante Alighieri. *Dante's Monarchia,* translated by R. Kay, Toronto: Pontifical Institute of Medieval Studies, 1998.

Catherine of Siena (Saint). *The Dialogue,* translated by S. Noffke, New York: Paulist Press, 1980.

Marsilius of Padua. *Defender of Peace,* translated by A. Gewirth, New York: Harper & Row, 1967.

CHAPTER 5

Bataillon, Marcel. *Erasme et l'Espagne: recherches sur l'histoire spirituelle du XVI° siècle,* Genève: Droz, 1998 (1937).

Guy, John. *Thomas More,* London: Arnold, 2000.

Hanke, Lewis. *Las Casas and the Spanish Struggle for Justice in the Conquest of America,* Institue of Latin American Studies, School of International Affairs-Columbia University, 1966.

Jardin, Lisa. *Erasmus, Man of Letters. The Construction of Charisma in Print,* Princeton, New Jersey: Princeton University Press, 1993.

Pastor, Ludwig (von). *The History of the Popes from the Close of the Middle Ages,* ed. Frederick Antrobus, London: Routledge and Kegan Paul/St. Louis Missouri: Herder Book, 1936–1961.

Screech, M. A. *Rabelais,* Ithaca, New York: Cornell University Press, 1979.

Texts

Erasmus, Desiderius. *Enchiridion militis Christiani. An English Version,* New York: Oxford University Press, 1981.

————————. *The Erasmus Reader,* edited by E. Rummel, Toronto: University of Toronto Press, 1990.

Las Casas, Bartolome (de). *The Devastation of the Indies. A Brief Account,* translated by H. Briffaut, Baltimore: Johns Hopkins University Press, 1992.

More, Thomas (Saint). *Utopia,* edited by S. Bruce, Oxford; New York: Oxford University Press, 1999.

————————. *Conscience Decides. Letters and Prayers from Prison written by Sir Thomas More between April 1534 and July 1535,* London: G. Chapman, 1971.

————————. *The Last Letters of Thomas More,* edited by A. de Silva, Grand Rapids, Michigan: W.B. Eerdmans, 2000.

Rabelais, François. *Gargantua and Pantagruel,* New York: Knopf, 1994.

Savonarola, Girolamo. *Prison Meditations on Psalms 51 and 31,* translated by J. P. Donnelly, Milwaukee: Marquette University Press, 1994.

Vitoria, Francisco (de). *Relectiones theologicae,* The Classic of International Law, 12, Washington D.C., 1917.

CHAPTER 6

Bedouelle, Guy & Roussel Bernard. *Le temps des Réformes et la Bible,* Paris: Beauchesne, 1989.

Bedouelle, Guy. *La réforme du catholicisme (1480–1620),* Paris: Editions du Cerf, 2002.

Chaunu, Pierre: *The Reformation,* edited by P. Chaunu, New York: Saint Martin's Press, 1990.

Febvre, Lucien. *Martin Luther. A Destiny,* translated by R. Tapley, London: Dent, 1930.

Jedin, Hubert. *A History of Council of Trent,* translated by E. Graf, London-New York: T. Nelson, 1957–1961, 2 vol.

Lecler, Joseph. *Toleration and the Reformation,* translated by T. L. Westow, New York: Association Press, 1960.

Lohse, Bernhard. *Martin Luther. An Introduction to His Life and Work,* Philadelphia: Fortress Press, 1986.

Lortz, Joseph. *The Reformation in Germany,* translated by R. Walls, London: Darton, Longman & Todd; New York: Herder & Herder, 1968.

Weber, Max. *The Protestant Ethic and the Spirit of Capitalism,* translated by T. Parsons, London, New York: Routledge, 2001.

Texts

Bascape, Carlo. *Vita e opere di S. Carlo Borromeo,* Milan: Nuovo Edizione Duomo, 1983.

Calvin, Jean. *Institutes of the Christian Religion,* translated by H. Beveridge, Chicago: Encyclopaedia Britannica, 1990.

Catechismus Romanus, The Roman Catechism, Boston, Massachusetts: St. Paul Editions, 1985.

Luther, Martin. *Luther's Works,* edited by J. Pelikan, St. Louis, Philadelphia, 1986.

CHAPTER 7

Benichou, Paul. *Man and Ethics. Studies in French Classicism,* translated by E. Hughes, Garden City, New York: Anchor Books, 1971.

Châtellier, Louis. *The Religion of the Poor. Rural Missions in Europe and the Formation of Modern Catholicism,* translated by B. Pearce, Cambridge, United Kingdom; New York: Cambridge University Press, 1997.

————————. *The Europe of the Devout. The Catholic Reformation and the Formation of a new Society,* translated by J. Birell, New York: Cambrigde University Press, 1989.

Galileo Galilei: Toward a Resolution of 350 Years of Debate, 1633–1983, edited by Paul Cardinal Poupard, with epilogue by John Paul II, Pittsburgh, Pennsylvania: Duquesne University Press, 1987.

Redondi Pietro, *Galileo heretic,* translated by R. Rosenthal, Princeton, New Jersey, Princeton University Press, 1989.

Texts

Campanella, Tommaso. *The City of the Sun: A Poetical Dialogue,* translated by D.J. Donno, Berkeley: University of California Press, 1981.

Francis of Sales (Saint). *Introduction to the Devout Life,* edited by Ch. Dollen, New York: Alba House, 1992.

Pascal, Blaise. *The Provincial Letters,* translated by A. J. Krailsheimer, Harmondsworth: Penguin, 1982.

Ricci, Matteo & Trigault Nicolas. *Histoire de l'expédition chrétienne au royaume de la Chine, 1582–1610,* Lille 1617, reed. Paris, 1975.

CHAPTER 8

Cassirer, Ernst. *The Philosophy of the Enlightenment,* translated by F. A. Koelln & J. P. Pettegrove, Boston: Beacon Press, 1965.

Hazard, Paul. *The European Mind: the Critical Years, 1680–1715,* New York: Fordham University Press, 1990.

Labrousse, Elisabeth. *Bayle,* translated by D. Potts, New York: Oxford University Press, 1983.

Minamiki, George. *The Chinese Rites Controversy: From Its Beginning to Modern Times,* Chicago: Loyola University Press, 1985.

Texts

Bayle, Pierre. *Ce qu'est la France toute catholique,* ed. by E. Labrousse, Paris: Vrin, 1973.

Correspondance Leibniz-Bossuet (1691–1702), in F. Gaquère, *Le dialogue irénique,* Paris: Beauchesne, 1966.

Rousseau, Jean-Jacques. *Emile,* book IV, translated by B. Foxley, London: Dent, 1993.

CHAPTER 9

Benichou, Paul. *The Consecration of the Writer, 1750–1839,* translated by Mark K. Jensen, Lincoln: Nebraska University Press, 1999.

Bowman, Frank Paul. *Le Christ romantique. 1789, le sans-culotte de Nazareth,* Genève: Droz, 1973.

Chadwick, Owen. *Newman,* Oxford University Press, 1983.

Maier, Hans. *Revolution and Church. The Early History of Christian Democracy, 1789–1901,* translated by E. M. Schossberger, Notre-Dame: University of Notre Dame Press, 1969.

Martina, Giacomo. *Pio IX,* Roma: Università Gregoriana, 3 vol., 1974–1990.

Texts

Möhler, Johann Adam. *Unity in the Church or the Principle of Catholicism: Presented in the Spirit of the Church Fathers of the First Three Centuries,* edited and translated by P.C. Erb, Washington, D.C.: Catholic University of America Press, 1996.

La condamnation de Lamennais, edited by M. J. Le Guillou and L. Le Guillou, Paris, 1982.

Rosmini, Antonio. *Of the Five Wounds of the Holy Church,* edited by H. P. Liddon, London: Rivingtons, 1883.

Newman, John Henry. *Apologia pro vita sua: Being a History of His Religious Opinions,* London: Oxford University Press, 1964.

_____. *Fifteen Sermons preached before the University of Oxford between 1826–1843,* Westminster, Maryland: Christian Classics, 1966.

CHAPTER 10

Le deuxième concile du Vatican (1959–1965), Collection de l'Ecole française de Rome, 113, Rome, 1989.

Hennesey John, *American Catholics,* New York: Oxford University Press, 1981.

Texts

Actes et documents du Saint-Siège relatifs à la seconde Guerre mondiale, Vatican, 1961–1981, 11 vol.

Tomos Agapis, Towards the Healing of Schism. The Sees of Rome and Constantinople: public Statements and Correspondence between the Holy See and the Ecumenical Patriarchate, 1958–1984, edited by E. J. Stormon, New York: Paulist Press, 1987.

Chautard, Jean-Baptiste. *The Soul of the Apostolate,* translated by Thomas Merton, Garden City, New York: Image Books, 1961.

Loisy, Alfred, "De la croyance à la foi" (1937), edited by E. Poulat, *Critique et mystique,* Paris: Le Centurion, 1984.

Meditation of Ermit, London, 1930. (Ch. de Foucauld)

Thérèse of Lisieux (Saint). *The Autobiography of St. Thérèse of Lisieux: The Story of a Soul,* Garden City, New York: Image Book, 1957.

CHAPTER 11

Carro, Venancio D. *La teologia y los teólogos-juristas españoles ante la conquista de America,* 2 vol., Salamanca: 1954.

Gernet, Jacques. *China and the Christian Impact. A Conflict of Cultures,* translated by J. Llyod, Cambridge, New York: Cambridge University Press, 1985.

Hanke, Lewis, *La lucha por la justitia en la conquista española de América,* Madrid, 1969.

Ricard, Robert, *The Spirituel Conquest of Mexico. An Essay on the Apostolate and the Evangelizing Methods of the Mendicant Orders in New Spain,* translated by L. Byrd Simpson, Berkeley: University of California Press, 1982.

Texts

Las Casas, Bartolome (de). *Obras escogidas,* edited by J. Perez de Tuleda, Madrid, 1957–1958, 5 vol.

Lecomte, Louis. *Nouveaux mémoires sur l'état présent de la Chine, 1687–1692,* reed. Paris, 1990.

Muratori, Ludovico Antonio, *Il cristianesimo Felice nelle Missioni de' Padri della Compagnia di Gesù nel Paraguai,* 2 vol., Venice, 1743–1749.

Ruiz de Montoya, Antonio. *The Spiritual Conquest Accomplished by the Religious of the Society of Jesus in the Provinces of Paraguay, Parana, Urugay,* St. Louis, Missouri: Institute of Jesuit Sources, 1993.

INDEX OF NAMES AND PLACES

Blondel, Maurice, 142, 197
Bloy, Léon, 198–199
Boccacio, 95, 97–98
Bocquet, Nicolas, 151
Bodin, Jean, 143
Boethius, 36–37, 49
Boel, Pieter, 149
Boizot, Claude, 76
Bogota, 221
Bohemia, 90, 125, 135, 144
Bolivar, 177
Bolivia, 231
Bologna, 76
Bombay, 221
Bonaventure, saint, 75–77, 80
Boniface VIII, pope, 85–86
Bonn, 45
   Landsmuseum, 45
Bordeaux, 86
Borgia, Caesar, 109
Borromeo, Charles, cardinal, 132–133
Borromeo, Federico, cardinal, 152
Bosco, Jean, saint, 187
Bose, monastery, 213
Bosse, Abraham, 156
Bossuet, 159–161
Boston, Museum of Fine Arts, 136, 192
Botticelli, Sandro, 86, 110–111, 114
Boullée, Étienne Louis, 165
Boulogne-sur-mer, Municipal Library, 34
Bourbons, 145
Burgundy, 95
Bouts, Dierick, 90
Boyvin, René, 125–126
Braga, 133
Brahma, 14
Bramante, 105
Bramantino, Bartolomeo, 115
Brentwood, California, Paul Getty Museum, 240
Brescia, City Museum, 40
Brazil, 200, 223, 232–233
Bresson, Robert, 218
Bridget of Sweden, saint, 88–89
Britto, Jean de, 235
Brunelleschi, Filippo, 98
Brussels, 186, 205
   Royal Library, 52, 91, 136
   Jesuit Provincial House, 138
Bry, Théodore de, 240
Bucer, Martin, 125
Budapest, 158
   Szepmuveszti Museum, 158
Buddha, 14, 237
Buenos Aires, 169
Buganda, 188
Bujumbura, 244
Buñel, Luis, 218
Bureau, Henri, 213
Burgos, 83

Burundi, 244
Busleyden, Jérôme, 101

Cabassi, C., 213
Caen, Museum of Fine Arts, 148
Caesarius of Arles, bishop, 30
Cajetan of Thiene, saint, 131
Calcutta, 223
California, 240, 248
Caligula, emperor, 11
Callistus II, pope, 72
Callo, Marcel, 207
Calvin, 121, 125–127, 148, 151
Cambridge, 217
   Fogg Art Museum, 184
Cameroon, 244
Camillo Benso, Count of Cavour, 177
Cannes, 30
Cano de la Pena, Eduardo, 226
Canossa, St. Sabinus Cathedral, 67
Canterbury, 41, 74
   cathedral, 41
Canton, 235
Cape of Good Hope, 102
Capo Verde, 103
Caravaggio, 117
Cardijn, Joseph, abbot, 205, 245
Caroline Islands, 200
Carolingians, 50, 52
Carthage, 27
Carthagena, 240
Casaldaliga, Pedro, 223
Cassiodorus, 36–37
Castiglione, Giuseppe, 169, 237, 238
Castille, 50, 62, 73, 83, 101, 226
Castres, 52
   Goya Museum, 52
   Cataldino, Joseph, 232
Catalonia, 66, 144, 240
Catherine de Ricci, saint, 112
Catherine II, 162, 169
Catherine of Siena, saint, 88–89, 210
Cauchon, bishop of Beauvais, 92
Cavour, 177
Celsus, 19
Cervi, Gino, 209
Ceuta, 102
Cevenatico, 213
Ceylon, 234, 235
Chacour, Abouna Elias, 221
Chagall, Marc, 216, 248
Chalais, 179
Chalcedon, 24, 27, 31
Chantilly, Condé Museum, 55
Charente, 68
Charlemagne, emperor, 28, 52, 53
Charles I, king of England, 144, 175
Charles II "the Bald," emperor, 52
Charles V, emperor, 129, 227, 229
Charles VII, king of France, 108

INDEX OF NAMES AND PLACES

Photo Credits

The numbers written in Roman numerals refer to chapters; those in Arabic numbers refer to illustrations. All illustrations not mentioned in these credits belong to the Archives of Editoriale Jaca Book (AJB).

Agence Grazia Neri, Milan: XI/46 (G. Rancinan/GLMR), 57 (F. Origlia/Sygma); AJB/Angelo Stabin: III/2, XI/30; AJB/BAMS photo Rodella: I/27, II/31, 31, IV/44, V/1, 3, VI/31, 38, VIII/14, 30, 31, IX/46, X/69, XI/35; AJB/Corrado Gavinelli: X/45, 58, 59; AJB/Cristina Esteras: VIII/24, XI/22; AJB/Davide Domenici: XI/11; AJB/Duccio Bonavia: XI/13, 14; AJB/Elio Ciol: I/33; AJB/Ermanno Leso (drawing): I/40; AJB/Fernando Lanzi: III/20, 36; AJB/Isber Melhem: I/2, 3, 20, 21, 38; AJB/Jaime Moncada: VIII/29; AJB/Lunwerg: III/21, 34; AJB/M. Llimargas: IV/9, VIII/16; X/28, 53; AJB/Mauro Magliani: I/23, 30, 37; AJB/Gustavo Landivar: VI/49; AJB/Isabel Cruz: VI/27; AJB/Mireille Vautier: V/30; AJB/Sandro Vannini: V/25, 26; Alinari/Giraudon: II/21, Alinari/Bridgeman: IV/56; Archivo Fotogramma, Bari: III/38; Apostolic Library, Vatican: I/1, 6, 24, III/9, 22, IV/46, 49, V/7, 28; Laurenziana Library, Florence: II/11; Éditions du Rouergue/Naili Samaan: X/7; Éditions du Rouergue/Jean Starcky: X/41; Excalibur, Milan: X/62, 63, 64, 65, 66, 67, 68; Franco Cosimo Panini, Florence: II/12, V/4; Giovanni Chiaramonte: XI/56; Instituto Portugês de Museus, National Museum of Antique Art, Lisbon: V/18; Jean-Louis Arbey: II/30; Kunsthistorisches Museum, Vienna: VIII/22; Luca Mozzati: IV/8; Matteo Rodella: X/70; Museum of Art and History, Fribourg: VI/21; Musée Poldi Pezzoli, Milan: V/41; Photothèque Zodiaque, Abbaye-de-la-Pierre-qui-Vire: I/36, III/25, 31, 32, 37, IV/1, 3, 11, 12, 13, 36, 38, 50, 51, V/6; Richard Bösel: VI/41, 42; RMN, Paris: VII/27 (G. Blot), VII/28 (G. Blot/C. Jean), IX/13, XI/25, XI/34 (Arnaudet), IX/21, 22 (H. Lewandowski); SIAE: IX/52, 55, 57, X/13, 26, 29, 34, 54, 55, 56, 61, XI/54.